THE GREAT POWERS AND
THE EUROPEAN STATES SYSTEM
1815–1914

The Great Powers and the European States System 1815–1914

F. R. Bridge and Roger Bullen

Longman
London and New York

Longman Group Limited London

Associated companies, branches and representatives throughout the world

Published in the United States of America by Longman Inc., New York

© Longman Group Limited 1980

First published 1980

British Library Cataloguing in Publication Data

Bridge, F. R.
  The great powers and the European states system, 1815–1914.
  1. Europe – Foreign relations
  2. Europe – Politics and government – 1815–1871
  3. Europe – Politics and government – 1871–1918
  I. Title   II. Bullen, Roger
  327.4   D363   79–41567

  ISBN 0–582–49134–7
  ISBN 0–582–49135–5 Pbk

Set in 10/12 pt V-I-P Bembo
Printed in Great Britain by
Richard Clay (The Chaucer Press) Ltd., Bungay, Suffolk

Contents

List of maps

Preface

As teachers of international history we think that a short survey of the relations of the European great powers from the defeat of Napoleon to the outbreak of the First World War would be useful. We have not sought to provide a detailed narrative, rather we have concentrated on the following questions: what rules were observed by the powers in their relations with each other?; what circumstances best suited their observance?; under what conditions were these rules modified and for what reasons did they occasionally break down?

In the preparation of this book we have secured much help and guidance particularly from Maureen Hastie, Derek McKay, Hugh Purse, Felicity Strong and Keith Wilson. A number of international history students at Leeds and London provided invaluable criticism. We would also like to record that over the years we have both derived great benefit from the seminars in nineteenth-century international history held at the Institute of Historical Research by W. N. Medlicott, James Joll and Kenneth Bourne.

F. R. BRIDGE
ROGER BULLEN

CHAPTER ONE

Introduction: The character of international relations 1815–1914

In the century between the Congress of Vienna and the outbreak of the First World War international relations in Europe were largely dominated by five great powers: Austria (after 1867 Austria-Hungary), France, Great Britain, Prussia (after 1871 Germany) and Russia. There was always a clear distinction between what contemporaries called 'first-rate powers' and 'secondary states', and there was rarely any doubt into which category any state should be placed. The great powers jealously guarded their status and were at all times disinclined to admit new members into their ranks. After her unification in the 1860s Italy liked to be regarded as a great power, but it was only in the capacity of an ally of the Central Powers after 1882, and as a member of the Concert dealing with the affairs of the Ottoman Empire that she could claim anything like equality with the other five. The dominance of the five or six powers over such a long period gave an underlying stability to international relations, a stability not found in either the eighteenth or the twentieth centuries. During the former both Spain and Sweden clung tenaciously to great-power status long after they had ceased to possess its attributes, and both Prussia and Russia effectively transformed themselves from second-class states into great powers. In the twentieth century great powers have fought to destroy each other, and the status of a European great power has ceased to have the same importance as it had before the First World War. The nineteenth century witnessed no such dramatic changes. In the upheavals of 1848–49 Austria came close to the brink of disintegration, but Russia rallied to her defence and preserved the five-power system. The four great-power wars of the mid century were not fought à l'outrance: the belligerents were concerned essentially with limited and localized objectives. Despite two defeats, in 1859 and 1866, Austria continued to be treated as a great power, and so did France after her military collapse in 1871. For the most part the great powers respected each other's status: they were accustomed to a great-power system, and strove to maintain it. There was a constant and conscious fear that its demise would bring untold disasters to them all. This was perhaps the most permanent consequence of Napoleon's bid for the mastery of Europe.

Throughout the nineteenth century the European great powers claimed for themselves special rights and responsibilities which they were unwilling to accord to other states. They usually consulted each other, although not the small states, on major issues. They regarded themselves as the guardians of the peace of Europe, and they assumed responsibility for the maintenance of order within their neighbouring states. It was the strongest second-class states which resented the existence of this 'exclusive club' of great powers. Their resentment was particularly evident at the Congress of Vienna when the four victorious powers treated states such as Sweden, Spain and Holland as inferior supplicants rather than as equal allies. The very fact that at the congress the previously vexed question of the precedence of diplomatic envoys was settled by the simple rule of 'length of service' attests to the new confidence of the great powers in their status: they no longer thought it necessary to prove their importance by squabbles over precedence at ceremonial occasions. In the years after 1815 German states such as Bavaria, Saxony and Hanover often found Austro-Prussian domination of the Germanic Confederation irksome. Indeed, during the revolutionary years 1848–49 they even tried to shake it off; but they failed largely because neither the Austrians nor the Prussians were prepared to tolerate such pretensions. For the most part, however, all the small states of Europe accepted the pre-eminence of the great powers and were content to place themselves under the protection of one or more of them. Moreover, just as the great powers claimed special rights for themselves, so the small states claimed that the great had special responsibilities for their well-being: they expected protection from external aggression and military assistance to suppress revolution. In some cases the great powers were expected to provide, either directly or indirectly, financial assistance to stave off public bankruptcy in small states. Many of the weaker states of Europe thus willingly cast themselves in the role of client states, and came to regard it as advantageous to be dependent on their great-power patrons.

Occasionally one or more great powers would find it necessary to 'discipline' a recalcitrant small state. In 1832 the British and the French had to take military action to force the Dutch government to accept the decisions of the London Conference on the delineation of the border after the separation of Belgium from Holland. In 1864 the Austrians and the Prussians were able to claim that their invasion of the two duchies of Schleswig and Holstein was intended to force the Danes to comply with the provisions of the Treaty of London of 1852. This was a stand which they knew the other powers would find it difficult to oppose. Similarly, in the later nineteeenth century, Austria-Hungary and Russia – equally claiming to act in defence of the territorial settlement established by the Concert at the Congress of Berlin – frequently threatened military intervention of a punitive or restraining nature against small states in the Balkans. In return for the protection they afforded the small states, the great powers expected a degree of obedience from them. It was not always forthcoming; for Portuguese governments it was almost a matter of principle to defy British governments which, on three separate occasions between 1826 and 1847, had to intervene to protect the Portuguese monarchy against rebel factions. In eastern Europe the close involvement of several rival powers, and the growing tension in the second half of the century, made drastic intervention of this kind an increasingly dangerous proposition; but Russia was certainly considering the use of force to maintain a puppet régime in Bulgaria in 1886–87; and armed intervention to re-establish an Austrophile régime in Serbia was discussed often enough in Vienna even in the twentieth century.

The only state which did not know its place in the hierarchy of power was the Ottoman Empire. Although it had extensive possessions in the Balkans and although the Treaty of Paris of 1856 formally admitted it to the Concert of Europe, it was never regarded as a European state. There was a general assumption that only Christian states could properly be regarded as members of the European community of nations. In 1897, for example, even Turkey's friends in the Concert agreed that Christian territory, once freed from Ottoman rule, could never be returned; and Turkey was not allowed to profit from her victory in her war with Greece. Ottoman governments oscillated between the most abject dependence on the great powers and defiance of them. In its relations with the European powers, the Ottoman Empire faced two almost insuperable problems: it could not please all the powers all the time, and it did not always know which one to fear most. It was these problems that were at the root of the Near Eastern conflict which eventually degenerated into the Crimean War and which continued to preoccupy the diplomatists of Europe until 1918.

From the Treaty of Chaumont (1814) onwards, the dominance enjoyed by the great powers was given increasingly formal recognition.

3

The Quadruple Alliance of November 1815 was specifically limited to the four great powers of the anti-French coalition. This was one reason why it was so much more important than the rival Russian-inspired Holy Alliance, which was signed by a motley collection of great and minor states. In 1818 France was formally rehabilitated as a great power, after defeat and occupation, by the creation of a new five-power concert. The clear notion behind both the Quadruple Alliance and the Concert was that there should be some formal and recognized procedure by which the great powers could maintain peace and the territorial *status quo,* which contemporary statesmen called 'the public law of Europe', and it usually took the form of conference diplomacy. Between 1822 and 1913 there were twenty-six conferences attended by representatives of all the great powers – the last of which, in London, lasted nearly eight months; and many more at which two or more great powers reached agreement. One of the principal assumptions of 'concert diplomacy' was that changes in the territorial order required the consent of the great powers. This doctrine was forcibly stated by Palmerston in 1846 when he wrote that it was impossible for any state to attempt to change the territorial order 'in a manner inconsistent with the Treaty of Vienna without the concurrence of the other powers who were party to that Treaty'. In the fifteen years from the Crimean War to the Treaty of Frankfurt this view of the purpose of the Concert was all but abandoned and peace treaties between belligerent great powers replaced it as the principal means of territorial revision. But the London Protocol of 1871 formally restated the principle that treaties could not be altered without the consent of all the signatory powers – an important issue in the crisis after the annexation of Bosnia nearly forty years later.

In practical terms the Concert of Europe could successfully allocate territory from one small or weak state to another. It could also provide the framework for the settlement of crises in which the powers were anxious to reach agreement. But it could not satisfy the territorial ambitions of great powers when these were in conflict with each other. Not one of the many suggestions for five-power discussion of territorial revision made between 1856 and 1871 was ever taken up and after 1871 the status of Alsace-Lorraine was an issue over which France and Germany differed so profoundly as to doom to failure any attempts at a compromise solution, let alone any general *entente* between the two powers. Equally, although in 1897 Russia and Austria-Hungary reached an agreement to co-exist in the Near East this was only possible on the basis of both powers renouncing any selfish territorial ambitions there. Much the same can be said of Austro-Italian agreements about the future of the Adriatic territories of the Ottoman Empire. In peacetime powers were reluctant openly to avow their expansionist objectives; only victory on the battlefield would give both force and righteousness to their demands. The successful operation of the Concert depended in fact upon a self-denying ordinance from each of the great powers. When two or more powers sought either treaty revision or territorial expansion and were prepared to bargain with each other on this basis, the concert could not control them. This did not mean that it ceased to exist, merely that it failed to operate in particular circumstances. It was quite frequently revived if the great powers were confronted by new issues on which they were disposed to compromise.

Almost immediately after the defeat of Napoleon informed observers of international relations began to distinguish between two categories of European great power. There were firstly those with exclusively European territory and interests, for example Austria and Prussia. Then there were those, such as Great Britain and Russia, with extensive possessions, influence and interests outside Europe. England owed her world power to her vast commercial interests in every continent, to her Indian empire and her overwhelming sea-power. Russia enjoyed the same status because of the vast and unknown size of her Asiatic possessions. It was, moreover, the growth of the French empire in North Africa after the occupation of Algiers in 1830 that placed France in the ranks of the world powers. In the 1870s the French reacted to their second defeat with a renewed emphasis on colonial expansion. Then, as in the 1820s and 1830s, many Frenchmen believed that their empire overseas would help provide France with the strength she needed to recover lost status and territory in Europe. By the late nineteenth century it was clear that the fears entertained by many continental diplomats earlier in the century that England and Russia would divide the world between them had proved unfounded. Nevertheless the world-wide rivalry of these two powers was certainly a constant element shaping their European alignments. The welcome if somewhat uneasy end of this struggle in the early twentieth century was an important factor in the British decision to stand by Russia in 1914.

The distinction between the purely European powers and the world powers was perhaps rather less significant before 1870. In the early nineteenth century Europe itself offered ample commercial opportunities for expanding economies. Moreover, there was very little reliance on raw materials produced outside Europe, and from the 1840s onwards railway building absorbed most surplus capital. In the period before 1870 England was the only great power to have an export economy geared to world-wide trade. Moreover, as far as the four continental powers were concerned, the dominant problems of international relations were European. Until the 1850s the European ruling élite was determined to ensure its own survival and to contain or destroy the challenges it faced from liberalism and nationalism. In the late 1850s and the 1860s their preoccupations were different but still European: the great powers concentrated on territorial expansion in Europe itself. Until 1870 the French certainly attached more importance to Italy and the Rhineland than they did to expansion in North Africa; as late as the 1860s the Russians were more concerned about retaining the congress kingdom of Poland than expanding their possessions in central Asia.

The only non-European issues which significantly affected the relations of the great powers in the first half of the nineteenth century arose as a result of the political instability of the central Asian states of Afghanistan and Persia and of the collapse of the authority of the Ottoman empire in its outlying provinces in central Asia and in North Africa. In central Asia the British feared that the Russians would eventually push southwards to threaten the British empire in India; in North Africa the British likewise believed that the French were intent upon expansion from Algiers to Egypt – all of which apprehensions marked British policy until the twentieth century. The effect of these British anxieties, however, was not to create new patterns of rivalry but to confirm and extend rivalries which already existed and which were European in origin. Neither the Prussian nor the Austrian governments shared the alarm of the British over the extra-European expansion of France and Russia. In the Atlantic the French never really attempted to exploit Anglo-American rivalry nor the British dread of American expansion into Canada. Although British governments sometimes feared that they might, French governments in fact never managed to establish close relations with the United States. For most of the century after the end of the War of 1812 the Americans were rather more suspicious of the imperial ambitions of the French in Central and South America than they were of the British. By the turn of the century the British had decided that a war against the United States was the one war they must never fight. Atlantic rivalry, which had played such an important part in Anglo-French relations in the late eighteenth century, was a negligible factor after 1815.

With the defeat of the Second Empire territorial gains on the Rhine ceased to be a practical proposition for the French; and Russia, having no longer to fear Napoleon III or a Crimean Coalition, at last gained security in both Poland and the Near East. These were but two of the factors leading the great powers to concentrate more of their attention on expansion outside Europe. The 1870s saw the spread of both a world-wide depression and of fears on the part of some governments – particularly those of Britain and Germany – that large annexations of territory by commercial rivals might be accompanied by the closure of markets hitherto open to them under the system of 'informal empire'. The 1880s and 1890s were marked by a spate of 'imperialist' activity – the partition of Africa and the intervention of the European Powers in China – all of which, however, was accomplished without serious danger of war, owing largely to Britain's and Germany's unwillingness to co-operate in defence of the 'open door' to trade. It is true that relations between Britain on the one hand and France and Russia on the other took a turn for the worse: indeed, to a very large extent Britain was the real target of the Franco-Russian alliance of the 1890s. But the extra-European activities of the great powers had not fundamentally altered their priorities: even those powers that were only semi-European never lost sight of their essentially European interests – the need to seek security in Europe by preventing any power or group of powers establishing a Napoleonic domination of the Continent. This continued to be the fundamental aim of their diplomacy.

In the last resort, great-power status was a reflection of economic, military and naval strength. The great powers were the largest, richest and most populous states. The ability to wage war on a massive scale was the ultimate test of great-power status. This was the simple and brutal reality underlying the complex edifice of international relations. In the French Revolutionary and Napoleonic wars each of the five great powers had put its status to the test. The fact that Austria and Prussia narrowly escaped destruction at the hands of the French, combined with the belief that they had been saved by the financial resources of the British and the military strength of the Russians, cast a long shadow over great-power relations until the Crimean War. It established the hierarchy of power which existed within the ranks of the great powers. In the years after the Congress of Vienna British financial and naval strength, and the military power at the disposal of the Russian emperor, were the decisive underlying factors in European diplomacy. It was these resources that the French knew they would have to match before they could contemplate an all-out attack on the Vienna settlement. The fact that it had taken the combined efforts of four powers to defeat France had given her a unique status within the new order, as the power least satisfied with the arrangements made in 1815, and the power with the greatest potential for disruption. In the decades after 1871 France was, of course, still a highly dissatisfied power. But in view of her

7

continuing diplomatic isolation and of the steady growth of Germany's demographic, industrial and military preponderance, she was in no position to challenge the 1871 settlement. Even so, this settlement lacked the moral validity of the treaties of 1815. After 1871 peace was maintained, not by the moral consensus of a conservative coalition comprising at least three and sometimes four great powers, but simply by the brutal fact of German military superiority over France – and it would last only so long as that superiority was maintained. Karl Marx gloomily predicted that the Treaty of Frankfurt would make war an institution.

In the first half of the nineteenth century none of the great powers made regular and precise estimates of each other's military and naval strength. For the most part they had very hazy notions of the military and naval resources at each other's disposal. There was, moreover, hardly any detailed forward planning by military leaders for future wars. None of the political leaders who took the decisions to go to war in the years from 1854 to 1870 attached decisive importance to the opinions of their military advisers. In the early nineteenth century the task of the military was to win wars after they had been declared. Before 1848 it was generally assumed that the next war would be a repetition of the last, a four-power coalition against France fought, like the campaigns of 1813 and 1814, in the west. In fact this war never materialized. When the great powers did fight in Europe in the late 1850s and 1860s it was with new weapons, a new technology, a new speed and smaller armies. Contemporary opinion was by no means certain in advance of the outcome of these wars; in 1866 and 1870 many military experts were convinced that the belligerents were evenly matched and that the wars would be long and inconclusive.

The speedy and catastrophic defeats of Austria and France seemed to portend a revolution in the role of the military in the formation of state policy. Prussia's victories had clearly demonstrated the importance of the efficient organization of manpower resources, their armament, and their speedy and effective deployment on the battlefield. After the wars of 1866 and 1870, efficiency and speed seemed more important than ever; and in succeeding years all the continental powers made frantic efforts to improve their war-making capacity. Conscription became the rule; general staffs were created to devise war plans and supervise other reforms on the Prussian model. The concentration on the building of strategic railways testified to the importance generally accorded to speed of mobilization. After 1871 military planning came into its own, and elaborate schemes were drawn up to cater for even the most improbable contingencies. The significance of this change should not be exaggerated. State policy still remained in the hands of monarchs and statesmen. Bismarck steadily and successfully set his face against a veritable stream of advice from Prussian and Austrian military planners in favour of a preventive war against Russia in the late 1880s; and in 1911 the emperor of Austria dismissed his chief of staff for persistently advocating war with Italy against the wishes of his foreign minister. But on occasions, when political and military leaders took the same view, the military could become more than the mere servants of the civilian authorities, and the emphasis placed by the military on the importance of detailed contingency plans could influence the course of events. The Franco–Russian military convention of 1892 formed the basis of the alliance of 1894. Blind faith in military advice as illustrated by the German government's decision to treat Russian mobilization as a *casus belli* had even more momentous consequences in July 1914.

In the exercise of their dominance over the European state system the great powers showed remarkable restraint, particularly in the decades from 1815 to 1856. They rarely acted arbitrarily or capriciously. It was not until the 1850s that any of the four victorious allies actually provoked a major diplomatic crisis. Most of the important problems of the pre-Crimean period were either provoked by small states or by dissident elements within small states. The great powers merely reacted to these crises, and attempted to prevent them from disturbing the peace of Europe. Nor was there any inclination among the four powers to exploit a local crisis produced by or within small states to embark upon an ambitious and forward policy which seriously and adversely affected the interests of other powers. The French were the exception to this rule: in Spain in 1823, in Belgium in 1830, and in Italy in 1848 they were intent upon securing important advantages for themselves. Until 1856, however, France was the only revisionist great power; her conduct was necessarily different from that of her satiated rivals. Moreover, French governments themselves provoked two major crises: in 1840 Thiers transformed a local Near Eastern conflict into a question of peace and war on the Rhine; and in 1852 Napoleon III successfully broke what he regarded as the deadlock of peace between the powers by an adventurous policy in the Near East. From 1856 to 1870 the other great powers also provoked crises, embarked upon wars of aggression, and exploited problems arising in small states in order to secure both political and territorial advantages for themselves.

Even so, the late 1850s and the 1860s proved to be an untypical interlude, an aberration. The decades after 1871 resemble those after 1815, with crises again being provoked by small states on the periphery of the continent while compromise and restraint characterized the diplomacy of the great powers. The latter had been unpleasantly reminded, by the bloodshed of the Commune in Paris, that the revolutionary hydra was not yet dead; and they were increasingly aware, as they became enmeshed in complex alliance obligations, of the potential extent of any conflict that was allowed to develop in Europe. It was only in the years after 1900 that some continental statesmen began to argue that the risks of war could be minimized and that war could solve problems which were otherwise insoluble. There was, moreover, amongst many German leaders a growing conviction that the cautious diplomacy of the post–1871 period had paid few dividends.

The Vienna states system, like the international orders which preceded and followed it, ultimately rested on the sanction of force. Yet the attitudes of the powers towards the use of force varied with circumstances. In general terms, for most of the nineteenth century, liberal opinion in England and France strongly condemned war as a crime against civilization; whereas in the military monarchies of central and eastern Europe war was always regarded as a noble activity, especially if it was for the defence of the sacred institution of monarchy against revolution. In particular instances, for example in the 1850s and 1860s, intellectuals in western and central Europe were prepared to justify war as an essential activity in the onward march of progress. But, on the whole, as far as the statesmen and diplomats of the nineteenth century were concerned, the use of force, both within the state and between states, was a necessary evil and the organization of war was an essential task of government. It was the only activity to which they gave their undivided attention and over which they sought exclusive control. The great powers issued threats of force with some frequency to each other and to small states. They were usually intended as an indication of the gravity with which a particular power viewed a crisis and the consequences which would follow if another power persisted in a line of policy of which it disapproved.

Throughout the period from 1815 to 1914 all the great powers, for many different reasons, regarded the prospect of a general European war with some apprehension. British governments believed that such a war would be long and expensive, the three eastern autocracies were convinced that it would probably result in the disintegration of the social order and provide their disaffected subject nationalities with an excellent opportunity for revolt. French governments before 1848 feared that a general war would inevitably see a revival of the four-power coalition against them or that it might provide the radical republicans with the ideal circumstances for a *coup*. Above all, before 1848 there was a general conviction amongst the great powers that a local conflict between two or more powers would probably degenerate into a general conflagration. This view derived from the conservative belief about the events of 1792: that revolutionary elements in France had deliberately dragged the European powers into war to imperil their social and political systems. The great dread of the social and political consequences of war acted as a powerful restraint on a ruling class which felt itself beleaguered and which was lacking in confidence. The revolutions of 1848 and the Crimean War both proved that wars could be localized and temporarily dispelled the fear of social collapse. Yet even then the dread of a general war remained strong. Those powers which in the 1850s and 1860s embarked on wars of territorial gain strove desperately to keep the wars localized, lest they be robbed of the fruits of victory.

The fall of the Second Empire and the bloody events of the Commune – both consequences of the war of 1870 – revived apprehensions about even localized war as the harbinger of revolution, at least in Europe east of the Rhine; and it was not long before doctrines of conservative solidarity reminiscent of the neo-Holy Alliance reappeared in the Three Emperors' League and the Three Emperors' Alliance. Further afield, the Central Powers' diplomatic links with Italy and Spain in the 1880s were conscious attempts to bolster up the monarchies in Rome and Madrid against 'the dangerous idea of a republican brotherhood of Latin races' centred on France. Franz Joseph's ambassador in St Petersburg was convinced that there was in Europe 'a great revolutionary subversive party just waiting for the crash and for the great conservative powers to weaken and exhaust each other' in war; and as late as 1913 Bercthold was warning the German emperor of the dangers that would assail the Central Powers if revolution broke out in Russia as a result of war. By the early twentieth century, however, the exponents of conservative solidarity had shifted their ground and were beginning to argue, as Bismarck had done in the 1860s, that the problem of defending the social and political order was one which each state must solve for itself and in its own way. This was certainly the view in Berlin and St Petersburg. In July 1914 even conservatives in Vienna were opting for violent solutions to local problems, albeit as a counsel of despair.

As a rule, however, nineteenth-century governments were content to seek their salvation in diplomacy. In 1815 the common obligation to uphold the treaty structure of Europe was given great emphasis by the victorious allies, who regarded the General Act of the Congress of Vienna as the foundation of the European territorial order. The British government came to hold an extremely legalistic attitude towards questions of treaty maintenance and treaty revision; and the eastern powers in the period from the revolutions of the early 1820s to the Crimean war were similarly disposed. There were specific reasons for this. The second Peace of Paris was, as far as the four victorious powers were concerned, the legal instrument by which France was contained. The allies' insistence on the sanctity of treaties was another means of emphasizing their determination to keep France within the limits imposed upon her in 1815. Secondly, each of the three victorious continental powers had made valuable territorial gains in 1814 and 1815, and these they were determined to retain. In fact, therefore, the four powers elevated their common interests into a matter of high principle. The eastern powers also attempted to use the binding character of treaties as a means of preventing any change of which they disapproved, whereas the British, who cared less for the maintenance of the existing political order and were prepared to contemplate limited reforms, argued that treaties could be revised with the consent of all the contracting parties: this was the basis of Palmerston's policy towards Belgium in 1830 and towards Italy in 1848. In the 1860s British governments went even further, arguing that treaties could be revised in the name of justice and humanity – it was on this basis that Britain recognized the new kingdom of Italy. But this new British formula was only selectively applied. Gladstone's attempt to revive it during the Near Eastern crisis of the late 1870s was only partially successful. Disraeli cared much more for the principle of contractual obligations.

The monarchs of the autocratic monarchies regarded treaties, particularly those which they had concluded with each other, as binding personal commitments which their honour and their duty towards God decreed that they must uphold. It was considerations of this sort that guided Nicholas I's approach to foreign policy. The French, by contrast, throughout the period from 1815 to 1870 consistently maintained that the treaties of 1815, which they condemned in their entirety, were an intolerable burden which they could not be expected long to tolerate. They claimed that France was not the only victim of the ambition and lust for conquest of the allies: the peoples of Italy, Poland and Belgium had also been sacrificed. Yet despite this general attack on the treaty structure, French governments found it convenient to pay lip service to the doctrine that the revision of treaties required the consent of the contracting parties: on three separate occasions between 1836 and 1863 French governments called for a congress of the powers to revise the Vienna settlement. In the late 1850s and 1860s the doctrine of treaty maintenance was either completely disregarded or cynically manipulated by those powers that sought treaty revision. Yet as soon as a state had made territorial gains, it sought to retain them by the revival of the principle of the binding character of treaties.

This was perhaps just one other respect in which 1871 marked the end of an interlude of upheaval and the return of the great powers to something resembling consensus. The London Protocol of March 1871, signed by all six powers, explicitly reaffirmed that treaties could not be legally altered without the consent of all the signatories – a principle that was successfully upheld when Russia had to submit the Treaty of San Stefano to the scrutiny of the Congress of Berlin in 1878; and one that proved a useful weapon in the hands of Austria-Hungary's opponents during the Bosnian crisis of 1908–9. Although Bismarck himself liked to say that treaties only had value so long as they suited the real interests of the contracting parties, in practice he had become the chief upholder of a European states system embodying the *status quo* of the Treaty of Frankfurt. As this was acceptable to all except France and as she alone was impotent to change matters, the European states system based on the Treaties of Frankfurt and Berlin, like that based on the Treaty of Vienna, in effect represented a tacit coalition against France. So long as France found no ally, the system was stable.

One of the most important elements in European diplomacy in the nineteenth century was the network of dynastic links, not only between the great powers, but also between them and the small states of Europe. Their effects were felt in several different ways. Firstly, there were the close family ties and personal friendships of the sovereigns of the great powers. The frequent meetings between the three autocratic monarchs were occasions for much diplomatic business to be conducted. No decade passed between 1815 and 1914 without at least one such meeting. The close family ties between the dynasties of Russia and Prussia were a significant factor within the alignment of the eastern powers. Both Alexander I and Nicholas I felt more closely attached to the Prussians than to the Austrians, and it was a matter of great regret to Nicholas that the Habsburgs refused for religious reasons to marry into the Russian imperial family. In the 1840s Nicholas I paid a state visit to Queen Victoria in order to consolidate the good relations he had established with the British during the Near Eastern crisis of 1839–40. Similarly Queen Victoria established close personal relations with both Louis Philippe and Napoleon III. The complex agreements on the Spanish Marriages were concluded during private visits between Queen Victoria and Louis Philippe. The affection felt by William I for his nephew, Alexander II, was a serious obstacle in the way of Bismarck's concluding the alliance with Austria–Hungary in 1879; just as the antipathy felt by Alexander III for William II helped to undermine the Reinsurance Treaty. Moreover the ill feeling prevailing between William II and Edward VII did nothing for Anglo-German relations after the turn of the century.

Secondly, there was throughout the period a sort of monarchical 'trades unionism', rooted in the belief that monarchs must stand together or they would fall together. Edward VII, for example, was largely instrumental in delaying until 1906 British recognition of the regicide government established in Serbia in 1903; and George V's private secretary was sternly reminding the foreign office, as late as 1912, of the necessity 'in present revolutionary times for sovereigns to hold together. . . . We made too much of the French republic.' The German government, certainly, was gambling on feelings of monarchical solidarity in St Petersburg when they advised the Austrians to strike quickly at Serbia after the Sarajevo assassinations. Earlier in the period, too, a Prussian monarch had written, when concluding an anti-revolutionary alliance with Austria in 1854: 'I shall not allow Austria . . . to be attacked by the Revolution without drawing the sword on her behalf, and this from pure love of Prussia, from self-preservation.' The propaganda of French republicans, who called for a 'war of the peoples of Europe against the kings of Europe', and the widespread belief of conservatives in the existence of a general revolutionary conspiracy, did much to foster such attitudes. The activities of the Second International (established in 1889) and a spate of anarchist assassinations of crowned heads in the decades around the turn of the century sustained these feelings into the twentieth century.

Thirdly, it was widely accepted that a dispute between two states could be settled by the mediation of a third sovereign. The Austrian emperor successfully solved a territorial dispute between the dukes of Parma and Tuscany in the 1840s, and in 1850 Nicholas I strongly urged the Austrians and the Prussians to compose their differences at Olmütz. In the later nineteenth century this practice was less in evidence. It was the republican President Roosevelt who mediated peace between the emperors of Russia and Japan in 1905. Nevertheless, the Hague Peace Conferences of 1899 and 1907 were summoned in response to the personal wish of the Tsar; and the emperor of Austria was instrumental in persuading the Germans to submit to arbitration the potentially explosive Casablanca dispute with France in 1909.

Lastly, the great powers used dynastic alliances to cement their political agreements and symbolize their co-operation. The alliance of France and Piedmont in 1859 for war against Austria included a marriage compact between a daughter of Victor Emmanuel and a cousin of Napoleon III. Neither Louis Philippe nor Napoleon III, who had gained their thrones by revolution, could secure marriage alliances with the ruling families of the other great powers; and they felt themselves outcasts. The monarchs of the other great powers did little to dispel these feelings. The animosity felt by Nicholas I towards both these monarchs affected Franco–Russian relations quite decisively. The Treaty of Björkö, signed on the occasion of an emotional meeting between William II and his cousin the Tsar in 1905, behind the backs of and contrary to the wishes of their foreign ministers, was an extreme and, not surprisingly, abortive example of dynastic solidarity. Nevertheless William was more successful in his approaches to his Russian cousin at Potsdam in 1910, a move of which his government approved. The dynastic links between the Hohenzollerns in Berlin and Bucharest were an important factor in Germany's Near Eastern policy throughout the reign of King Carol, from 1866 to 1914: the fact that his heir was married to an English princess was the source of helpless gloom and resignation in Berlin. In the last resort, however, close family ties and monarchical solidarity were never allowed to stand in the way of a determined pursuit of state interests. There was undoubted truth in the remark made by Gorchakov in 1870: 'We are no longer in an epoch where family ties can lead to such great results as those of an alliance.' Moreover it must be remembered that in the course of the nineteenth century more monarchs lost their thrones as a consequence of the ambitions of fellow monarchs than as a result of revolution.

In the assumptions of their foreign policies and in their analyses of international relations the great powers differed significantly. The concept of the balance of power was hardly ever used except by British governments. The continental powers certainly did not consciously seek to uphold it. In the period before 1848 the three autocratic monarchies were determined that preponderant strength should be on the side of the forces of order and on the side of the coalition against France. The dominant concept of their foreign policies was 'security' against the great dangers that confronted them. In the 1880s and 1890s the maintenance of peace and the *status quo* depended on a preponderance of power centred on a conservative German empire and its associates, rather than on any genuine balance of power. Even in the era of two balanced blocs after 1907 it may be argued that behind Britain's devotion to the idea of the balance of power lay the harsh reality of a desperate need to stand well with France and Russia as much as any fear of Germany. Indeed, in so far as the continental states took the British theory of the balance of power into account, it had long been their custom to point to its inconsistency. Both the French and the Russians had insisted after 1815 that the aim of the British government was to create a military deadlock on the continent (which they then called a balance), while at the same time they jealously guarded their own naval hegemony. In fact, therefore, the association of the idea of the balance of power with British policy served to discredit it in the opinion of many continental statesmen. It was regarded as a justification for opportunism at a time when the conservative powers felt that a rigid adherence to fixed principles and loyalty to war-time allies were the surest means of maintaining the *status quo*.

In the 1850s and 1860s all the continental states, with the exception of Austria which took refuge in her treaty rights, began to justify the need for treaty revision and territorial expansion in terms either of the existence of unnatural coalitions against them or of national self-determination. In fact, therefore, both the Russians and the Prussians adopted after the Crimean War the very arguments which before the war they had so strongly opposed. The Russians adopted the French argument, that the humiliating treaty of 1856 had been imposed upon them by an 'unnatural coalition' which could not survive; the Prussians borrowed and modified the revolutionary doctrine that the state must fulfil the national aspirations of the German people. In the late 1860s the French abandoned the principle of national self-determination which they had earlier championed, and began to base their foreign policy on the old eighteenth-century notion of compensation: if other powers gained territory, then so must France. These two decades of aggressive policies, of hastily devised arguments for diplomatic expediency and short-term alliances for precise offensive objectives proved no more than an interlude. By the 1870s most governments – except the French – re-affirmed their commitment to the *status quo*. The British did not believe that the great changes of the 1860s rendered obsolete their attachment to the balance of power. For the most part, they had regarded it as directed against the expansion of France and Russia. There were many British statesmen who were convinced that the emergence of a large Germany strengthened a balance which had been weakened by the restless policies of Nicholas I in the Near East and Napoleon III in Italy and on the Rhine.

Russia and Austria-Hungary returned to the principles of the neo–Holy Alliance as early as 1873, partly out of mistrust of Germany. When the latter power also declared for the *status quo* the stage was set for a whole series of conservative agreements in the 1870s and 1880s. These were intended like those of the period 1815–54 to be more or less permanent and to safeguard the lasting interests of the signatories in maintaining stability and order. Once again France was treated as the pariah and Great Britain was loosely linked to some of her erstwhile allies of the Fourth Coalition. It was only when Germany became a source of anxiety to her neighbours in the 1890s, that a counter-system of alliances developed. All the alliances concluded by the great powers in the years after 1879 with the exception of the Anglo-Japanese alliance of 1902 were strictly defensive – whatever suspicious observers may have thought. These alliances were intended to represent certain vital interests; and it was the clash of these interests which ultimately produced a European war in 1914. Nevertheless the curious fact remains that not one of the agreements concluded in the previous forty years came into operation to transform the Austro-Serbian conflict into a general war.

In the century after the Congress of Vienna the foreign policies of the great powers were formulated and executed by a very small number of men. In 1815 only in England and France was there anything like a public and informed discussion of foreign policy. Yet by the 1860s even the Russian government was alive to the necessity of presenting a clear picture of its foreign policy to educated opinion, and in Austria and Prussia the press commented regularly on foreign affairs. By the time of the Franco-Prussian war all the great powers had adopted the practice of using newspapers as a means of influencing and regulating public opinion on international affairs. In central and eastern Europe the conduct of policy remained for the most part under the tight control of the sovereigns and their principal advisers. A report on the Russian foreign ministry in the 1830s described it as 'merely the faithful executor of the intentions of the Tsar'. It was only in England and France that the principle of ministerial control of foreign policy was properly established. In France this was abandoned under the Second Empire, and Napoleon III exercised as much personal control over the making of foreign policy as did Alexander II of Russia. After the 1905 revolution, liberal and Pan-Slav elements were able to exercise pressure – sometimes effectively – on the Russian government through the Duma and the press. In constitutional Austria, as late as 1911, the emperor could declare that the foreign minister was simply '*Mein Minister*' carrying out '*Meine Politik*', and neither the Austrian nor the Hungarian parliament ever acquired a voice in the making of foreign policy.

Many foreign ministers retained their positions for decades. Metternich directed Austrian policy from 1809 to 1848 and Nesselrode served as Russian foreign minister from 1816 to 1856. His successor, Gorchakov, occupied the post for twenty-five years. Palmerston exercised a decisive influence over British foreign policy either as foreign secretary or as prime minister for almost a quarter of a century between 1830 and 1865, just as Salisbury did in the last quarter of the century. The foreign ministries of the powers were extremely small organizations, and as a rule ministers did not expect the permanent officials to provide them with political advice. For the most part they were clerks and copyists who performed menial tasks. The emergence of permanent official advisers on foreign policy was everywhere a development of the late nineteenth century. The aristocratic and landowning background of most nineteenth-century diplomats and their shared cultural and social assumptions did much to establish and maintain a unity of outlook and common code of ethics amongst the diplomatic corps in the capitals of the great powers. Many diplomats, like foreign ministers, remained at their posts for decades: Barons Brunnow and Bunsen were respectively Russian and Prussian ambassadors in London from the 1830s to the late 1850s; Baron Calice represented Austria-Hungary at Constantinople from 1880 to 1906, and his successor, Markgraf Pallavicini from 1906 to 1918. The diplomats whom the great powers accredited to each other were always respected figures in the social and political life of the European capitals: Count Mensdorff, Austro-Hungarian ambassador at London from 1904 to 1914 was on intimate terms with his 'cousins' King George V and King Ferdinand of Bulgaria. In 1848 the provisional government in France decided to send prominent republicans as its envoys abroad, but Lamartine soon realized that this was a mistake and replaced them with more socially acceptable men. The diplomatic service of the Third Republic could also find use for a count or an admiral in posts like St Petersburg. Diplomacy was not regarded in the nineteenth century as a profession separate from politics. Many of the leading statesmen of Europe had at some stage of their careers been diplomats, Guizot, Clarendon, Bismarck and Bülow being notable examples. Ambassadors and envoys at the courts of the great powers certainly played an important part in the settlement of disputes, particularly in conference diplomacy. Their role was, however, usually restricted to the arrangement of details. It was this and the drafting of treaties that constituted what contemporaries regarded as 'the art of diplomacy'.

The steady improvement in communications that occurred in the nineteenth century, largely as a consequence of steamships, railways and the telegraph, did not in fact greatly alter the responsibilities of diplomats, at least as far as Europe was concerned. Major decisions about the relations of the great powers had always been taken at the highest level, although diplomats outside Europe were sometimes in a position to interpret more widely the political instructions they received from their governments. The main effect of better communications was to quicken the pace of diplomacy. Most of the great-power crises of the pre-Crimean War period lasted at least several months, and some for more than a year. It took the British and the Russians nearly nine months to reach agreement in 1839–40 on the settlement of the Egyptian-Turkish dispute. This was partly because it required at least eleven days for dispatches to be exchanged between the British and Russian capitals. It was not uncommon for minor diplomatic problems to drag on for several years, and in fact to be buried in volumes of correspondence. Ottoman governments were particularly prone to use this method when harassed by the great powers – witness their largely successful rearguard actions against the attempts of the powers to introduce reforms in Macedonia and Armenia in the late nineteenth and early twentieth centuries. In the post-Crimean War period crises were shorter and frequently accompanied by the exchange of recriminations between governments in newspapers and in parliamentary assemblies. There was much more emphasis on domestic propaganda and on casting opponents in the role of the aggressor: in 1914 each of the belligerent governments was able to persuade its subjects that it was fighting a defensive war. All realized that, in war, the mobilization of domestic resources, human as well as material, was vital: speed and surprise were at a premium, but the role of communications in sustaining the war effort and boosting morale was no less essential. The peace terms, too, which followed the great wars of the mid nineteenth century, were also quickly negotiated: both the Truce of Villafranca, which ended the war in northern Italy in 1859, and the preliminary Peace of Nikolsburg after the Austro-Prussian war of 1866, were negotiated in less than three weeks. This was possible because of improved communications, and urgently necessary if the intervention of other powers were to be prevented. But these were changes of form rather than of substance. Even in the decades after the Treaty of Frankfurt, despite the increasing prevalence of professional advisers in the foreign ministries of the great powers, the old *esprit de corps* and the cosmopolitan outlook of the diplomats, and the common 'unspoken assumptions' of the decision-makers about the nature and purpose of the European states system, survived. In fact, the European states system was still essentially that of the Congress of Vienna on the very eve of the First World War.

CHAPTER TWO

The creation and the evolution of a new order 1815–1830

The European states system created in 1814 and 1815 and thereafter described as the Vienna system was defined in the negative. It was an explicit rejection of the hegemony of one power, of constant warfare and of revolution. These were identified as the elements of disorder in European society. Fear of these forces of destruction was shared by the leading statesmen of Austria, Great Britain, Prussia and Russia long before these powers came together in the fourth and final coalition against France in 1813. When it was established the allies regarded it as more than a military alliance for the defeat of France. They believed that it stood for the law of nations against the will of a conqueror; that it was as much concerned with re-establishing order within states as order between states; and that it enjoyed the right of protection over the small states of Europe. It was the British and the Russians who were the most anxious to give the alliance against Napoleon a sense of moral purpose. It was in the abortive Anglo-Russian alliance negotiations of 1805 that this question was first discussed: then Alexander I had declared that England and Russia were the only two powers capable of liberating Europe from Napoleon and creating a new international order based on binding treaties and acknowledged rights. This was indeed an accurate assessment. The next half-century in international relations was dominated by these two powers. It was they who brought the coalition into existence and held it together; they who contributed most to the destruction of the Napoleonic empire; they who shaped the essential features of the peace settlement; and it was around them that the other great powers grouped in the four decades from the Congress of Vienna to the Crimean War. Equally it was only in the period after 1856 when the British and the Russians, for a variety of reasons, stood aside that the other powers could demolish the international system which they had created and sustained.

It was almost a year after the French invasion of Russia in 1812 that the Fourth Coalition emerged in the form in which it was to triumph over Napoleon. It was the Russians who began the new offensive in the east. Alexander I and his military advisers decided to pursue the retreating Grand Army and push it back as far west as possible. When the Russians began the struggle they had no allies. Their initial successes against the French brought the Prussians into the war in February 1813 following the Treaty of Kalisch. The Prussians believed that an alliance with Russia against France was the only means of recovering their position as a great power in Germany, a position which Napoleon had effectively denied them. The Austrians, who were invited to join the alliance, found the decision more difficult: in the event of victory over Napoleon they would certainly increase and consolidate their power in central Europe; in the event of defeat they feared that they would suffer further losses and cease to be a great power. In June 1813 Great Britain signed treaties of alliance with Prussia and Russia at Reichenbach. This linked the British offensive in the west which was already well under way in the Iberian Peninsula, where Wellington and his army had put the French on the retreat, with the new offensive in the east. The British could not fight the war in eastern Europe, but they could and did pay for it. The new three-power alliance and a series of reverses for the French army in May altered the position of the Austrians. They could no longer afford to remain neutral. Metternich, the Austrian foreign minister, offered to end the war by armed mediation; this was intended to destroy the French empire in central Europe but not the power of France in the west. In this way the Austrians hoped to balance the antagonisms of their two great rivals, France and Russia. When mediation failed, the Austrians had no alternative but to decide which power they feared most, France or Russia. The British entry into the alliance tipped the scales in favour of working with Russia to restrain France. In a four-power alliance Metternich believed that he could rely on the British to support Austria's recovery in central Europe. The Austrians entered the war in August 1813; in mid October the allies destroyed Napoleon's position in Germany at the battle of Leipzig. By December he was forced to retreat into France itself. The French empire was in ruins; Alexander I, and not Napoleon, was the effective master of Europe from the Vistula to the Rhine. The Russian army, subsidized by British gold, had by the end of 1813 emerged as one of the dominant forces in European politics. It was to remain so for the next forty years.

Military success brought the coalition to the verge of diplomatic collapse. It was the Austrians and the Russians who were the most suspicious of one another and who came into conflict over two quite fundamental problems: the disposal of Polish territory after the war, and the conduct of the war in the west. The future of Poland was the more intractable Austro-Russian dispute. Alexander I wanted as much Polish territory as he could get, and for this reason he posed as the liberator of Poland. He did not want an independent Poland; he sought a large Poland under Russian control – his aim was to gain Polish territory which Prussia and Austria had formerly possessed. The Prussians were quite willing to agree to this as long as they were adequately compensated elsewhere; but in Vienna Russia's Polish ambitions aroused strong misgivings. The Austrians feared for themselves, not for the Poles: they believed that Austria would be as threatened in the future by the extension of Russian power in eastern Europe as it had been in the past by French expansion in the west. Metternich wanted security for Austria, not the exchange of one overwhelming menace for another. In the short term the two allies could find no solution to this problem; the most they could do was to agree to postpone their differences and this underlying conflict affected Austria's attitude to the conduct of the war itself. She feared the diplomatic consequences of the Russian military advance, and therefore held it up in the hope of forcing concessions out of her ally. In January 1814, however, inter-allied negotiations entered a new phase when Castlereagh, the British foreign secretary, arrived at the military headquarters. He changed the emphasis from conflict in the east to a search for an agreement in the west. This was a logical step; it was the only hope of saving the alliance from disintegration, and whereas eastern Europe had been liberated Napoleon still refused to accept defeat in the west and was attempting to organize a new offensive. Moreover, for Great Britain the most pressing objective was the destruction of French power and the containment of France. Castlereagh saw more clearly than Metternich that Russia's pretensions would have to remain unchecked until those of Napoleon had been destroyed. This was his most important contribution to allied diplomacy in the crucial period from January to May 1814. It enabled him to achieve some agreement with his allies on the two issues of paramount importance to Great Britain, a final offensive against Napoleon and the peace terms to be imposed on France.

In February 1814 the allies made a final offer to Napoleon. They proposed that France should be confined within the borders of 1792. This offer, known as the 'Troyes basis' assumed that Napoleon would remain the ruler of France after the war. The purpose of the war was still to contain France, not to depose Napoleon. Napoleon instructed his representatives to prolong the negotiations in the hope that either the military situation would change or the coalition would begin to disintegrate. This desperate gamble revealed his failing grasp of reality. His refusal to treat these negotiations seriously sealed his fate; it turned the allies against him and undermined his position in France. In Paris a group of important politicians, led by Talleyrand, concluded that the emperor himself was now the only obstacle to an honourable peace; and in March the allies too resolved that they would no longer negotiate with Napoleon or any member of his family. They realized that Napoleon would never regard a peace settlement as more than a temporary truce. What the allies wanted was a lasting peace with France.

On 9 March 1814 the four allies signed the Treaty of Chaumont. They soon came to recognize it as the keystone of the new order in Europe. Between 1814 and 1818 they renewed it on four separate occasions, Wellington proudly claimed that by this treaty the four powers assumed the right of protection over the peace of Europe. This meant no more than that the allies intended it to become a permanent league for the containment of France. This was its real significance. The treaty established precise conditions for the last phase of the war effort. Each of the allies was to provide 150,000 men, and Great Britain agreed to pay an additional subsidy of £5 million for the conduct of the war in 1814. For the first time since the War of the Spanish Succession the British were making a massive military as well as financial commitment to a war in Europe. The power which Castlereagh exercised in the counsels of the allies in 1814 and 1815 was based as much upon Britain's military contribution to the war as upon her financial strength. Secret articles annexed to the treaty established the main features of the postwar settlement in the west: the containment of France within the borders of 1792, the union of the former Austrian Netherlands with Holland, and the creation of a large block of Prussian territory on the east bank of the Rhine. After this agreement, the allies renewed the military offensive. The Russians had for some time argued that Paris should be the goal of the allied armies. With their capital occupied by their enemies, the French would be forced to accept whatever terms the allies were disposed to offer to them. This aim was quickly realized. At the end of March 1814 the allied forces, with Alexander I at their head, entered the French capital. The war, to all intents and purposes, was over. The appointment of a Russian general in April 1814 as military governor of Paris symbolized the total collapse of Bonapartism and the complete defeat of France. The way was now clear for the reconstruction of the European territorial order.

The new states system in Europe was long in the making. The

negotiations lasted from April 1814 until November 1815. There was a short gap from July to November 1814 when the allied leaders dispersed to attend to their domestic affairs, but otherwise they were in almost continuous negotiation. The new territorial order was made in three distinct stages. The first Peace of Paris of May 1814, with its secret articles, amounted to a western settlement. At the Congress of Vienna between November 1814 and March 1815 the allies redrew the frontiers of eastern and central Europe. Finally, after the collapse of Napoleon's attempted comeback and his defeat at Waterloo, the allies modified the settlement with France in the second Peace of Paris of November 1815. In April 1814 the Prussians suggested that the allies should settle all the outstanding territorial questions at the same time. This was rejected by the other three powers because they feared that it would result in the collapse of the alliance and would enable France to exploit their differences to secure more favourable peace terms. Castlereagh was determined that Austro-Russian differences in eastern Europe should not postpone or endanger the containment of France in the west, and the Russians themselves were convinced that they would be better placed to press their own claims after France was chastened and confined. The two major territorial problems raised by the defeat of Napoleon – the containment of France and the partition of Poland – were kept separate. To some extent this worked to the disadvantage of the Russians, because the British government had already achieved its major objectives before it opposed those of Russia in the east. On the other hand, the Russian demands on Poland owed their force to the fact that the country was already occupied by the Russian army. This fact would have determined the outcome of the negotiations on Poland whenever they took place.

The restoration of the Bourbons was inevitable once the allies decided to depose Napoleon. The really important question was what form it would take. The Charter of 1814 by which Louis XVIII recovered the throne of his ancestors established a constitutional monarchy not dissimilar to that which then existed in England. From the allied point of view the old dynasty and the new constitution were the best they could hope for. The main emphasis of the Peace of Paris (30 May 1814), however, was on the containment of France; little reliance was placed on the good intentions of its new rulers. The allies imposed upon France a revised version of the 'Troyes basis'; France was confined within the borders of 1792. The French retained the ancient conquests of Richelieu, Mazarin and Louis XIV but lost most of those of the Revolution and Napoleon. The Bourbons could not resent the loss of what they had never possessed. Most of the colonies lost to Great

Britain in the colonial wars of the 1790s were restored except Tobago, Mauritius and a few other small islands. Many contemporaries were astonished at the moderation shown by the allies. The real damage to French power in western Europe in May 1814 was, however, concealed in separate articles annexed to the main treaty. In the main text of the treaty France was left a great power; in the annexes she was deprived of some of the most important attributes of great power status. She was denied influence over her small neighbours, secure lines of defence for her capital city and frontiers which she could easily dominate. In fact, France was surrounded by a series of hostile buffer states; containment and not dismemberment was the keynote of the western settlement. Austria controlled northern Italy, adding Venetia to Lombardy; the kingdom of Piedmont was strengthened by the acquisition of Genoa and linked to Austria by a treaty of defence. The southern Netherlands were united with Holland, and in June 1814 the British agreed to pay £2 million towards the cost of erecting barrier fortresses along the Franco-Dutch border. Prussia received large tracts of territory in the Rhineland, and it was assumed that she would maintain a large part of her army in these new provinces. Thus the three frontiers which French armies had regularly crossed in the eighteenth century were strengthened against French aggression. The French soon realized the extent of the change, and bitterly condemned the terms imposed upon them. It was their exclusion from their traditional areas of influence which they resented as much as the loss of the territory they had briefly possessed under Napoleon.

The Congress of Vienna (Oct. 1814–June 1815), held forty-one sittings before the General Act of the Congress was signed. A great deal of its work was done in specialist committees; the principal representatives of the great powers concentrated on the major problems of territorial redistribution. At the outset the four allies of Chaumont made two important procedural decisions which vitally affected the deliberations of the congress. First, they included France in their discussions. Whereas the Peace of Paris was negotiated between the four allies, the eastern settlement was the work of the five great powers. Second, the small states who had joined the alliance against Napoleon were excluded from the meetings of the big five. This was a clear reflection of the belief that great powers had special rights and obligations and that they alone could guarantee the security of the new order. Even within the ranks of the great powers there was a marked sense of hierarchy: the Russians expected the Prussians to follow their lead, and the British acted in a similar way towards the Austrians. France could and did attempt to join one or other of these informal combinations within the alliance, but when Talleyrand, the French representative at Vienna, tried to act independently the four allies closed ranks against him.

Between November 1814 and January 1815 the proceedings of the congress were dominated by the Polish-Saxon issue. The Russians proposed that they should take virtually the whole of Poland, including Prussia's former Polish territories, and that Prussia should be compensated by the acquisition of Saxony. The Prussians were ready to fall in with this plan because they preferred German to Polish territory, and because the Prussian king was guided by a deep sense of loyalty to Alexander I, whom he regarded as the saviour of his kingdom. The Austrians put forward three principal objections to this plan: the acquisition of so much of Poland would immeasurably strengthen Russia and enable her completely to dominate eastern Europe; it would make Austria's Polish province of Galicia dangerously vulnerable to both political and military pressure from Russia; Prussia would acquire a commanding position in north Germany which would enable her to challenge Austria's traditional leadership of the German states. Castlereagh supported these objections because he feared that the Russian proposals would wreck his plan for an independent central Europe, able to resist aggression from both east and west. He called this the balance of power; what he really meant was a Europe shaped to safeguard British interests which were the containment of France and Russia and the maintenance of peace. Talleyrand supported the British and the Austrians largely because he saw the chance to divide the alliance permanently and thus enable France to break out of her isolation. Throughout December 1814 the two great-power alignments hardened over the Polish-Saxon question, especially after a British attempt to detach Prussia from Russia failed. In the first week of January 1815 Great Britain, France and Austria signed a secret defensive alliance ostensibly preparing for war, the contents of which were leaked to the Russians. In fact it was more of a final bid to force the Prussians to make concessions on Saxony. This they did a few days later. Castlereagh and Metternich then abandoned the French in order to reach an agreement with their two allies. In the compromise of January 1815 it was agreed that Prussia would get only two-fifths of Saxony, and Russia agreed to concede Polish territory to Prussia and Austria which together contained over a million inhabitants. The rest of Poland was to form an independent kingdom with a separate constitution, ruled over by the Russian emperor. By this agreement the Russians secured the lion's share of what Austria and Prussia had previously enjoyed after the partitions of 1792 and 1795. After the Russians it was the Austrians who gained most from the agreement; the principle of the partition of Poland between three powers was re-established and the reduction of Prussia's Saxon gains appeared to safeguard Austria's leadership of Germany. Castlereagh's chief consolation was that the alliance of the four powers had survived a major disagreement. He could not claim that Russia's power in eastern Europe had been effectively reduced because it rested on her military strength which was hardly affected by her renunciation of a little Polish territory. Moreover, Russian influence could only be excluded from central Europe if Austria and Prussia were prepared to co-operate with England against her and were content to rely on their combined military strength to keep Russia as well as France at bay. This remained an open question.

The central European arrangements made after the Napoleonic Wars proved to be the weakest feature of the new order. The weakness arose out of the fact that Austrian power was over-stretched. She was made into a buffer state defending the *status quo* against future French aggression from the west and Russian aggression from the east. This conception of Austria's role was Anglo–Austrian; the Austrians wanted to recover and consolidate their position in central Europe, but it was the British who decided that this must have some general purpose. It was Castlereagh rather than Metternich who made Austria into a European necessity. In the south Austria was strengthened by the recovery of Lombardy and the acquisition of Venetia. This, together with a complex network of treaties and dynastic links, gathered all the Italian states together under Austrian auspices. The dual purpose of these arrangements was to bring order to Italy and to keep the French out of the Italian peninsula. In Germany, Austria was placed at the head of the new confederation. This was intended to secure to Austria the co-operation of all the other German states, including Prussia, and to enable her to contain France on the Rhine and to keep Russia within her new limits in Poland. The onus of defending the new order against potential aggressors in the traditional areas of conflict was thus placed squarely on Austrian shoulders. She did not have the means to sustain this burden. Unlike Great Britain, she did not have a rich and developing economy; she was a backward agrarian state with poorly developed financial institutions. Unlike Russia, Austria did not have vast reserves of manpower from which to create a large army. The central problem of the Vienna states system was how to strengthen Austria to enable her to fulfil the tasks which had been imposed upon her. Castlereagh and Metternich tried to solve this question by leading the four-power alliance and using it to control both France and Russia. When this failed Metternich was forced to rely exclusively on Russia to keep the empire intact and defend the monarchy against the revolutionary threat from below and the French threat from the west. When this also failed Austria was vulnerable to her enemies.

In the work of the peacemakers there was a clear recognition of the dependence of order between states on the maintenance of order within states. They were all convinced that revolution was the scourge of their times. They were equally convinced that the forces of revolution were no respecters of frontiers; 'one revolution', declared Castlereagh, 'was made the means of giving birth to another'. Moreover, war between states fulfilled the purpose of revolutionaries because it exposed the social and political order to great dangers. Gentz, Metternich's principal adviser at the congress, was certainly right when he declared that the 'wider object' of the peacemakers was to contain the 'restlessness of the masses and the disorders of our time'. The problem which faced the representatives at Vienna after they had completed the territorial reconstruction of Europe was how to work for the maintenance of order in the future. In one respect the solution was simple. In 1815 each of the four allies regarded France as the principal source of danger to both peace and order; she was the home of revolution and the power least satisfied with the new territorial arrangements. The continued existence of the four-power alliance was therefore the best security against these dangers. Yet the maintenance of the alliance raised two further questions: first, the form it was to take; and second, in the aftermath of the disagreements between the allies at Vienna, which power, Great Britain or Russia, would dominate it. These two questions were never separated. Indeed, in the next decade the Anglo-Russian struggle for the leadership of the new Europe virtually came to dominate all other issues. In November 1815 the British and the Russians made different proposals for the continuation of the alliance. Castlereagh's Quadruple Alliance of November 1815, with its provision under Article VI for periodic meetings of the powers, was an attempt to provide a practical basis for co-operation. He clearly intended that within this arrangement England and Austria would have a special and dominant relationship which would enable them to control Russia as well as to contain France. On the problem of revolution, Castlereagh's approach was pragmatic; the powers could consider each problem as it arose. Alexander I's Holy Alliance was more widely based; it was open to all Christian monarchs, and it emphasized the need for monarchical solidarity against revolution and war. In part the vagueness of this alliance was a reflection of the fact that Alexander, unlike Castlereagh, had evolved no clear strategy with which to pursue Russian aims in the postwar world. When it became

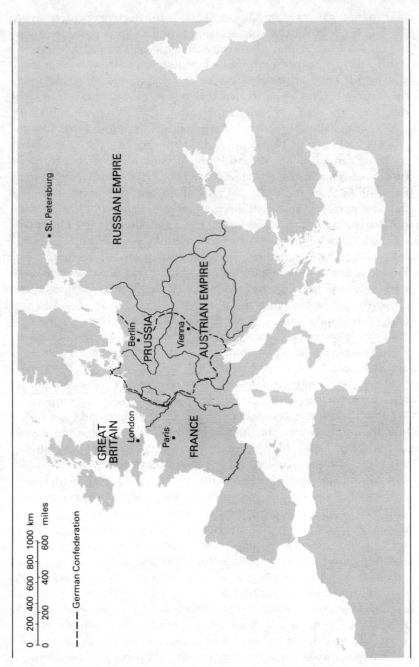

Map 1   Europe in 1815

clear to him that the Holy Alliance was not an effective counterpoise to the Quadruple Alliance he all but abandoned it and proceeded to contest British influence within the alliance which Castlereagh had created.

Napoleon's escape from Elba and the renewal of the war in the west, which ended with his final defeat at Waterloo in June 1815, had given the four powers a much needed unity of purpose after their disagreements on the Polish–Saxon question. In November 1815 the last act of the allies before they dispersed was to punish France for the crime of rallying to Napoleon and attempting to destroy the peace settlement of 1814. The second Peace of Paris was different from the first in three major respects. The borders of France were reduced from those of 1792 to those of 1790; an allied army of occupation was imposed upon her; and the Bourbon government, restored for a second time, was forced to pay an indemnity of 700 million francs. Thus in the second treaty the principle of containment was applied more harshly than in the first and France was made to pay for her war guilt. The French commissioners appointed to negotiate with the allies refused to sign the treaty claiming that France could never be reconciled to further territorial losses; but when the allies refused to yield Louis XVIII was obliged to appoint a new government which would accept the new treaty in its entirety. Confronted by the unity of the four allies, the French had retreated: a pattern often repeated in the years between 1815 and 1848.

After the Congress of Vienna it was apparent to contemporary observers that there was a new hierarchy of power in Europe. The hegemony of France was destroyed and Great Britain and Russia were now the dominant powers. Both were peripheral powers, with interests and possessions outside Europe. Beyond this, they had very little in common. Drawn together by their common antipathy to Napoleon, they were beginning after the defeat of France to drift apart largely because of their rival pretensions to the leadership of the new Europe. There was only one possible basis for continued co-operation between them: a determination to keep France in check. Great Britain owed her strength to her fast developing economy, her extensive overseas trade and her unrivalled naval power. In 1814 and 1815 Castlereagh had jealously guarded Great Britain's undisputed mastery of the high seas at the same time as he sought to contain the power of France and limit the expansion of Russia. It was this more than anything else which gave the Russians a community of interest with defeated France. Both resented what they regarded as Britain's double standards, maintaining her own naval hegemony while attempting to restrain the military power of her rivals. Great Britain's political system and her interest in developing and extending her world-wide commerce set her apart not only from Russia but also from her other allies. The British were not particular as to the means by which peace and order were maintained in Europe provided that they were maintained, as a necessary condition for their economic and commercial expansion, whereas the continental allies placed much greater emphasis on the maintenance of existing political and social structures. There was therefore a fundamental difference of priorities between the British and their continental allies. Moreover, in the decades after Waterloo, there was an increasing distrust in Europe of British commercial policy. It was generally regarded as aggressive, and the British government was suspected of willingness to sacrifice political principles for commercial expediency.

Alexander I was the autocratic ruler of a vast and backward state which maintained the institution of serfdom in an almost medieval form. Russia owed her power to her huge army. In 1813 and 1814 the Russian army had marched across Europe to the astonishment of most contemporaries. The memory of the invincible Russian army and the belief that in Russia there was an almost limitless reserve of manpower created a fear of Russian power which was not destroyed until the Crimean War. It obsessed western statesmen and diplomats, and entirely coloured their attitude towards Russia. Some of them regarded Russia as a state which existed for the sole purpose of making war. In Europe England and Russia competed for diplomatic preponderance, for prestige and the allegiance of the other great powers. It was only in the Near East that there was a direct clash of interests between them. The Ottoman Empire in south-eastern Europe, the Near East and North Africa was untouched by the peacemakers; they had not attempted to reconcile their potential clash of interests in these areas. Yet in the history of the Vienna states system Near Eastern problems played as great a part in the relations of the powers as European issues. Until the Crimean War Anglo-Russian relations revolved around three questions: rivalry in Europe, a common interest in the containment of France, and a conflict of interest in the Near East. It was only when the two powers were able to cope with these problems that the 1815 order was secure.

Although both Austria and Prussia recovered their positions as the leading great powers in central Europe, and indeed increased their possessions, neither power felt itself to be completely independent and secure. The Prussians feared a French attack across the Rhine, which they were convinced they could not face without Austrian and Russian support. In the short term the Prussians felt that their new responsibilities in the Rhineland weakened rather than strengthened them. The king and his ministers were acutely conscious of the fact that they owed their recovery to the coalition, and in particular to Russia. In the years after Vienna the Prussian government posed only one question about its foreign policy: which power should it look to for support? In practice Prussian policy was torn in two directions: a strong sense of the importance of dynastic connections inclined the Prussians towards Russia (the two ruling families were closely connected), but an equally strong feeling of German solidarity drew them towards Austria. The Prussians were therefore always energetic advocates of an Austro–Russian understanding directed against France. This was their ideal alignment. In the decades after Waterloo Metternich feared France and Russia equally; the diplomatic combination he feared most was a Franco–Russian *rapprochement,* because this would expose the weakness of Austria and, he assumed, would eventually result in a direct attack upon her. Although it was natural for Metternich to gravitate towards England for support against both France and Russia, this had the disadvantage of pushing the Russians towards the French. Metternich's ideal was close relations with England combined with good relations with Russia. Together the three powers could co-operate for the containment of France. This was a position he was only rarely to achieve. For most of his career as a diplomatist Metternich had to content himself with second best. It was internal problems which forced Metternich to change his policy. By the early 1820s Austria faced a third and new threat: revolution. The emergence of this threat, which Metternich regarded as the most dangerous of the three, resulted in the transfer of Austria's diplomatic dependence from England to Russia. This was a more logical foreign policy. Russia, with her vast military power, could guarantee Austria against France and the revolution. Moreover, Metternich believed that he could always rely on Great Britain to oppose Russia in the Near East without previous concert with Austria. The constant search by Prussia and Austria for support, for either implicit or explicit guarantees against their enemies, was an admission of their low rank in the hierarchy of the great powers. On questions of general European interest they willingly submitted themselves to their more powerful allies.

In the last resort each of the four allies feared France more than they feared each other. The French feared the continued existence of the coalition against them and their consequent isolation above all else. This balance of fear was for decades the great stabilizing factor in the Vienna states system. The French realized that they could not regain their complete independence until the allied army of occupation was removed from French soil, and until the coalition against them had begun to disintegrate. French governments also recognized that they could not attempt to undo the 1815 settlement until there was another power equally interested in the same task. The basic aim of French foreign policy was to find a revisionist ally. This in itself was an admission of decline. Napoleon had defied the rest of Europe; his successors did not think that they were able to do so. This was an accurate assessment of the new position in which France was placed. Yet she remained a formidable power, certainly stronger than either Austria or Prussia. Like Russia she had a large and powerful army, although under the Restoration and July Monarchies it was considerably smaller than it had been under the Empire. Like Great Britain she had a naval tradition and overseas commercial interests. Even if in 1815 she did not have a large navy, she had the financial resources and the dockyards with which to build one. Until the 1850s her economy was growing at a faster rate than that of the other continental powers, and Russia was the only great power with a larger population. The problem of French foreign policy was how to create the conditions that would enable her to use this strength. While the coalition against her existed, France was forced into playing the same role as Austria and Prussia; she had to attach herself to either England or Russia. Unlike the two German powers, however, France sought an alignment not for security but to break out of isolation and to begin to destroy the Vienna settlement. The ultimate aim of French foreign policy was to regain the leadership of Europe which she had lost to England and Russia in 1815.

In the decade after the Congress of Vienna the relations of the great powers were dominated by five major problems. From the outset the Anglo-Russian struggle for the leadership of the alliance was the dominant issue. This was no more than the extension into the postwar world of a conflict which had emerged at the congress itself. It was as much a struggle for prestige as it was a clash of real national interest. Secondly, the question of who was to lead the alliance was clearly linked to the debate about the nature and purpose of the alliance. Should it be permanently restricted to the four victorious allies, or should it be extended to include France? Was the alliance intended to be no more than the framework within which the allies consulted each other on common problems, or should the allies use the alliance as the means to establish principles for common action and as the ultimate sanction for action itself? This was never an abstract debate. It was always discussed in the light of the third major problem: the continued existence of the revolutionary spirit in Europe and the many insurrections that took place in small states. By the early 1820s a fourth problem had emerged:

revolution within the Ottoman Empire, which raised wider issues of conflict between the great powers in the Near East. It was over this problem that Anglo-Russian tension was most acute. Lastly, it was impossible to separate these four problems from the attempt by France to recover from the disasters of defeat and occupation. French policy-makers sought to exploit all the tensions between the four allies to promote their own recovery. They were determined to join the great-power alliance because they were convinced that they could more easily destroy it from within. The interaction of these five problems resulted in the collapse of the alliance by the mid 1820s.

For Castlereagh and Metternich the Quadruple Alliance had several distinct purposes. The four allies could continue to co-operate for the containment of France. Both men were convinced that vigilance in the west was vital for the maintenance of peace. Secondly, co-operation amongst the four powers would keep alive the spirit of unity which had proved so valuable in the years between 1813 and 1815. These were the open and acknowledged ends of the alliance to which all four members could subscribe. In addition to these aims, however, the British and the Austrians sought to use the alliance as a means to disguise their restraint of Russia. Both Metternich and Castlereagh had reached the conclusion at Vienna that Russia was a restless and ambitious power, and they feared that in 1815 her aspirations had not been entirely satisfied. In their opinion Russia was the victorious power least content with the new order in Europe. They were certainly more suspicious of the Russian emperor's advisers (men such as the Corfiote Capodistrias) than they were of the emperor himself. They counted on Alexander's undoubted sympathies for his fellow monarchs and his fear of revolution to keep Russia within the alliance. In short, the aim of Castlereagh and Metternich was to make use of an informal network of personal relationships built up during the peace negotiations to direct the formal alliance of the four victorious allies in the postwar world.

The Russians were, from the outset, well aware that two of their allies were working against them. After the Congress of Vienna Russian policy became markedly anti-British, and there was a growing conviction at St Petersburg that the British were determined to deny Russia her rightful place in the postwar world. The Austrians were seen less as the source of the new anti-Russian spirit in Europe than as the agents of England on the continent. Alexander I, guided by Capodistrias, rapidly reached the conclusion that the balance of power established in 1815 was a false balance because there were no restraints on the naval expansion of England whereas France, and indeed Russia herself, were surrounded by buffer states. The immediate objectives of

Russian postwar policy were to frustrate Anglo-Austrian attempts to capture the leadership of the alliance and to organize an informal grouping of powers which was capable of limiting the naval and commercial expansion of England. In the pursuit of this anti-British policy the Russians looked to the French. If France was admitted to the alliance she, with Russia, could form a powerful counterpoise to the Anglo-Austrian *entente*. Moreover, if Prussia continued to follow a Russian lead the Russians would be in a majority of three. Austria would then realize the futility and the danger of opposing her continental allies, and if she then abandoned England the influence of the latter in continental affairs would immeasurably decline. France, with her naval, commercial and colonial traditions and her naval dockyards, was the only power able effectively to begin to challenge Britain's mastery of the high seas.

The French responded eagerly to Russian overtures; they seemed to suggest a real conflict of interest within the coalition, and this the French were eager to promote. The governments of the Restoration Monarchy saw Russia as the natural ally of France; together the two powers possessed overwhelming military strength which would enable them to revise the settlement of 1815 to suit their own interests. For the next fifteen years the French believed that a new Tilsit could replace the General Act of the Congress of Vienna. In fact, however, the Russian approaches to the French always meant less than the French imagined. The Russians wanted the French to follow their lead, not to establish a new partnership which would restore to France the hegemony she had formerly enjoyed in the west. The real difference between the two powers was that whereas the Russians were largely satisfied with the new territorial order and merely sought to reshape the alignments of the powers, the French always saw the reshaping of alignments as a prelude to territorial revision. There was therefore always a significant gulf between the two powers. The most important basis of co-operation between them was their mutual determination to reduce British influence in Europe. The years from 1815 to 1822 were the heyday of Franco-Russian co-operation. It was in the conference of ambassadors at Paris which was responsible for the supervision of the allied army of occupation in France that the Russians first manifested their opposition to England, their irritation with Austria and their friendly disposition towards the defeated power. In 1816 and 1817 they openly championed the French in their determination to reduce both the size and the duration of the army of occupation. In 1818 the rivalries and tensions within the alliance were transferred from the conference of ambassadors at Paris to the larger stage of congress diplomacy.

The four congresses held between 1818 and 1822 were convened under Article VI of the Quadruple Alliance of November 1815. There was no clear understanding between the powers about what the congresses were for, merely an agreement that they should be held. Each congress was preceded by intense diplomatic preparations and followed by searching examinations of their consequences, which were just as important as the congresses themselves. Congress diplomacy produced few surprises; for the most part the powers knew what would happen before the congress met. This was why the British in the end refused to attend them. The original intention of the congresses was to demonstrate allied unity on matters of common concern. This presupposed that a basic identity of interest would always triumph over temporary differences of outlook. This was not the case. The Anglo–Russian struggle for the leadership of Europe was already the dominant fact of alliance politics before the first congress met. It was inevitable that it should also dominate the congress. The ostensible motive for the congress of Aix-la-Chapelle which met in 1818 was to determine how and when to end the allied occupation of France. Underlying this, however, was a much more important issue. Both the French and the Russians wanted to transform the alliance; they wanted to substitute a five-power alliance, which they hoped ultimately to direct against England, for four-power control of France. The Franco–Russian argument for the extension of the alliance was presented in the guise of monarchical solidarity: France must take her place as a bastion of order, as an additional guarantor of monarchy against revolution in the new Europe. Metternich and Castlereagh clearly realized that Russian support for France was an expression of their irritation at Anglo–Austrian control of the alliance and an attempt to undermine it. The conflict was settled by a compromise. Castlereagh and Metternich suggested a renewal of the Treaty of Chaumont against France combined with the admission of France into the congress system. In this way four-power co-operation for the maintenance of the treaties of 1815 and five-power co-operation for the maintenance of peace and order could exist side by side. Clearly the object of the British and the Austrians was to strengthen the links that existed between them and Russia and to stress the need for continued vigilance to maintain the Vienna settlement in the west. But their basic aim was to forestall the emergence of a Franco–Russian *entente*. In his contacts with French diplomats Metternich placed great emphasis on the unpredictability of Alexander and the ambiguity of Russian policy. At St Petersburg he impressed upon Alexander that France was a dangerous element in great-power relations because of the instability of her governments and the revolutionary elements which still existed in French society. In the two years from 1818 to 1820 one of the main tasks of Anglo-Austrian diplomacy was to keep France and Russia apart.

The revolutions of 1820 added a new dimension to great-power conflicts. They raised in an acute form the question: for what purpose did the alliance exist? The leaders of the conservative continental monarchies were convinced that the questions of peace between states and order within states could not be separated. The effect of the debate on the purpose of the alliance was to begin the reshaping of the informal alignments between the powers which led to the collapse of the alliance and congress system. The Italian revolutions of 1820 forced Metternich to reconsider the priorities of his foreign policy. Since 1815 he had sought British co-operation to restrain Austria's two great rivals, France and Russia. He now needed support against a third and potentially more dangerous enemy: revolution. Metternich attached great significance to the unity of the powers in the face of revolution. If Austria suppressed the Italian revolutions in the name of the alliance, the other powers could not exploit the revolution to weaken Austria, as he feared the Russians and the French might attempt to do. He believed that this anti-revolutionary policy would strengthen the alliance, and in no way threaten Anglo-Austrian co-operation. In fact it was the British who refused to allow Metternich to use the alliance as an instrument for the suppression of revolution. He was thus forced to the conclusion that the Anglo-Austrian *entente* did not serve all of Austria's needs. This led him to turn to the Russians for support against his new enemy in Italy. If the Russians would co-operate with Austria against the revolution, this would be a great security for the Habsburg monarchy. It would isolate France and keep Russia firmly attached to the *status quo* powers. Even if England did not give Austria wholehearted support against the forces of revolution, the two powers could still work together on other issues, particularly the restraint of Russia in the Near East. In effect Metternich was attempting to hold the alliance together, use it against revolution, and regroup the powers around Austria. In the early 1820s it was Austria's manifest weakness that secured for Metternich such a prominent role in great-power diplomacy.

It was the British and the Russians who frustrated Metternich's plan. Neither power was prepared permanently to concede such a leading position to Austria. When the British reached the conclusion that they could no longer depend on Austria, they abandoned her. The Russians exploited Austria's difficulties in order to separate her from England. Metternich could not lead when others would not follow. In their separate ways, the British and the Russians solved Metternich's problems for him. In his State Paper of May 1820 Castlereagh outlined British objections to the use of the Quadruple Alliance for the suppression of revolution. In his opinion each great power ought to act within its own sphere of influence according to its own interests. Austria was perfectly free to deal with the Italian revolutions as she chose, but there could never be a general right of interference in the internal affairs of small states belonging to the alliance of the great powers. Castlereagh knew that neither his cabinet colleagues nor the British parliament would consent to continued membership by Britain of an alliance used for this purpose. If they were to remain in the alliance, it must be restricted in its scope, and if Anglo-Austrian co-operation was to remain the cornerstone of British policy, Austria must abandon both her attempt to work with Russia against the revolution and her plan to transform the alliance. This was the position Castlereagh came reluctantly to adopt between May 1820 and his death in the summer of 1822. The Russians, like the British, were forced to reconsider their attitude towards the alliance and towards Austria. The revolutionary upsurge of the early 1820s which disturbed Germany, Spain and Portugal as well as the Italian states profoundly affected Alexander I. He was genuinely alarmed by the violent attacks on and virulent criticism of monarchical authority. He came to see all revolutionary activity as inspired by French ideals and even organized in France itself. His enthusiasm for a *rapprochement* with France gave way to suspicion of her. This, combined with Austria's new and friendly attitude towards Russia, disposed him gradually to abandon France and to draw closer to Austria. This was a significant shift of emphasis in Russian policy; the emperor began slowly to turn his attention away from his grandiose scheme of attempting to create a combination of naval powers against England to the narrower but more realistic objective of working with Austria to reduce, perhaps even exclude, British influence on the continent. Alexander realized that by supporting Austria's interpretation of the alliance Russia could gain security for the existing order in eastern Europe and at the same time wreck the Anglo-Austrian *entente*. It was these quite fundamental changes of British and Russian policy which emerged from the complex diplomacy of the years from 1820 to 1822 and which centred around the congresses of Troppau, Laibach and Verona.

It was the French who took the lead in proposing a congress of the powers to discuss the revolution in Naples. They saw it as a means of bringing Anglo-Austrian differences out into the open, of moving closer to Russia and of undermining Austrian influence in Italy. For the government in Paris the real question at issue was the recovery of

France, not the maintenance of peace and order. Although Castlereagh was opposed to a congress, Metternich was anxious to secure the widest possible support for Austria's anti-revolutionary policy in Italy. He supported the French proposal. When the congress met at Troppau in October 1820 there was a prolonged struggle between the French and the Austrians for the support of Alexander I. He came to the congress with two proposals, both drawn up by Capodistrias. The first was to secure a general statement of principle that the alliance of the five powers had a right to intervene in the internal affairs of all states. This proposal was designed to alienate the British. Secondly, he hoped to secure a further statement that reforms within small states were admissible so long as they received the assent of the allies. This proposal was designed to provoke the Austrians who were opposed to any concessions to the Italian revolutionaries. When it became apparent that the Austrians were prepared to abandon the British to work with him to secure the first proposal, Alexander dropped the second and the French, whose influence in Italy the reform proposal was primarily intended to support. The Troppau Protocol, which was signed by the Austrians, Prussians and Russians on 19 November 1820, uncompromisingly asserted the right of the alliance to intervene in the internal affairs of the states of Europe where order was disturbed and where the government was unable to defend itself against its domestic enemies. It reflected a real identity of interest between the three eastern powers. Each regarded the suppression of revolution as essential to its survival. This common fear drew the three powers together, and for the next three decades it was capable of overriding their differences on other issues.

Both the British and the French refused to sign the Protocol of Troppau. After its publication the congress was adjourned until such time as the three powers had decided in the light of further investigations what to do in Italy. The congress resumed in January of 1821, to discuss how Austria should proceed to suppress the Italian revolutions. Metternich received from his two allies a mandate to intervene in an area where Austria's interests were paramount. This was a real admission of weakness; the actual intervention, which severely strained Austria's limited financial resources, was a further reminder to Metternich of the perilous position of Austria. Although the congresses of Troppau and Laibach fundamentally weakened British leadership of the alliance, Austrian intervention in Italy strengthened her control of the peninsula, a development which the British were at all times anxious to promote. It was British prestige rather than British interests which was adversely affected by the congress. The French, by contrast, suffered a direct setback to their hope of recovery. All hope of a *rapprochement* with Russia was dashed, and Austria's reassertion of her dominance in Italy destroyed French expectations of acting as the patron of an active reform movement in the peninsula. In April 1821 news reached the representatives at Laibach of the revolt of the Greeks against Turkish rule. Metternich was appalled at this fresh manifestation of the revolutionary spirit. He was concerned lest the Russians should adopt a different attitude to revolution in the Ottoman Empire than to revolution in Europe. There was a number of outstanding conflicts betweeen Russia and Turkey, and the Greeks were fellow Orthodox Christians struggling to free themselves from barbarian rule. Metternich urged on Alexander the necessity for a common front on the Greek question. He was not, however, content to rely solely on Russia's assurances of co-operation with her allies in the Near East. There was clearly a need to revive the Anglo-Austrian *entente* for the restraint of Russia in the Near East. Moreover, the revolution organized by a group of army officers in Spain against the absolutism of the restored Bourbon Ferdinand VII had for over a year been demanding British and Austrian attention. Although they might not see eye to eye over what should be done in Spain, both powers were anxious to prevent French intervention, and Metternich was determined to prevent the Russians from using the Spanish question to widen the breach between England and Austria. Despite their recent differences, the two powers still had a common interest in preventing a forward policy by Russia in the Near East and by France in western Europe. It was these common anxieties that led Metternich and Castlereagh to meet at Hanover in October 1821. The two statesmen effectively co-ordinated measures for the restraint of Russia in the Near East; having committed Alexander to an actively anti-revolutionary policy in Europe, Metternich, with Castlereagh's assistance, strove to dampen his sympathies for the Greeks. On the Spanish question Metternich and Castlereagh agreed on the need to restrain France. Beyond that, there was no possible basis for further agreement. Metternich's position was anomalous: he had secured Russia's assent to the general principle of intervention and to its application in Italy; he now sought to secure Russian adherence to the British doctrine of non-intervention in Spain. This was an inconsistency which the Russians were determined to exploit.

Castlereagh's death before the congress of Verona and the appointment of George Canning as his successor did not decisively affect the outcome of the congress. The separation of England from the alliance was virtually completed by Castlereagh in his last months at the Foreign Office. It was the Russian government which, before the congress met, insisted on the application of the principles of the Protocol of Troppau to Spain. Alexander argued with perfect consistency that if the Greek revolt was part of the universal conspiracy against order, so was the Spanish. The Russians knew for certain that this would widen the breach between England and Austria, and that it could even result in the British severing their connection with the alliance. The French hoped to defy their former enemies over the Spanish question; with England divided from her continental allies, and the other three powers anxious to see the destruction of the Spanish revolution, there could be no better opportunity for the dramatic reassertion of French power in western Europe. Metternich saw his role at Verona as the mediator of the conflicts of the powers: to satisfy the Russians on the point of principle, to cause the least offence to England, and to restrain the French from acting on their own. He attempted to persuade the representatives at Verona, who met from October to December 1822, to send simultaneous notes of protest to Madrid, but to take no further action. After long and difficult negotiations Metternich seemed to succeed. The four continental powers adopted the course he proposed. It was only the British who held aloof. Canning still refused to recognize any right of the alliance to interfere in the internal affairs of Spain.

Almost immediately after the congress Metternich's compromise diplomacy collapsed. The French government realized that its representatives at Verona had been duped by Metternich. Montmorency, the foreign minister, resigned and was replaced by Chateaubriand who was determined to pursue an independent policy towards Spain. One of his first acts as foreign minister was to refuse to present the French note of protest at Madrid simultaneously with the other three powers. By the spring of 1823 the postwar edifice of co-operation was in ruins: England was separated from her allies, France was acting alone in Spain, and the three eastern powers refused to take any measures to prevent the French army from crossing the Pyrenees. The congress system did not cause any of these differences, it merely failed to provide a framework within which they could be patched up.

The failure of congress diplomacy did not mean that the powers ceased to co-operate, nor did they lack the means by which their more occasional need for joint discussion and common action could be given a regular form. In fact congresses were replaced by conferences of ambassadors which were usually held in the capitals of the great powers. Between 1815 and 1822 the powers convened both congresses and conferences; after 1823 the conference as an instrument of co-operation came into its own. It proved to be much more effective than a congress, firstly because the willingness of a power to send a representative to a conference was in itself an indication of the desire to seek a peaceful solution to a particular problem, and secondly because conferences dealt with specific issues of pressing concern rather than ranging over a wide variety of topics. Lastly, conferences did not need the participation of all the powers; there were several three-power and four-power conferences in the period between the collapse of the congress system and the outbreak of the Crimean War. Congresses, by contrast, were regarded as meetings of all the great powers. In the 1850s and 1860s Napoleon III sought to revive congresses at the expense of conferences. He thought the former were much grander and likely to achieve more than the latter. His attempt was unsuccessful because the other powers, although willing to negotiate with each other on particular problems, were not prepared to discuss more general issues when they knew in advance they could not agree.

In terms of the evolution of great-power alignments, the period of congresses achieved a great deal. France was firmly brought within the new international order; from 1818 onwards there was a five-power, rather than a four-power, system in operation. This change was smoothly accomplished, and although the French certainly sought to destroy the new international order they were forced to work within its limits until they felt strong and confident enough to break out of it. The collapse of the congress system did not mean that the four powers had ceased to work together to contain France within the borders imposed by the second Peace of Paris. Secondly, the attempts of the British and the Russians to dominate and control the alliance were virtually brought to an end with the collapse of the congress system. In 1824 and 1825 the Russians vainly tried to pretend that the congress system could continue to exist without British participation, but they were soon forced to abandon this pretence. The Anglo-Russian struggle was essentially a conflict of prestige which both combatants lost; neither could dominate and lead the other four permanently. Both powers were forced to recognize their joint dominance of the new European order and to concede to each other predominance in particular areas. Great Britain tacitly acknowledged Russian supremacy in eastern and central Europe, while Russia acknowledged Great Britain's dominance in the west. It was only in the Near East that there was a direct conflict of interest between the two powers. Lastly, the most significant result of the three congresses of Troppau, Laibach and Verona was to effect by peaceful means the transfer of Austria's dependence from England to Russia. This made better sense for Austria; as a west-European naval power, England could not afford Austria the support she needed except in the Near East, or in the event of a full-scale European war provoked by France. She could be of no real assistance to Austria in central Europe where support was most needed. The Russians, by contrast, with their vast military power, could. By the mid 1820s the Russians were playing the role in eastern and central Europe which Castlereagh and Metternich had tried to prevent them from assuming at the time of the Polish-Saxon crisis. The fears they then entertained were not realized; Russia sought to dominate eastern and central Europe not as a prelude to further expansion but to protect Russia and Poland from the eastward spread of western liberal and revolutionary ideas. The protection she afforded Austria and Prussia consolidated rather than weakened the territorial order of 1815.

For the British government the collapse of the congress system and the Anglo-Austrian *entente* was not a serious blow. Britain's position was unchanged and the essential objectives of her policy – the containment of France in the west and Russia in the Near East – remained equally unchanged. Canning's task was to find new means to achieve the objectives which Castlereagh had set out. He substituted the policy of direct agreements with France and Russia for the policy of indirect control formerly exercised through the Anglo-Austrian *entente*. This was a perfectly adequate substitute where Great Britain's naval power could be brought to bear. The greatest danger to Britain's power and interests, the emergence of a Franco-Russian alliance which could certainly have dominated the continent, was avoided when Austria replaced France as Russia's principal partner on European questions. Austria's weakness made her an imperfect instrument of British policy on the continent, and the co-operation of the two powers had tended to push Russia and France closer together. Until the revolution of July 1830 the French continued to pay court at St Petersburg and to believe that the Russians would eventually conclude some sort of an agreement with them. In fact, however, the Russians were no longer interested.

In April 1823 a French army of 100,000 men crossed the Pyrenees to suppress the Spanish revolt. The British had no means to prevent it; they had no army of their own and no ally in central Europe who would threaten France's eastern frontier. Canning was therefore forced to concentrate on limiting French action. He did so in three ways: he demanded assurances from France that the occupation of Spain was purely temporary, that the territorial integrity of Portugal would be respected, and that the French would make no attempt to recover either for Spain herself or indirectly for themselves the rebel Spanish colonies in South America. Once the French army was in the peninsula, the key issues for Great Britain were the maintenance of British ascendancy over Portugal and the protection of British trade with Latin America. On the South American question Canning turned to the United States of America for support. This bold stroke did not have any effective results; the Americans did not want to act as the junior partner of Great Britain and they feared British influence and trade in South America more than they feared any designs that France might entertain. Denied the co-operation of any other power, Canning turned to direct negotiations with the French, and in October 1823 he reached an agreement with them, enshrined in the Polignac memorandum, which safeguarded British interests in Latin America.

In the crisis over Spain and the South American colonies the strengths and weaknesses of Great Britain's position were clearly revealed. In Spain itself she was powerless; in Portugal, where she had a naval squadron stationed in the Tagus, she could negotiate from a position of strength. Over South America where she could, if necessary, use her overwhelming sea power to prevent a Franco-Spanish naval expedition from attempting to cross the Atlantic, she was invincible. The French invasion of Spain made the British government more jealous of its influence over Portugal, and in 1826 Canning sent a small British force to Lisbon to protect the Portuguese constitutionalists against the absolutist factions which were assisted and encouraged by Spain. By the late 1820s the Anglo-French struggle for influence in the Iberian peninsula had become one of the most important sources of conflict between the two western powers. At the same time, however, both powers recognized a common interest in preventing the absolutist powers of eastern Europe from interfering in the affairs of the two peninsular monarchies. In 1826 Canning rejected Metternich's suggestion that the five great powers should hold a conference on Portugal, yet later in the same year he visited Paris and had frank discussions on Portugal with the French government. The division of Europe into two separate great-power systems, an Anglo-French struggle for dominance in the west and the co-operation of the three powers under Russian leadership in eastern and central Europe, was apparent in the mid 1820s. It merely became more marked in the early 1830s. The division could not and did not apply to the Near East, where the interests of Great Britain and France, the two great Mediterranean naval powers, could under no circumstances be ignored. In 1824 and 1825 the Russians attempted to break the deadlock on the Greek question in negotiations with Austria and Prussia at St Petersburg. In 1826 they abandoned this approach in favour of direct co-operation with England and France.

The Ottoman Empire in Europe was untouched by the peacemakers in 1815. What discussions there were on Near Eastern problems merely revealed the great clash of interests between them. The great powers were agreed as to what was happening in the eastern Mediterranean and the Balkans: Ottoman authority was in decline, Turkey's treatment of her Christian subjects was barbarous, and there was little central authority exerted over the outlying provinces. The reason why there was an eastern question throughout the nineteenth century was that the great powers could not agree on what to do about these problems. In the absence of any previous understanding, they only reacted to problems when they had reached crisis proportions. The only exception to this was in the early 1850s when the French actually provoked a Near-Eastern crisis.

After the failure of Ypsilanti's attempt to lead a revolt amongst the mainland Greeks in April 1821, a new revolt broke out in the Morea. This was much more serious; as long as the Greek rebels had control of the islands and the sea routes of the Aegean, the Morea was difficult of access to a Turkish army. The Greek question in international relations arose because the Turks failed to crush the revolt quickly. It soon became a matter of great concern to the powers. Both the British and the Russians had a great deal of maritime commerce passing through the Aegean. There was considerable intellectual sympathy in western Europe for the Greeks who were assumed to be the heirs of ancient Greek civilization. In Russia there was religious sympathy for fellow Orthodox Christians and Russo–Turkish relations were already bad as a consequence of Turkey's failure to fulfil her obligations under the Treaty of Bucharest of 1812. In 1824 the Russians proposed a conference of the powers at St Petersburg to discuss a plan for creating three autonomous Greek principalities. The Greeks themselves, as well as the other powers, were opposed to it, the Greeks because it did not go far enough, the powers because it went too far. The British in particular saw it as a Russian plan to weaken Turkey and create Russian client states. In 1825 the Sultan called upon the assistance of his vassal, Mehemet Ali, the ruler of Egypt, who had a fleet which could transport troops to the Morea. The Russians suggested another conference at St Petersburg to discuss the issue. Canning refused and Metternich instructed his ambassador to oppose any action directed against Turkey. It was in the context of the failure of the conference proposal and the advance of the Egyptian forces that the Russians abandoned the attempt to work with Austria in favour of direct co-operation with England. Russia's European policy remained unchanged; Austria now relied on Russia to protect her against France and the revolution in Europe, and Russia could safely work without Austria in the Near East as long as she respected her Balkan interests. The Russians saw no inconsistency between a rigid response to revolution in Europe and a flexible response to revolution in the Near East; both policies suited their interests.

When Canning said he was prepared to 'talk Greek' to the Russians, he meant that he was not prepared to allow them to act alone in the Near East. Equally, Canning was determined to ensure that Turkey was not humiliated and weakened, and that the Greeks were not massacred by the Egyptians. In effect he was forced to look for some permanent solution to the Greek question. In April 1826 the British and the Russians reached an agreement, the St Petersburg Protocol, which provided for the creation of an autonomous Greek state under Turkish suzerainty; it also contained a vague clause about intervention should it become necessary for the powers to prevent a Turko-Egyptian suppression of the revolt. The French were the only other power who were prepared to join the British and the Russians in giving effect to the agreement. It gave them an opportunity to demonstrate the recovery of their power in the Mediterranean and to keep on good terms with Russia. The Austrians and the Prussians refused to act against a sovereign in defence of rebels. A three-power treaty was signed at London in July 1827. The Turks refused the mediation of the powers, and this posed the problem of how to protect the Greeks without embarking on hostilities towards Turkey. This was an impossible dilemma. In October 1827 the navies of the three powers destroyed the Turko-Egyptian fleet at Navarino. The Turkish reaction to this changed the nature of the issues in the Near East. Canning had tried to separate the Greek question from the Russo-Turkish disputes arising out of the Treaty of Bucharest. The Turks repudiated a recent agreement with the Russians on these questions and began a Holy War of Moslems against Russia. The Austrians and the Prussians were appalled by the war in the Near East; both blamed the Russians but neither was in any position to manifest disapproval in a positive way. Wellington, who became prime minister of Great Britain in 1828, some months after the death of Canning, believed that Navarino had shown the danger of forcing events; his policy was to wait upon them. It was the French who attempted to link the war in the Near East with the rivalries of the powers in Europe. In the autumn of 1829, just before the Russians concluded peace with Turkey, Polignac, the French prime minister, proposed to the Russians a plan for territorial revision in western Europe and the Near East: Russia would make extensive gains at the expense of Turkey, France at the expense of the united Netherlands. The Russians gave no encouragement to the proposal; they wanted neither war nor territorial revision in Europe, and they did not believe that the other powers would attempt to rob them of the fruits of their victory over Turkey. In September 1829 the Russians and the Turks concluded peace at Adrianople; Russia acquired territory in Asia and at the mouth of the Danube and, even more important, extensive rights of protectorate over the Danubian principalities. In 1814 a Russian army had occupied Paris; in 1829 the same army was within a few days' march of Constantinople. It was the military power at the disposal of the Russian emperor that excited the fears of the rest of Europe. Russia's triumph in 1829 added immeasurably to British suspicion of her. In the next decade Nicholas I was regarded as the new Napoleon, ambitious, restless and totally unscrupulous.

It was only after the Russo–Turkish war had ended that the three signatory powers to the Treaty of London could finally settle the Greek question. This they accomplished by conference diplomacy in the years from 1829 to 1831. They arranged the borders, drew up the constitution of the new state and defined its relations with Turkey. In 1830 the French, denied the territorial revision they wanted in western Europe, turned to North Africa and, on the pretext of suppressing piracy in the western Mediterranean, bombarded and occupied Algiers. The British government was alarmed by this action. They saw it as an indirect attack on their Mediterranean naval supremacy, which indeed it was. Thwarted on their northern and eastern borders, and faced with mounting criticism at home, the French government sought adventure in the Mediterranean. In the decade from 1820 to 1830 it had been Mediterranean issues that dominated the relations between the great powers: first Italy, then Spain, then Greece and lastly North Africa. The political and territorial order created in 1815, from France in the west to Poland in the east, seemed stable and secure. The revolutions of 1830 in France, Belgium, and then in Italy and Poland, revealed how illusory this security was. In the early 1830s the four erstwhile allies of Chaumont had to make renewed efforts to contain France and to maintain order in Europe. Although divided on many other issues, they continued to share a common fear of French aggression. The steadfast allegiance of the four powers to the basic aim of the Vienna settlement ensured its survival.

CHAPTER THREE

From revolution to war
1830–1854

The revolutions of 1830 were all protests against particular aspects of the peace settlement of 1814–15. The new order which the monarchs and statesmen of the great powers had imposed upon the states of Europe was condemned by liberals and nationalists as an old order, incapable of satisfying the aspirations of the peoples of Europe. This conflict of ideas which the revolutions of 1830 brought sharply into focus was, in the long run, more important than the revolutions themselves. By the end of 1832 the great powers had managed to contain the revolutions, but within forty years the idea of nationalism had totally destroyed the Vienna settlement. The peacemakers had worked on the assumption that states existed on the basis of dynastic rights and binding treaties. This was what they called the public law of Europe. From the 1830s onward a new class of politicians began to argue that states owed their existence to the will of the people, and that the existing treaty structure enslaved the peoples of Europe. This was a profound conflict which admitted of no compromise and which could not be brushed aside. Liberal nationalists were confident that in the long run they would win the struggle of opinion. In fact, however, the problem was solved in a way that they had not anticipated: in the 1850s and 1860s some of the conservative monarchies ceased to cling to the treaty structure of Europe, separated liberalism from nationalism and appealed to the people over the heads of middle-class liberal politicians to legitimize their actions. In the 1830s, however, the conservative powers strove to maintain the existing order within their states and in international relations.

In the late 1820s the three eastern powers had drifted apart. Prussia had strongly disapproved of Russia's Near Eastern policy, and Metternich had actively opposed it. To many observers it seemed that the Emperor Nicholas had abandoned the recently-established policy of close co-operation with the two German powers when he indicated his willingness to work with England and France on the Greek question. In reality the neo-Holy Alliance, as the Troppau grouping was often called, was almost unaffected by these differences in the Near East. Throughout the crisis the Russians carefully avoided any action which could be construed as an attack on Austria's Balkan interests. Moreover, both the Austrians and the Prussians remained alive to the need for Russian support against France and the revolution in Europe. Neither power felt able to dispense with it. Russia's apparent strength enabled her to offend her allies without seriously undermining her relations with them. Her guarantee to support them against their enemies was not withdrawn during the Near Eastern crisis of the late 1820s. The French revolution of July 1830, raising as it did the spectres of both revolution and war, quickly revived a sense of unity amongst the three allies. In August 1830 they issued the 'Chiffon de Carlsbad' in which they pledged themselves to maintain the 1815 settlement and warned the new regime in France to respect the established order in the rest of Europe. This was a measure of protection for central and eastern Europe rather than a challenge to France in the west. The three powers realized that they could not destroy revolution in France. Throughout the crisis of the early 1830s their aim was to prevent revolution from spreading eastwards.

The decision of the four erstwhile allies of Chaumont to recognize the government of Louis Philippe in France (the Orleans Monarchy) was essentially a bid for peace. They indicated their willingness to live with the new order in France if it would live with the existing order in the rest of Europe. The British government was the first to accord formal recognition to Louis Philippe; the Austrians and the Prussians quickly followed its example. Prussia wanted peace on the Rhine and Austria sought assurances that the new regime would recognize her dominant position in Italy. It was only the Russians who held out; they did not fear France to the same extent as the other three powers. To Nicholas, Louis Philippe was no more than a 'vile usurper'. However, by January 1831 he gave in and recognized the Orleans Monarchy. By delaying recognition for six months he had clearly manifested his dislike of the new liberal order. It was Franco-Russian relations which were the most decisively altered by the French revolution of 1830. Whereas the Bourbon Monarchy had regarded Russia as its most likely ally, its successor saw Russia as its most inveterate enemy. The link between St Petersburg and Paris, which by the late 1820s was already tenuous, was now completely severed. It was not repaired until after the

49

Crimean War. It was England and Austria who benefited most from the new antagonism between France and Russia; they no longer had to fear a Franco-Russian *rapprochement* for the revision of the 1815 settlement in Europe and for a forward policy by Russia in the Near East. Russia under Nicholas I was indisputably ranged amongst the *status quo* powers.

The appointment in November 1830 of a Whig government in England, committed to a measure of parliamentary reform, was regarded by many European conservatives, such as Metternich, as an event not very different in its consequences from the French revolution of July. It was regarded as another onslaught on the established order. Liberal politicians were quick to take up the theme that the great powers were divided by the character of their political institutions into two rival groups: an eastern autocratic alignment and a western liberal *entente*. In England and France prominent politicians publicly suggested that their governments had a common interest in defending liberal ideas and institutions wherever they were struggling to establish themselves, and that they shared a common hatred of absolutist forms of government. This was the origin of the so-called 'liberal alliance' of the 1830s. Both British and French governments shared an exaggerated fear of Russian power and both were convinced that Russia entertained expansionist objectives in the Near East. Their criticisms of absolutism were mainly directed against the Russian autocracy, particularly after its suppression of the Polish revolt of 1830. Attacks on the Austrian and Prussian versions of autocracy were much less frequent and less strident in tone. Each power saw the other as a potential ally against Russia. Nevertheless, the new Whig government was just as anxious to contain France within the borders of 1815 as its Tory predecessors had been. Palmerston, the new foreign secretary, believed that this could be achieved by working with France rather than against her. This policy was Canning's legacy, to which the Whigs added a small dose of liberal sentiment. Palmerston found it easier to work with France in the early 1830s than Canning had in the mid 1820s. In foreign policy the revolution of 1830 was a setback for France. The new French government was acutely conscious of the great danger of isolation; it realized that one false step could easily revive the four-power coalition against France. The dread of isolation forced the new regime temporarily to abandon French revisionist objectives, and to work with Great Britain to avoid isolation. Palmerston exploited French weakness to the full; he attached strict conditions to his willingness to work with France: in Europe she must respect the Vienna settlement and in the Near East she must follow a British lead.

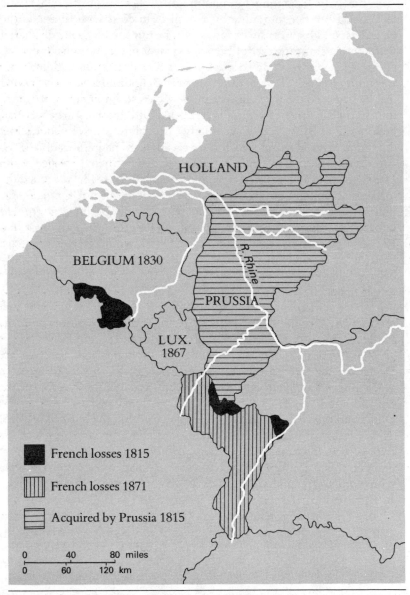

Map 2   *The Low Countries and Rhine frontier 1814–71*

In the early 1830s England was in an ambiguous position. She was separated from her four allies by a clash of interest with Russia in the Near East and by a conflict of ideology in Europe, yet she still shared with them a common fear of French expansion. She was also linked to France by a common dread of absolutism. Palmerston exploited this ambiguity to great effect in the crisis over Belgium. He rightly claimed that he had used the three eastern powers to restrain France and France to restrain the three eastern powers. In August 1830 disturbances had broken out in Brussels that eventually turned into a movement against the union with Holland which the peacemakers had effected in 1815. After the revolution in Brussels the Dutch government appealed to the Prussians, who as a result of arrangements made in 1815 garrisoned the fortress of Luxembourg (a possession of the House of Orange), for military assistance to suppress the revolt. The Berlin government refused to act without British approval. Wellington was convinced that Prussian intervention on the side of the Dutch would give the French a pretext for counter-intervention to protect the rebels, and he rightly believed that once the French army was in Belguim it would take a war to get it out. It was he who committed the British government to a negotiated settlement of the dispute by conference diplomacy in which the French were invited to participate. Like the recognition of Louis Philippe, this was a bid to maintain peace in the west.

The London conference opened in November 1830. By late December the five powers had agreed that Belgium should form an independent state. Palmerston's argument was that separation was the only solution calculated permanently to settle the dispute between the Dutch and the Belgians and to keep France within the borders of 1815. This, combined with the self-denying ordinance by which each of the five powers renounced any claim on Belgian territory (which in practice affected only France) was what persuaded the eastern powers reluctantly to accept that a popular revolt could result in treaty revision. In January 1831 the five powers assigned to Holland the frontiers of 1790, agreed to negotiate with the German Confederation a separate status for Luxembourg, and established the principle that the new kingdom of Belgium would be a neutral state, guaranteed by the five powers. Neutrality was intended to be the substitute for the barrier fortresses of 1814, most of which were demolished. In this way France was committed by new treaties to her own containment. Had the Dutch immediately accepted these terms, the Belgian question would have been settled by three months of conference diplomacy. Their refusal to do so prolonged the Belgian crisis for another two years and postponed the final settlement until April 1839 when all the parties involved signed the Treaty of London. In 1831 and 1832 the British and the French twice used force to coerce the Dutch into accepting the settlement. On both occasions the French attempted to gain something for themselves. With their troops actually in Belgium they felt in a better position to demand concessions. It was Palmerston who opposed them with the threat of war. Throughout the Belgian crisis England was the only great power which was not prepared to treat it as a matter for compromise. Palmerston insisted that such vital interests of security for Great Britain were at stake that no important concessions could be made to either the French or the Dutch. The eastern powers were forced to abandon their policy of suppressing popular revolts by vigorous great-power intervention in order to work with Great Britain for the containment of France, and the French were forced to relinquish their territorial ambitions to avoid the prospect of isolation and, perhaps, war.

Whereas the French government was convinced that a challenge to Great Britain on Belgium involved great dangers, in Italy the same restraints did not apply. Austrian policy was markedly anti-French and Metternich made no secret of his dislike of the new regime. Moreover, Austria in Italy was a weaker opponent than Great Britain had been in the Low Countries. In central Italy France sought to exert her legitimate influence as a Catholic power, which the non-Catholic powers were in no position to deny. Lastly, French objectives in Italy were political rather than territorial: they wished to act as the patron of the reform and anti-Austrian movements within the Italian states. The great-power conflict produced by the revolutions of 1831 in the Papal States and in the two outposts of Habsburg despotism, Parma and Modena, was less serious than the crisis over Belgium. There was no question of territorial revision, and the French were not prepared to go to war to uphold the doctrine of non-intervention in Italy. All they wanted was a striking diplomatic success. They were disposed to think that they could achieve it, first because Russia was preoccupied by the revolution in Poland and could give only moral support to Austria, and second because the Whig government in England would not assist Metternich to shore up petty absolutisms in Italy. Austria without allies was the one rival the French felt they could confidently take on. They hoped to prevent Austrian intervention to suppress the revolts in central Italy by threatening counter-intervention. Metternich was not, however, prepared to abdicate Austria's authority in the peninsula. He did not want a war over Italy any more than the French did, but he was convinced that, whatever happened, Austria must defend her interests and her great-power status. In March 1831 Austrian troops entered the Papal States; the French retaliated by a naval occupation of the papal port of Ancona. The government in Paris declared that when Austria evacuated her troops, France would withdraw her frigates and marines. This did not occur until 1838. Yet French intervention in Italy was much more of a domestic than a diplomatic triumph. The recovery of conservatism in Italy under Austrian auspices was achieved despite the French, the Pope was horrified that a Catholic power should openly champion his domestic enemies, and the three eastern powers, alarmed by French action, agreed in 1833 on measures to forestall such counter-intervention in the future. French action in Italy was a policy of gestures rather than of confrontation. The major consequence these gestures secured was the strengthening of the conservative alliance against her.

In Poland, as in Italy, the new monarchy in France sought to appear as the patron of the oppressed. There was a large number of Polish émigrés in Paris and it suited the government, taunted by its republican opponents for its failure to liberate the enslaved peoples of Europe, to adopt a radical stand on an issue which fundamentally it was powerless to affect. Moreover, the Poles, like the French, had a case against the treaties of 1815, and all French governments from the Restoration to the Second Empire thought it looked less selfish to emphasize the grievances of others. In November 1830 a revolt broke out in Warsaw which quickly spread to the rest of Russian Poland. The French began to act as if there was a Polish question in European diplomacy; they condemned Russia's suppression of the revolt and suggested a meeting of the great powers to decide what measures of reform they should advise Russia to adopt in Poland. There was in fact no Polish question in European diplomacy, any more than there was an Irish question. The disaffected subjects of the strongest powers might gain much sympathy abroad, but they could not expect other states to take up arms on their behalf. By their protests to the Russians over the treatment of the Poles the French merely strengthened the repugnance in which Nicholas I held France. Palmerston received a deputation of Polish émigrés in London; he made clear his sympathy for them but equally he pointed out that he could do nothing for them. The British position was unequivocal: Russia ruled Poland by established treaty rights which accusations of misrule could not undermine. To attack them would be to strike a blow at the existing order throughout Europe. For the British government Russian control of Poland was an integral part of the international order which contained France in the west. In the last resort there was no possible basis for Anglo–French co-operation on Poland. On this issue, as in Belgium and Italy, the French government pursued a policy which appeared to be radical but which in fact fell far short of a direct challenge to the Vienna system.

The Near Eastern crisis of 1832–33 was a direct consequence of the Greek revolt. In late 1831 Mehemet Ali invaded Syria, which he claimed as the reward promised him by the Sultan for the assistance which the Egyptians had been asked to give the Turks in the Morea. In April 1832 the Sultan declared war on his vassal. This was followed by several months of negotiations in which both sides unsuccessfully attempted to gain the support of the European powers. In December 1832 the war was renewed and the Turks were decisively defeated at Koniah. The Sultan then turned to the British government to save the Ottoman Empire from disaster. Palmerston did not really appreciate the gravity of the crisis in the Near East. He was reluctant to intervene, if only because to do so would require increased naval expenditure to fit out more ships, and this was regarded as impossible for a government committed to financial retrenchment. In the early nineteenth century British governments sought to maintain Great Britain's status as a great power by threats of increased expenditure rather than by actual increases. This was a powerful deterrent when the other powers could not afford to build large navies. Palmerston was equally reluctant to follow an Austrian lead and allow the crisis to be settled by conference diplomacy at Vienna. By these decisions he unwittingly paved the way for a Russian triumph. The Turks, desperate for support, turned to their former enemies. Nicholas I readily offered the assistance which the British had refused. He had good reasons for doing so. He saw the crisis in the Near East as part of the revolutionary upsurge which had already disturbed Europe. To support Turkey against her rebel subject was consistent with his European policy of containment. Secondly, Nicholas was anxious to prevent the collapse of Turkey; in 1829 an imperial committee had reported to the emperor that it was in Russia's interest to support Turkey until such time as her collapse could be fully exploited by Russia. Lastly, Nicholas wanted to prevent Mehemet Ali from taking Constantinople and installing himself as Sultan. He did not want an energetic and reforming ruler in control of the Ottoman Empire. Essentially Russian policy was directed towards the maintenance of the *status quo,* a weak Turkey always susceptible to Russian pressure. By the spring of 1833, with the Egyptian army only 150 miles from Constantinople, the Turks were dependent on Russian naval and military assistance. In July of that year this dependence was formally confirmed by the Treaty of Unkiar Skelessi. The treaty, which was to last for eight years, was a pact of mutual assistance in case of attack. In a secret article Russia relinquished her right to call on the assistance of Turkey in return for Turkish agreement to close the Straits to foreign warships. This too was a Russian attempt to maintain the *status quo;* it confirmed a long-standing tradition of Ottoman policy that the Straits were closed to warships of all nations. It applied as much to Russia as it did to the other powers. The British and the French were greatly alarmed by the treaty. They believed that the Russians had acquired the right to open and close the Straits at will, and Palmerston was genuinely convinced that the new Russian policy was a prelude to the partition of the Ottoman Empire. He refused to accept Nicholas's assurances that the treaty represented no fundamental change in Russo-Turkish relations. He and his cabinet colleagues could not conceive of a situation in which Britain and Russia were pursuing identical policies in the Near East.

After their triumph in the Near East, the Russians turned their attention to central Europe. Once again they sought to strengthen the *status quo* by specific agreements. Nicholas I realized that in order to place his relations with Austria on a secure footing he would have to offer Metternich assurances on the two great issues over which he was suspicious of Russian policy: the Near East and Poland. Nicholas and Metternich met at Münchengrätz in September 1833 and quickly concluded an agreement. The two powers agreed to act together to preserve the existing dynasty in Turkey, to defend the Sultan against the attacks of Mehemet Ali, to consult each other if the Turkish empire were to collapse, and mutually to guarantee their Polish possessions. This unequivocal Russian commitment to the maintenance of the existing order was intended to allay Metternich's fears that Russia sought expansion at the expense of her two weak neighbours. A month later the three eastern powers signed the Convention of Berlin, which was essentially a renewal, albeit in a modified form, of the principles of the Protocol of Troppau. Whereas Münchengrätz witnessed the Near Eastern and Polish agreements, the Berlin Convention established the basis for the future relations of the three powers in central Europe. This was in reality no more than the renewal of the Russian guarantee of support to Austria and Prussia against the revolution and France. They agreed to assist their fellow monarchs to suppress revolution and bound themselves to prevent the counter-intervention of a fourth power. It was this clause that was the most important result of the French occupation of Ancona. The Russians were well content with the various agreements they had concluded: 'all this seems to me', wrote the emperor, 'to insure our security and our defensive position'. The great strength of the eastern alignment was the inequality of power within it; both the Austrians and the Prussians were dependent on Russian support in case either or both were attacked by France or were overwhelmed by revolution. In German affairs, particularly where the stability of the smaller German states was concerned, and in the affairs of the Confederation, Prussia was expected to follow an Austrian lead. In the last resort, the alignment was held together by Russia's willingness to respect Austria's interests in the Near East and by her vast military power. Palmerston, however, was convinced that 'the military organization of Russia's political fabric renders encroachment upon her neighbours almost a necessary condition of her existence'. He was determined to destroy the new Russian position in the Near East and to create a counterweight to Russian power in Europe. In the early 1830s the British government was convinced that the Russians posed an even greater danger to the peace of Europe than France.

The British and French governments reacted differently to the triumphs of Russian diplomacy in 1833. The French were more alarmed by the Convention of Berlin, which they believed was specifically directed against them; the British saw the greatest danger in the Near East where Turkey had been made unnaturally dependent on her most dangerous enemy. Talleyrand, the French ambassador in London, and leading members of the cabinet in Paris were convinced that the difference of outlook could be overcome by a general defensive alliance between the two powers whereby France would assist Great Britain to defend her interests in the Near East, and in return the British would support the French in Europe. Talleyrand's alliance proposal was rejected by Palmerston. Although he wanted French assistance against Russia in the Near East, he did not want to give the French security in Europe. The alliance which the French proposed would have placed the two governments on equal terms. Palmerston's aim was to perpetuate French fear of isolation and thus render them permanently dependent on British goodwill. He was convinced that, once free from this anxiety, the French would revive their territorial ambitions. In fact, Palmerston sought to do in the west what Nicholas had done in the east: exploit the weakness and fears of his potential allies to force them to accept an agreement on his terms. In this Palmerston eventually succeeded. In January 1834 he finally refused the general alliance which the French offered. In March he offered instead a limited agreement designed to serve what were essentially British interests in the Iberian peninsula. The triumph of Russian diplomacy in 1833 in the Near East and eastern Europe was followed in 1834 by the triumph of British diplomacy in the west. There could be no doubt that these two powers dominated the European states system.

Canning's intervention in Portugal in 1826 had only been successful in the short term. After the immediate danger to the pro-British regime was past, the British marines were withdrawn, and in the following year the Portuguese government fell victim to those forces against which Canning had tried to protect it. By 1828, when the French withdrew their army of occupation from Spain, old-style absolutism had been restored in both Spain and Portugal. The two rulers, Ferdinand VII in Spain and Dom Miguel in Portugal, looked to the three eastern powers for financial support and political guidance, particularly after the July revolution in France and the appointment of a Whig government in England. In the early 1830s the British and French lost their positions as the patrons of the peninsular monarchies. Between 1830 and 1834 Palmerston made several attempts by diplomacy to destroy Dom Miguel and his absolutism in Portugal. But all his efforts to champion the constitution of 1826 and to restore Queen Dona Maria to the throne failed. Ferdinand VII's determination to maintain absolutism throughout the peninsula was the greatest obstacle in the way of Palmerston's Portuguese policy. The death of Ferdinand VII and the succession of his infant daughter Isabella II changed both peninsular politics and great-power relations in the Peninsula. The late king's brother, Don Carlos, who was an exile in Portugal, refused to recognize his niece as Queen of Spain and began to gather together an army to invade Spain and claim the throne. The Spanish Regent, Queen Cristina, turned to England for support and offered to assist in the destruction of Portuguese absolutism in return for British assistance in destroying the Carlist challenge to the new order in Spain. It was as a result of these realignments that the Quadruple Alliance of 1834 was created.

Palmerston's aim was to associate France with the new treaty but to exclude her from the actual military and naval operations in Portugal. The French had little alternative but to accept the offer, first because they wanted an agreement with England and second because they saw British intervention in Portugal as a precedent for French intervention in Spain. Moreover, some French ministers hoped that some time in the future this limited treaty could be transformed into a defensive alliance. In late April and May 1834 British and Spanish forces quickly destroyed the military bases of the two pretenders in Portugal. The constitution of 1826 was restored and both Miguel and Carlos were forced into exile. Within two months Carlos returned to Spain and joined the Basque revolt. To the provincial insurrection was now added a disputed succession and a war of ideas, between Madrid liberalism on the one hand and clerical absolutism on the other. From the outset the eastern powers supplied the Carlists with arms and money, usually channelled through the lesser absolutist states. In July 1834 the British and French signed additional articles to the Quadruple Alliance in the hope of cutting off supplies to the Carlists and strengthening the new liberal regime at Madrid. Palmerston argued that although the letter of the treaty had been fulfilled by the expulsion of the pretenders from Portugal, the spirit of the treaty demanded that the two great-power signatories to the treaty were morally obliged to assist Spain to destroy the challenge of Carlism. From the outset Palmerston was determined that the new alliance should have a wider significance; 'the new confederacy of the west', he claimed, counterbalanced the 'triple league of the despotic powers'. The British government regarded its rivalry with Russia as the main problem of its foreign policy. 'There is', wrote Palmerston, 'the same principle of repulsion between Russia and us that there was between us and Bonaparte.' In the 1830s Russophobia became an important element in shaping British attitudes towards Europe. It combined a hatred of absolutism with a deep-rooted belief that Russia was an expansionist and aggressive power. The Russian government, by contrast, was never as overtly anti-British as the British were anti-Russian. As far as Nicholas was concerned, his main enemy was 'the revolution', and he regarded France as the principal source of all revolutionary excitement. The Russians were far more anti-French than anti-British. Moreover, both the British and the Russians sought by separate means to maintain the territorial order, the British in the west, the Russians in central and eastern Europe. Equally, both powers strove to maintain internal order, the Russians by resolute opposition to political change, the British by promoting limited change from above. In fact the gulf between Great Britain and Russia was not nearly as great as Palmerston supposed. The French soon realized that their British ally was as determined as the eastern powers to contain them. In the late 1830s they set out to destroy both the western liberal and the eastern autocratic alignment, and to create a new one centred around themselves.

In both England and France there were powerful influences opposed to the liberal union of the west. The Tory opposition in England condemned Anglo-French co-operation as a disastrous betrayal of the national interest, and in Paris many leading politicians regarded it as involving the sacrifice of French honour and prestige to purchase the goodwill of England. The French resented British attempts to place themselves on a footing of equality with France in Spain. Although many French politicians were in fact opposed to the intervention of the French army in Spain to end the civil war, they sought jealously to guard their sole right to intervene and their political ascendancy at Madrid. The very issue on which the union of the two powers was cemented by treaty obligations became a matter of constant conflict between them. In the Near East too British and French policies were beginning to diverge. Palmerston was convinced that Turkey must be released from her unnatural dependence on Russia, while by the mid 1830s the Orleans Monarchy was beginning to cultivate good relations with Mehemet Ali. Moreover, throughout the 1830s the British anxiously watched French expansion in Algeria, and were determined to oppose further French conquest of North African territory. By the late 1830s French Mediterranean policy had reverted to its former anti-British bias.

In 1836 Thiers, during his first ministry, attempted to reshape the European policy of France. This initiative was grounded in the recognition that England as much as Russia was a barrier to French recovery. He believed that Austria and Prussia were as much prisoners of their alliance with Russia as the French were of their alignment with England. His aim was to secure some sort of an agreement with either or both. This was a French bid to assert her equality with her two great rivals: France must create her own alignment rather than remain the junior partner of another power. The favourable response which Thiers's initial overtures met in Vienna was merely a ploy on Metternich's part. He sought a public affirmation by the French of their dissatisfaction with the liberal alliance. This would destroy the illusion entertained by liberals and revolutionaries that they were protected by the two liberal powers, and Metternich hoped that it would incline England to look to her erstwhile allies for support against France. He had no intention of beginning alliance negotiations with the French. Foiled in his attempt to detach the German powers from Russia, Thiers attempted to repeat the tactics of Chateaubriand and demonstrate French military power in the west by a slow build-up of French forces in Spain. This too was essentially anti-English. He wanted France to have all the credit for the destruction of Carlism, which was the surest way of reasserting French dominance at Madrid. In the autumn of 1836 this policy also collapsed as a result of disagreements within the French government and between Thiers and the king. By the beginning of 1837 the British and the French had ceased to co-operate in western Europe. Palmerston readily acknowledged this but he held on to the *entente* in the belief that it could still serve British interests in the Near East.

In the five years between the Treaty of Unkiar Skelessi and the outbreak of the second Mehemet Ali crisis, the Near East was a source of constant, if low-key, tension between the powers. The basis of Palmerston's belatedly-formulated Near Eastern policy was to strengthen the Ottoman Empire to enable it to resist attack from either

Mehemet Ali or Russia. He hoped that an extensive programme of reform would revitalize and transform it into a modern and efficient state, able to look after its own interests. While it remained vulnerable to its enemies the British were prepared to afford it the protection it needed. Although the Russians had no desire to strengthen Turkey, neither were they prepared to allow Mehemet Ali to precipitate its collapse. In so far as they were both opposed to Egyptian expansion, there was a real community of interest between the British and the Russians. All that was needed for actual co-operation was for the Russians to make clear the anti-Egyptian basis of their policy. Moreover, by the late 1830s both powers realized that no lasting settlement could be achieved in the Near East without some agreement between them. Palmerston was certainly prepared to work with the Russians in a great-power conference if they would abandon the Treaty of Unkiar Skelessi.

The Near Eastern crisis of 1839–41 was precipitated by Turkey. The Sultan, who had long sought revenge for his earlier defeat, declared war on Mehemet Ali in April 1839. Within six weeks the Ottoman empire was on the verge of collapse. In June the Egyptians inflicted the crushing defeat of Nizib on the Turkish forces. This, combined with the death of the Sultan, Mahmud II, the succession of a sixteen-year-old boy and the sinking of the Ottoman fleet produced panic at Constantinople. After an unsuccessful attempt to reach agreement with Mehemet Ali, the Turks saw no alternative but to allow the great powers to intervene, and in August 1839 the Porte empowered them to reach a settlement on its behalf with Mehemet Ali. The first phase of the crisis – armed conflict in the Near East between Turkey and Egypt – was over. In the second and longest phase, the future of the Near East was only one of the problems involved.

In the period from August 1839 to November 1840 great-power diplomacy was dominated by the interaction of three problems: the search for a settlement in the Near East, the role of France in the European states system, and the future of great-power alignments. When the French raised the threat of war, it was on the Rhine and not in the Near East. Moreover, it was the French who prevented a speedy settlement of the second Mehemet Ali crisis by the concerted action of the five powers. By the autumn of 1839 the French began to argue that Mehemet Ali must not be robbed of the fruits of his victories, and that the expansion of Egypt did not of necessity threaten the security of the Turkish empire. The British claimed that this was a complete *volte-face* on the part of France. In fact it was only a question of emphasis. Since .the mid 1830s the French had regarded their close relationship with

61

Mehemet Ali as an integral part of their Mediterranean policy. Thiers, who returned to office in 1840, was not prepared to abandon Mehemet Ali and follow a British lead in the eastern Mediterranean. Palmerston regarded the French proposal that Mehemet Ali should retain Syria as compatible neither with the strengthening of Turkey nor with safeguarding the land routes to British India. The Anglo-French *entente* which Palmerston had never openly repudiated despite its breakdown in western Europe, in case it might be needed to restrain Russia in the Near East, had completely collapsed. It no longer served any British interest. Palmerston then turned to Metternich for support. He believed that Britain and Austria could co-operate in the Near East despite their different outlooks in Europe. Metternich gladly responded to Palmerston's approach; he saw it as an opportunity for Austria to take the lead in a search for a settlement in the Near East, and to pave the way for the revival of the old four-power alliance. It was the Russians who denied Metternich the chance of such a diplomatic triumph. In September 1839 Nicholas I sent a Russian diplomat, Baron Brunnow, to London to seek Anglo-Russian co-operation for the settlement of the Near Eastern crisis.

In 1839 the Russians, like the French, changed the emphasis rather than the direction of their Near Eastern policy. Stability and order remained their basic objectives. The imperial government had already abandoned its right under the Treaty of Unkiar Skelessi to assist Turkey when it agreed, in August 1839, to seek an international settlement to the crisis. In fact the state of Russian finances was such that she could not afford to assist Turkey; the greatest army in Europe was immobilized by an empty treasury. In 1841 the treaty would expire, and it was apparent to the Russians that the British government was determined to frustrate any attempt to renew it. This meant that the Russians had to seek other means to prevent the collapse of Turkey and to keep the Straits closed in time of peace to foreign warships. In addition to these Near Eastern objectives, Nicholas and his foreign minister, Nesselrode, sought to destroy the Anglo-French *entente* in Europe, isolate France and contain the forces of revolution by the revival of the four-power combination of Chaumont. This was his traditional policy in a new form. Palmerston's response to Brunnow's overtures was immediate and favourable. Just as Canning had worked with Russia on the Greek question to achieve a settlement acceptable to both powers, so Palmerston was prepared to do the same in the second Mehemet Ali crisis. In January 1840 Great Britain and Russia agreed to work together to confine Mehemet Ali to Egypt.

Throughout 1840 there were several determined attempts from

within the British cabinet to frustrate Anglo-Russian co-operation. Some of Palmerston's cabinet colleagues regarded the preservation of the Anglo-French *entente* as vastly more important than the question of whether Egypt or Turkey should possess Syria. In March 1840 Thiers formed his second ministry; he was disposed to believe it more likely that Palmerston would be forced by his colleagues to make concessions to France than that France would be forced to watch while Great Britain and Russia coerced Mehemet Ali. This was a serious miscalculation. In July 1840 the British and the Russians, supported by Austria and Prussia, concluded a series of agreements on the Near East. The new Anglo-Russian accord was given a solid basis by their mutual resolve to close the Straits to foreign warships in time of peace. This, like the Treaty of Unkiar Skelessi, confirmed the traditional practice of the Ottoman Empire. The four powers also agreed the terms they would offer Mehemet Ali if he submitted to them in ten days: the hereditary rule of Egypt, and the possession of southern Syria for his lifetime only. If, however, he refused these terms, the four powers resolved to drive him out of Syria and confine him to Egypt. If it became necessary to enforce the latter terms, Great Britain and Russia, the two naval powers, would undertake the task. Confronted by the Anglo-Russian accord, the French hoped to salvage something for Mehemet Ali and to recover their fast diminishing prestige by changing the issue. They began to suggest, first by hints and then by direct menace, that the coercion of Mehemet Ali could mean war on the Rhine. This alarmed the Austrians and the Prussians who would bear the brunt of any French attack. Palmerston's pro-French colleagues urged the necessity of concessions to Mehemet Ali in the Near East to avoid war in Europe. Both Palmerston and Nicholas stood firm, the former because he believed that the French were bluffing, the latter because he knew that if the French attacked on the Rhine the British would offer him subsidies to put his army on a war footing. In August 1840 the British, Austrians and Russians began the coercion of Mehemet Ali against a background of war fever in Europe. By September some French newspapers were assuming that war was inevitable. It was at this point that Louis Philippe abandoned Thiers and the prospect of war and sought a new ministry which would work for peace. It was not difficult to find a new government which regarded peace in Europe as more important to France than the possession of Syria by Mehemet Ali. On 4 November the British Mediterranean fleet bombarded and captured Acre; as a result Mehemet Ali evacuated Syria and on 27 November accepted the terms offered by the four powers. With the change of government in France and the submission of Mehemet Ali, the crisis was effectively over. In June 1841 an agreement was concluded between the five powers on the Straits which confirmed the provisions of the agreement of July 1840. It was Austria and Prussia, rather than Great Britain and Russia, who were most anxious to bring France back into the Concert. Their real concern was not the Straits but peace on the Rhine.

After the crisis was over, the Russian government offered the British a formal agreement which would place their co-operation on a permanent basis. It was a straightforward alliance proposal which was intended to be the final link in the chain of Russia's agreements. Palmerston politely refused it on the grounds that the two powers had a sufficient community of interest, in the containment of France and the maintenance of order in the Near East, to ensure good relations in the future. Russia's position in Europe was undoubtedly strengthened by the outcome of the crisis. Her relations with her two central European allies remained unchanged; to this united front of absolutist powers the Russians could add a new stability in the Near East and good relations with England. The fall of Melbourne's Whig government and the formation of a new Tory ministry under Peel, with Lord Aberdeen at the Foreign Office, did not jeopardize the improvement in Anglo-Russian relations. The Tories had been consistent critics of the liberal alliance, and had always urged a united front of the four allies of Chaumont to maintain peace and order. Aberdeen, however, soon came to the conclusion that good relations between England and France were as necessary as good relations between England and Russia. If the two great powers of western Europe remained at loggerheads it was quite possible that one of their many conflicts of interest, inflamed by the mutual hostility of public opinion in both countries, could lead to war. Aberdeen did not seek to revive the liberal alliance of the 1830s, which had in reality been directed against Russia, but to create an atmosphere of trust and understanding in which disputes could be avoided. His attitude was shared by Guizot, the new French foreign minister. He believed that Thiers, by bringing France to the brink of war, had also brought her to the verge of another revolution. Stability and order within France herself required peace between the powers, and the best way to achieve this was by sympathy and understanding between the leading statesmen of Europe. Whereas Thiers had attempted to defy the other powers, Guizot tried to persuade them to respect France. His aim was to reconcile France to the Vienna settlement and to her new status in Europe, and to reconcile the other great powers, particularly the autocratic monarchies, to the new order in France. He, like Aberdeen, was convinced that peace and stability in the west demanded good relations between France and England.

By the end of 1843 both Aberdeen and Guizot spoke of the existence of an *entente cordiale* between England and France. This was no more than an understanding between themselves, supported by a growing intimacy between the British and French royal families. In neither country was the new *entente* popular. It was strongly criticized in the parliaments and press of both countries, it was never wholeheartedly supported by all the members of the British and French cabinets, and it was frequently thwarted in its execution by British and French diplomats. The *entente* was in fact an extremely fragile instrument of co-operation. Its fragility was revealed on virtually every issue on which the two ministers sought to reach a compromise. The British were outraged by the treatment accorded to the British consul, Pritchard, in the Friendly Islands after the French annexation in 1842. This dispute dragged on for several months, and Peel publicly described French policy in the Pacific as 'a gross insult' to Great Britain. In 1844 the two powers clashed over Morocco; the British suspected the French of attempting to take control of the country whereas the French claimed that they were merely pursuing Algerian rebels who were using Morocco as a base for their activities. The Moroccan crisis of 1844 coincided with the visit of the Russian emperor to England, which was intended to demonstrate and consolidate the cordial relations which existed between the two powers. As far as Europe was concerned, the two powers soon found common ground; they both feared the growth of French naval power in the Mediterranean, and the Russians were easily convinced that the *entente cordiale* was not directed against them. On the Near East the two governments held discussions in early June which were confirmed in a memorandum of September. They agreed to co-operate if Turkey seemed to be on the point of collapse or was attacked by another power. This was no more than an agreement to do in the future what they had done in 1840. In the event of the complete collapse of Turkey, they pledged themselves to establish a basis for joint action. These discussions mostly reflected Russian anxiety about the state of the Ottoman Empire, but they also revealed the willingness of the two powers to discuss issues of common concern in a frank and open manner. Having settled their outstanding differences by the Straits Convention of 1841, all the two powers could do was to establish a fund of goodwill upon which they could draw when future differences arose.

In late 1844 and 1845 Aberdeen and Guizot tried to breathe life into their ailing *entente* by an exchange of views on Spain. The result was a series of informal agreements. The ostensible problem was the choice of husbands for the young Queen of Spain and her sister, the heiress to the throne. The real issues at stake were French prestige and the division of influence in the Iberian peninsula between the two great powers. Guizot was determined to secure from Aberdeen a clear admission that France was the great-power patron of the new liberal order in Spain. At the same time he was willing to concede that English influence should predominate at Lisbon. In the late 1830s and the early 1840s Anglo-French rivalry in Spain had fastened itself upon the conflicts within Spanish politics between the *Moderados,* the pro-French party, and the *Progresistas,* the pro-English party. In 1844 a *coup* by *Moderado* politicians and army officers destroyed the *Progresista* ascendancy established, under British auspices, in the late 1830s. Guizot wanted to arrange marriages for the Queen and her sister which would consolidate the *Moderado* hegemony at Madrid and thus strengthen the links between France and Spain. This would demonstrate that France, like the other great powers, enjoyed influence over her smaller neighbours. Aberdeen was content to follow a French lead on Spanish questions, thereby implicitly recognizing the predominance of France at Madrid. Unlike Palmerston, he saw no need to contest French influence in Spain. Aberdeen's only qualification was that France must not dictate to Spain on the marriage question. In 1845 he agreed to the marriage of the Queen's sister to the Duke of Montpensier, son of the King of the French, after the Queen had married and produced an heir. His insistence that the marriage should be delayed was an attempt to make the marriage merely a Bourbon family arrangement rather than a political issue.

In 1846 Guizot's policy on the Spanish marriages was threatened on two fronts. The Spanish government began to resent French dictation on the question, and in June the Peel government in England fell and was replaced by a new Whig ministry led by Lord John Russell, with Palmerston again at the Foreign Office. The latter was not prepared to accept the fundamental assumption of Aberdeen's policy that France should enjoy an indisputable preponderance at Madrid. He adopted a policy on the marriage question which enabled him to appear to be the champion of Spanish independence when in reality he was attempting to undermine French influence at Madrid. Guizot feared that he, like Thiers in 1840, would be outmanoeuvred by Palmerston. He abandoned the agreement he had concluded with Aberdeen and hastily concluded a double-marriage pact: the Queen of Spain would marry a Spanish Bourbon of impeccable *Moderado* credentials and at the same time her sister would marry Louis Philippe's son.

Palmerston was greatly alarmed by the arrangement. After an unsuccessful attempt to prevent the marriages, he concluded that the *entente* was in ruins and that England must look to the eastern powers to help curb the ambitions of France. Guizot believed that, in view of the hostility of England, he must cultivate good relations with Austria to prevent the isolation of France. From the autumn of 1846 to the revolutions of 1848 Great Britain and France were not only engaged in a bitter war of words and a struggle for influence over the small powers in the west, but they were also competing for the goodwill of the eastern powers. Palmerston looked to Russia, and to a lesser extent Prussia, for support, whereas Guizot concentrated his efforts on gaining the goodwill of Metternich. The autocratic powers exploited this competition for their support. In the autumn of 1846 they extinguished the republic of Cracow, the last enclave of Polish independence, which had been a constant source of irritation to them. They claimed that it was the centre of Polish revolutionary activity, a danger to peace and order in eastern Europe. Although both the British and the French governments protested against the suppression of Cracow, their protests were muted and independent. Neither wished seriously to offend the eastern powers.

In the last year of his long stewardship of the Austrian Empire, Metternich enjoyed a more central role in European diplomacy, a role which had been denied him since the congress of Verona. He owed this importance not to his skill as a diplomat but to the many serious problems which Austria faced. The challenge to Austria's authority in central Europe began in 1847. In 1848 the nature of the challenge was to change from protest to revolution, and to extend from a few to virtually all areas within Austrian influence. Metternich for his part sought to isolate each of his problems and to deal with them by a combination of coercion and diplomacy. This was his final legacy to the Habsburg monarchy. His successor Schwarzenberg was to restore Habsburg authority in 1849 and 1850 by using the same tactics. In 1847 the two areas of crisis were Switzerland and Italy. In several Protestant cantons of the Swiss Confederation there were demands for radical reform of the Federal constitution, and in several Italian states there were protests against rising prices and inefficient government. Both problems could have been settled by Austro-French co-operation. Throughout the early part of 1847 Guizot claimed that he was just as anxious as Metternich to maintain stability and order in these areas. In fact, however, Metternich found it extremely difficult to persuade Guizot to work with him openly against the so-called forces of disruption. The French government wanted order restored in Switzerland under French rather than Austrian auspices, and moderate reform from above under French patronage rather than repression by Austria in central Italy. Fear of revolution in central Europe did not unite France and Austria: it merely intensified the competition between them. The French were never really prepared to ignore any opportunity to weaken Austria. In Paris Austria's difficulties were always regarded as France's opportunities. There were, moreover, domestic reasons why Guizot could not work with Austria alone; to do so would allow his critics in the Chamber to claim with justice that he had destroyed the *entente cordiale* and aligned the liberal monarchy with a reactionary power. On Switzerland, Guizot saw a way out of this dilemma by attempting to lead a concert of all the powers. If France took the initiative, Guizot, not Metternich, would earn the credit for pacifying Switzerland, and in a combination of five the presence of England would guard him against the charge of working exclusively with the absolutist powers. In fact it proved impossible to create a concert of five on the Swiss question; the four continental powers openly sympathized with the Swiss conservative cantons, the *Sonderbund,* whereas the British government took the side of the radicals. Only Franco–Austrian intervention in the autumn of 1847 could have saved the *Sonderbund* from defeat. Guizot did not contemplate intervention until it was too late, and after the radicals had triumphed he could not permit unilateral Austrian intervention to rob them of their victory. By December 1847 the radicals were in a position to push through the Federal reforms they wanted, and both Guizot and Metternich were forced to accept that their Swiss policies had failed. Metternich was quite right when he said that Austria and France had worked against each other rather than with each other.

Italian problems in 1847 were much more serious than the *Sonderbund* crisis; Palmerston was convinced that they could lead to war. He feared that the intervention of the Austrian army in the central Italian states would result in French counter-intervention, and that the two armies would inevitably clash. By the end of the year the Austrians, the French and the British were each trying separately to prevent revolution and war in Italy. Metternich was determined to preserve Austria's dominance in the peninsula. As far as he was concerned there could be no alteration of the 1815 settlement and no compromise with reform movements which attempted to undermine the sacred principle of monarchical authority. Although he was prepared to consider the possibility of some modification in the administration of the two Austrian provinces of Lombardy and Venetia, he was nevertheless reconciled to the fact that repression might become a necessity. In the autumn of 1847 the British government sent a cabinet minister, Lord Minto, on a roving mission to Italy to urge the Italian rulers to reform their governments and the Italian reformers not to provoke Austria into military action. The British bid for the patronage of the Italian reform movements forced Guizot to make a counter-bid. French diplomats in the peninsula urged Italian liberals to look to France for guidance and support. The Austrians resented both French and British interference in Italian affairs, and the French resented the intrusion of the British. Guizot regarded the anti-Austrian and the reform movements in Italy as exclusively under French direction. This pattern of great-power rivalry in Italy was interrupted, first by the February revolution in Paris and then by the Italian revolutions themselves. In 1848 it was the British government which took the initiative in the search for a new order in Italy which was both anti-Austrian and anti-French.

The French revolution of 1848 revived for a second time the fear that a revolutionary regime in France would attempt to destroy the 1815 settlement by a war of conquest and liberation. The fact that the new government was republican seemed to the autocratic powers to increase the danger. Nicholas I went so far as directly to warn the new government against intervention in Italy. In their propaganda the republicans had consistently called for a war of the people of Europe against the kings of Europe. Lamartine's denunciation of the treaties of 1815 immediately after he assumed the post of head of the provisional government was regarded by many as a clarion call to war. Yet it soon became evident that republican France sought peace. Lamartine was in much the same position as Louis Philippe and his ministers had been in 1830: it was necessary to condemn the 1815 settlement to appease French public opinion, but it was equally necessary to respect the treaties in order to avoid war. War would have pushed the revolution leftwards, which the moderate republicans were extremely anxious to prevent; they believed that it would almost certainly result in the defeat of France and the imposition of a far harsher settlement than that of 1815. Lamartine's circular, published in March 1848, was accompanied by private assurance to British politicians that the republic wanted peace. The four powers reacted to the revolution in France in 1848 just as they had done in 1830; they would not offend the new régime as long as it kept within its own frontiers.

In March the events of 1848 ceased to follow the pattern of 1830. On 13 March Metternich fell from power in Vienna, and with him collapsed the central authority of the Habsburg monarchy. In Hungary and Italy the revolutionary leaders turned their backs on Vienna and sought a separate future. Later in March, after riots in Berlin, the Prussian king, Frederick William IV, conceded constitutional reforms and appointed a new liberal ministry which declared that 'Prussia merges into Germany'. The only two great powers untouched by revolution were Great Britain and Russia. This fact brought the diplomatic dominance they had long enjoyed into even sharper relief. For the next three years Palmerston and Nicholas I were the diplomatic arbiters of Europe. Neither the British nor the Russians had one policy towards the great upheavals of 1848. They would have had if the revolutions had directly attacked their vital interests or if all the revolutions had been republican movements determined to destroy the institutions of monarchy and aristocracy in an attempt to construct a new social order. In those cases they would have defended themselves and the principle of monarchy. The diversity of the revolutions elicited flexible responses from both powers. The Russians in particular were prepared to wait upon events; throughout 1848 Nicholas adopted the pose of patient vigilance. He did not become 'the *gendarme* of Europe', the defender of the old order, until 1849 when the conservative forces in central Europe had already recovered their confidence and the political initiative from the divided revolutionaries. Palmerston, on the other hand, in Italy and to a lesser extent in Germany, sought to guide the forces of change and modify the territorial order of 1815. His efforts were much less successful. Nevertheless, both Britain and Russia in their separate ways sought to prevent a European war arising out of the revolutions. They were determined to localize all the revolutionary and military conflicts and to prevent the intervention of any great power except themselves. In this they succeeded; the three wars of 1848–49, in Italy, in Hungary and in the two duchies of Schleswig and Holstein, were all kept distinct. Only in one, that in Hungary, were two great powers involved, and they fought on the same side.

Although Great Britain and Russia urged peace in the spring and summer of 1848, the revolutionary governments did not heed their advice. The German liberals attempted to incite the Poles to fight a war of liberation against Russia; they hoped that this would divert Russian attention while they attempted to reconstruct Germany. This was a false start, and the failure of the Polish revolution to materialize created consternation amongst high-ranking German liberals. They feared that Nicholas I would use his military power to destroy the revolution in Germany. It was the Italians who unleashed the first war of 1848. It was not strictly a revolutionary war, although the Italians found it convenient to depict it as such. In reality it was a war of aggrandizement of one monarch against another. Charles Albert, the king of Piedmont, sought to exploit the revolutions in northern Italy to acquire the two Austrian provinces of Lombardy and Venetia. He was the first monarch since Charles X to seek territorial expansion as an antidote to revolution in his own state. In the next two decades others were to follow his example. In March and April a motley collection of regular troops and volunteers from other Italian states achieved some successes against the Austrians. In May the provisional governments of Lombardy and Venetia voted for union with Piedmont. These events convinced Palmerston that Austrian rule in Italy was bankrupt, and that the only chance of preserving the intended objectives of the Vienna settlement in Italy – a stable order free from French control – was by the creation of a new northern kingdom under the house of Savoy which would include Lombardy and Venetia. Palmerston offered British mediation between the belligerents on the condition that Austria would hand over her Italian possessions to Piedmont. He had high hopes for his projected settlement; it would end the war, strengthen northern Italy against France, safeguard British interests in the Mediterranean and enable the Austrians to concentrate on the recovery of their power in Hungary. It was, however, overtaken by events in northern Italy, over which Palmerston had no control. In July the Austrian forces, commanded by Radetzky, inflicted a major defeat on the Italians at Custozza; on 9 August Charles Albert concluded an armistice with the Austrians. The French government was greatly relieved by the collapse of the Italian war effort. Cavaignac, who had emerged as the strong man of the revolution after the June days in Paris, did not want the fragile republic embroiled in a war with Austria, nor did he wish to see the Italians expel the Austrians without the assistance of France. This would mean revision of the 1815 settlement without French gains which would be a serious blow to the republic. In August Palmerston tried to salvage something from his plan for northern Italy by devising a scheme by which Great Britain and France would prevent Austria from recovering Venetia. This failed when his cabinet colleagues and Queen Victoria refused to support it.

The example set by Piedmont in taking up arms against the treaties of 1815 was followed by Prussia in northern Germany. The two duchies of Schleswig and Holstein, although predominantly German in population, were ruled by the king of Denmark. In April the inhabitants appealed to their fellow Germans for asssistance to expel the Danes. The Prussian army entered the duchies, and by the end of April the Danish army had retreated into Denmark. The Prussians claimed that this was not an old-style war of conquest but a new-style war of liberation: a foreign king would be replaced in the duchies by a German prince. The Danes took their stand on treaty rights, and appealed to Great Britain and Russia to uphold the integrity of the Danish monarchy. The Russians merely denounced the attack by one monarch on the possessions of another, but they would not use their troops to defend Denmark or chastise the Prussians. Palmerston's response was more positive: he insisted that the Prussians should evacuate the duchies although, unlike the Russians, he had no means at his disposal to force them to do so. On northern Germany, as on northern Italy, the British had decided opinions; Palmerston believed that he knew what was best for both Austria and Prussia. His predecessor, Castlereagh, had realized that in central Europe Great Britain could not have an effective policy without allies. Palmerston had an ambitious policy but no allies; his various schemes consequently came to nothing. Although within a few months the Prussians withdrew from the duchies, this was not as a response to the British request that they should do so. The withdrawal of his army was Frederick William's way of separating himself from the German liberal movement. This was not an isolated act of defiance by the Prussian king but part of the growing conservative reaction against revolution. In the last months of 1848 the old ruling elites in Europe recovered their confidence and then used military force to recover their authority. As far as the territorial order of Europe was concerned, the revolutions of 1848 had had far less direct impact than the revolutions of 1830. A new state, Belgium, had emerged out of the upheavals of 1830; in 1848 the old frontiers were everywhere restored.

The recovery of monarchical and autocratic authority did not immediately result in the restoration of the old order in central Europe. In 1849 France ceased to be the only revisionist power; other states attempted to increase their power by jettisoning the work of the peacemakers. Both Austria and Prussia put forward extensive schemes of reconstruction for Germany, and Piedmont made a second bid for expansion in northern Italy. The old order was restored only after Austria had defeated Piedmont at Novara, recovered Hungary with the assistance of Russia, and eventually abandoned her own plan for the reorganization of Germany. Mainly with Russian backing, she had forced the Prussians to accept the revival of the German Confederation. The complete recovery of Austria was the most important development of the years 1849–51. It could not have been achieved without Russian military and diplomatic assistance. The moral of 1848 was that revolutionaries could not modify the settlement of 1815 by agreement amongst themselves; the moral of post-revolutionary diplomacy in the years from 1849 to 1851 was that the great powers could not do so either by agreement. In both Italy and Hungary short, localized wars were necessary to complete the recovery of the old order. British and French attempts to persuade the Austrians and the Piedmontese to settle their differences by negotiation failed, and in

March 1849 Charles Albert, pushed on by his radical parliament, renewed the war in northern Italy. Within a week he had been defeated at Novara, and he abdicated in favour of his son, Victor Emmanuel. Austria could defeat Piedmont, but England and France would not allow her to dismember so weak an opponent or to punish her harshly. The consequences of defeat for a small state with powerful protectors were less traumatic than for great powers. Piedmont could make war because she enjoyed immunity from disaster. This was an important asset which Cavour was later to exploit. Austria had to content herself with inflicting a mild rebuke on Piedmont in the form of a war indemnity which was finally agreed upon in August 1849. Moreover, even before the northern Italian question had been settled, the French had seized the opportunity provided by Austria's preoccupation in Hungary and Germany to exploit the problems in central Italy. In November 1848 Rome had turned against the Pope. In April 1849 Louis Napoleon Bonaparte, who had become president of the Second French Republic in December 1848, sent an army to the gates of Rome. He could not decide whether to act as a good Catholic and restore the Pope or to pose as a good republican and protect the republic. This was a secondary aspect of the question; the real purpose of the expedition was to enable France to assert her power at last in the peninsula after having missed the opportunities for intervention afforded by two wars in northern Italy. In June 1849, after new elections in France had returned a majority of pro-clerical deputies, the French army destroyed the republic and restored the Papacy. The temporal power of the Pope now rested on the permanent presence of French troops in Rome rather than on the occasional intervention of Austria. In 1832 France had challenged Austrian influence in the Papal States; in 1849 Austria was in no position to challenge France. In effect, therefore, the French expedition to Rome significantly reduced Austrian influence in Italy. This was a profound change which was to have far-reaching consequences within a decade.

In Hungary the Austrians could not easily recover their authority without Russian assistance. The Hungarian question in 1849 was exclusively an Austro-Russian concern; neither the French nor the British wished to see Austria lose Hungary: without it she would have ceased to be a great power, and then there would have been no bulwark in central Europe to contain the expansion of Russia. Hungarian independence had no champions because it would have destroyed the system of five great powers. Changes in the hierarchy of power and small adjustments of territory in western and central Europe were developments which the powers were prepared to contemplate, but far-reaching changes in eastern Europe were opposed by all the powers.

Great Britain and France feared that the collapse of Habsburg power in eastern Europe would strengthen Russia, Prussia feared that it would permanently concentrate the attention of Austria on her German interests. The Russians saw successful Hungarian defiance of Austria as a terrible precedent which the Poles might attempt to follow. In April 1849 the Austrian army was expelled from Hungary. In June the Russian army intervened in Hungary to save the Austrian empire from dissolution. The Hungarian question only became a matter for the five powers after the revolution had collapsed. Kossuth and the other leaders of the revolt fled to Turkey, whereupon the Russians demanded their extradition. This resulted in the most serious Anglo–Russian disagreement since the mid 1830s. The British government was convinced that the Russians were using the refugee question to browbeat Turkey while the other powers were preoccupied by European questions. Louis Napoleon did not repeat the mistake of Thiers and separate France from England on a Near Eastern issue. In fact the two powers co-operated closely in stiffening Turkish resistance. Yet soon after the refugee question was satisfactorily settled, the Anglo–French accord collapsed when Palmerston intervened at Athens in support of the complaints of the Maltese Jew, Don Pacifico, a slight to both France and Russia, the other two 'protecting powers' of Greece. Although both the British and the French were profoundly disturbed by the increase in Russian power and prestige after the intervention in Hungary, neither was prepared to set aside their own conflicts to combine against Russia. In both London and Paris Austria was by 1850 regarded as little more than a client state of Russia. It was generally assumed that on all but local questions she would follow a Russian lead.

It was only in Germany that the crisis provoked by the revolutions of 1848 was prolonged beyond the end of 1849. In 1849 it was a four-sided conflict between Austria, Prussia, the liberal parliament of Frankfurt and the Middle States each with its own scheme of reconstruction. The latter two dropped out of the struggle when the king of Prussia contemptuously refused the crown of a 'small Germany' excluding Austria, offered by the liberal deputies of Frankfurt, and when Prussia insisted on dominating rather than assisting the efforts of the Middle States to reform the *Bund* on a federal basis. The Austrians proposed an empire of seventy millions which included all the non-German possessions of the Habsburgs and in which Prussia would play an insignificant part. The Prussians put forward a plan for a small Germany from which Austria would be excluded and which the government at Berlin would easily dominate. Both powers rejected a return to dualism. The Prussians pressed ahead with their plan for a new Germany, formed the Erfurt Union and in May 1850 held a congress of German princes at Berlin. It was the Austrians who changed the nature of the struggle when they temporarily abandoned their plan for a reconstructed Germany. Almost immediately they gained the support of the lesser German princes who saw the institutionalized rivalry of Austria and Prussia in the Confederation as the best guarantee of their own independence. Moreover, it brought the Russians, who had hitherto tried to remain neutral, over to their side. Nicholas wanted to repeat the tactics of the early 1830s and recreate the united front of conservative powers against France and the revolution. In order to achieve this Austria and Prussia must settle their differences, and by offering to revive the Confederation of 1815 the Austrians had – so the Russians believed – shown an admirable willingness to compromise. By the end of 1850 the Russians were actively supporting the Austrian argument that the disturbances in the state of Hesse should be suppressed by the forces of the Confederation and not by those of the Erfurt Union. The Prussians had to decide whether they would resist Austria by war or yield to her by diplomacy. There was a war party in Berlin, but the king took the final decision to concede; he feared republican France more than he feared Austria, and he particularly regretted the estrangement between Russia and Prussia. The Prussians 'surrendered' at Olmütz in November 1850: the Erfurt Union was dissolved and the Confederation of 1815 immediately restored. At first sight the Prussians had lost everything. In fact they had gained a great deal since 1848. In the revived three-power alliance Prussia was certainly treated as the equal of Austria, whereas in its earlier existence Prussia had been regarded as the least of the three. Moreover, if war had come, Prussia would probably have been forced to concede territory to France on the Rhine to purchase her neutrality. The king believed that this would have been a greater calamity than an agreement with Austria. Moreover the Prussians could take consolation from the fact that at Dresden in 1851 the Austrians again failed to secure much support for their plan of an empire of 70 millions. Prussia was in no way weakened by her surrender; she had merely abandoned one plan for a new Germany, not her pretensions to its leadership.

The complete restoration of the 1815 order in central Europe and the revival of the three-power conservative alliance was above all a setback for republican France. Her Bonaparte president was denied the opportunity of seeking an alliance with another revisionist power, and there could be no doubt that the purpose of the Russian-dominated alliance was to isolate and contain her. Moreover, the fact that the new ruler of France was a Bonaparte enabled the Russians to create alarm at Vienna and Berlin about the intentions of France. It was easy for them to argue that sooner or later the nephew would attempt to emulate the uncle. By raising the spectre of war on the Rhine the Russians hoped to discipline their recently revisionist allies. Their fears were not well grounded. Louis Napoleon's aims in foreign policy were limited. He did not want a war of revenge against the four allies of Chaumont such as was advocated by some Bonapartists and most left-wing republicans. He merely sought a modification of the territorial order in the west and equality with England and Russia in the hierarchy of the great powers. In fact he entirely adopted the assumptions, aspirations and fears of his Bourbon and Orleanist predecessors. Like them, he resented the containment of France and the loss of status and prestige which the military defeat of 1815 implied; he shared their fear of isolation and their dread of a war in which France would be opposed by the other four powers. There was nothing new in his programme. Louis Napoleon used a few Bonapartist slogans to make his policy look different, but they were mainly for domestic consumption. In 1830 Louis Philippe said the Orleans Monarchy wanted peace; in 1848 Lamartine said the Republic sought peace; in 1852 Napoleon III said the Empire meant peace; they all meant that France would not go to war until she had secured allies to guard against the danger of another defeat.

It was his search for equality with Great Britain and Russia that led Napoleon III to take up the Near Eastern question. He had made a false start in Europe early in 1852 by appearing to threaten the independence of Belgium shortly after the *coup d'état* which made him Emperor. This had united the four powers against him. Palmerston raised the cry of French aggression to draw the four allies of Chaumont together. By turning away from Europe to the Near East Napoleon III sought to isolate and challenge Russia whom he regarded as the main obstacle to the recovery of France. He did not think in terms of war; he expected merely a conflict of prestige. In Europe the other four powers combined against France; in the Near East Prussia had no interests and neither Great Britain nor Austria had any interest in strengthening Russia. It was the contentious problems of the Near East which attracted Napoleon III. He chose to challenge Russia for two reasons: first, Nicholas I was extremely hostile towards France and the new imperial régime. After Napoleon's assumption of the imperial title Nicholas refused to address him as brother which was customary practice between sovereigns. Second, Napoleon III accurately assumed that the anti-French emphasis of the Russians was an attempt to provide the revived Holy Alliance with a unity of purpose which it would otherwise have lacked. Without Russian support Austria was weak, and freed from Russian control Prussia might revive her German ambitions. Moreover, the issue on which Napoleon III fixed his attention, the guardianship of the Holy Places, was likely to divide Austria, a Catholic power, from Russia, the leading Orthodox state. At the beginning of 1852 the French government demanded that the Ottoman government should hand over the keys to the Holy Places in and around Jerusalem to the Catholic monks, thus denying the Orthodox monks the protecting role they had for some years exercised. This demand was followed by a series of overt threats; by the end of the year the Turkish government conceded.

The unconcealed irritation of the Russians with the triumph of French diplomacy at Constantinople was just what Napoleon III wanted. If the Russians had not reacted in this way the French would have worked hard for nothing. The Russian Emperor saw behind the conflict of prestige over the guardianship of the Holy Places a struggle between 'order' and 'revolution'. His aim was to strengthen the forces of order by a serious blow to French prestige. He would humiliate France in the Near East by demonstrating that Turkey feared Russia more than she feared France and that she must concede more to Russia than she had to France. In February 1853 Nicholas sent Prince Menshikov on a special mission to Turkey, first to demand the dismissal of the minister who had bowed to French pressure over the Holy Places, and second to secure the recognition of Russia's right to protect the Christian subjects of Turkey, the Russian interpretation of the Treaty of Kutchuk Kainardji of 1774. Prior to Menshikov's departure Nicholas had tried to reassure both the British and the Austrians that he would respect their interests in the Near East. In January 1853 he assured Seymour, the British ambassador, that if Turkey collapsed Great Britian would receive a fair share of the partition. This was a renewal of the assurance he had given to Aberdeen, who had become prime minister in 1852, on his visit to London in 1844. In fact, however, the Menshikov mission provoked a Near Eastern crisis in which the British and the Austrians as well as the French became deeply suspicious of Russian policy. As this crisis developed, the conflict of prestige between France and Russia was relegated to second place. The Turks resisted Menshikov's demands, and in May 1853 he left Turkey after the complete failure of his mission. In July the Russians occupied the two Turkish provinces of Moldavia and Wallachia and declared that they would withdraw only when the Turks conceded the demands which Menshikov had been instructed to make.

Both the British and the Austrians were alarmed by Russia's action, the Austrians because the occupation of the principalities gave the Russians control of the mouth of the Danube, the most vital trade route of the Habsburg empire. The British could see no other explanation for Russia's occupation of the principalities than a determination to pursue a forward policy in the Near East. It seemed to many of the Whig members of the coalition government that their belief that strong despotic monarchies inevitably sought expansion was well grounded. At the outset of the crisis both powers wanted a settlement which would enable the Russians to withdraw without damage to their prestige and by which Turkey could concede something to Russia without affecting her independence. In 1840 conference diplomacy had solved the Near Eastern crisis; in 1853 the Austrians were convinced that it could do so again. There was, however, a fundamental difference between the two crises: in 1840 the powers were responding to a crisis provoked by Egypt, whereas in 1853 two great powers, the French and then the Russians, had themselves provoked the crisis. There was a profound difference between deciding on terms which Great Britain and Russia were agreed they would impose on Mehemet Ali and finding a solution to a Russo–Turkish conflict. The conference could only succeed if the Russians were prepared to retreat. It met at Vienna in July 1853; the representatives drew up the Vienna Note which contained the concessions which the powers thought Turkey could reasonably be expected to offer the Russians. The Turkish government afterwards insisted upon amendments, and in September the Russians declared that the Vienna Note gave them all they had demanded. This 'violent' interpretation destroyed the Concert. Having in fact retreated, the Russians were determined to make it look as if they had not done so. When diplomacy failed, the British and the French turned to naval action which was the only way they could demonstrate their determination to defend Turkey. They had already advanced their fleets into Turkish waters. In September 1853 they ordered them through the Dardanelles. By opposing the Russians the British could not escape co-operation with France. Napoleon III realized that the British were trapped: if they advanced, France could advance with them; if they retreated, France would replace them as the protector of Turkey against Russia.

While the two western powers drew closer together, the Russians tried to make a dignified retreat through the Holy Alliance. What Nicholas would not concede to the Concert of Five which included revolutionary France he could freely offer to his conservative allies. The Russians proposed to the Prussians an alliance against France in Europe, and assured the Austrians that they would evacuate the principalities after the Turks had made some minor concessions. This was too little for the Austrians and too much for the Prussians. Austria would not feel secure until the Russians were out of the principalities, and the Prussians did not want a war in Europe in which they would bear the brunt of the fighting. This deadlock in great-power diplomacy was broken by the Turks who declared war on Russia on 4 October 1853. Four days later the British cabinet decided to send their fleet up to Constantinople; it took the decision in ignorance of the fact that the Turks had already declared war. Its intention was to protect Turkey against Russia; its effect was to encourage her to begin hostilities. On 30 November the Russians destroyed the Turkish fleet at Sinope. This was a perfectly legitimate act of war but in the British and French press it was portrayed as a massacre. From the autumn of 1853 onwards there was war fever in Great Britain and France. Neither the British nor the French governments could ignore the fact that public opinion wanted a decisive setback for Russia and the humiliation of the Russian despot. War was the only means to achieve these ends. In January 1854 the British and the French governments declared that the purpose of their fleets in the Black Sea was to protect Turkish shipping and to confine the Russian fleet to its base at Sebastopol. In other words, Russia must not make war on Turkey even though Turkey had declared war upon her. This was not a last bid for peace: it was a demand for victory, without having to fight for it.

The Russians reluctantly assumed that these measures would inevitably result in Great Britain and France entering the war in the Near East. They therefore made a final effort to secure their position in Europe before the hostilities began. Nicholas sent Prince Orlov on a special mission to Vienna and Berlin to ask the two German powers for their armed neutrality. The Austrians and Prussians refused this reversal of roles: the purpose of the Holy Alliance was that the Russian army should protect Austria and Prussia in Europe, not that their armies should protect Russia in the Near East. The failure of the Orlov mission was a turning-point not only in the Near Eastern crisis but also in the history of Europe: it confirmed the collapse of the Holy Alliance which for three decades had been the great bulwark of order in eastern and central Europe. The unity of the three conservative monarchies under Russian leadership had held France in check and given the Vienna treaty structure its security and strength. When Orlov returned to St Petersburg empty-handed one of the essential props of the Vienna system had disappeared. In February 1854 Great Britain and France sent an ultimatum to Russia, demanding her withdrawal from the principalities: an action which the Russians had taken more than six months before was thus chosen as the *casus belli*. It was the Russian victory at Sinope which was the really decisive event, but the western powers could not legally object to this. Instead they chose an issue which made Russia appear the aggressor. When the Russians rejected the ultimatum the Crimean War began.

It was the British and the Russians who sacrificed most by their refusal to compromise in 1854. The Crimean War brought to a close the era of Anglo–Russian domination in Europe. Great Britain, by fighting with France in the Near East, and Russia, by fighting against her, both conceded equality to her as a Mediterranean power. During and immediately after the war the French asserted a dominance in Europe which was made possible by the collapse of the Holy Alliance and then by the defeat of Russia. Moreover, French participation in the war made the issues at stake as much European as Near Eastern. Both the British and the Russians wanted a Near Eastern war which would not affect adversely the European treaty structure. They both fought for limited and localized objectives. The French, by contrast, fought for essentially European ends: to confirm the destruction of the Holy Alliance, to deal a decisive blow to Russia's power and prestige in central Europe – in other words to create the conditions which would make revision of the 1815 settlement possible. Moreover, the outbreak of the Crimean War altered fundamentally the pattern of great-power relations. In the west France was no longer forced into a subordinate relationship with England. The liberal alliance of the 1830s was based on French fear of isolation in Europe; the alliance of the mid 1850s was based on equality in the Near East which the French intended to convert into primacy in Europe once the war was over. In eastern and central Europe the Russians had for three decades raised the spectre of French aggression on the Rhine and in Italy in order to persuade Austria and Prussia to follow their lead. This device worked only as long as the Russians made the maintenance of peace and order in Europe a higher priority in their foreign policy than the pursuit of their own interests in the Near East. The Crimean War reversed the order of priorities. The Russian obsession with their Near Eastern position changed their attitude towards France. From the early 1820s to the mid 1850s the Russians were determined to oppose French revision in Europe; after 1856 they saw it as a force to be exploited in the pursuit of their own revision in the Near East. By destroying the pattern of great-power relationships on which the Vienna treaty structure rested the Crimean War made territorial revision in Europe possible. Although not a shot was fired in Europe, it was certainly one of the most important European wars of the nineteenth century.

CHAPTER FOUR
The collapse of the Vienna system 1854–1871

Forty years of peace between the great powers were followed by fifteen years of intermittent warfare. Between 1854 and 1870 all the great powers fought at least one war; Austria, France and Prussia each fought three. The object of all these wars, with the exception of the Crimean War, was the piecemeal destruction of the Vienna settlement. Each of the wars was followed by important territorial changes; the single most extensive revision of the map of Europe between the Congress of Vienna and the Versailles settlement of 1919 took place in 1866. In the 1830s and 1840s liberals and nationalists had condemned the Vienna settlement as reactionary, designed by the forces of dynastic conservatism to serve their own interests, yet in the 1850s and 1860s it was the conservative monarchies that actually destroyed it. They did so quite deliberately. Aggressive wars of national reconstruction and the identification of victory on the battlefield with national pride and regeneration were the means by which monarchical conservatism gave itself a new lease of life. Before the revolutions of 1848 the governments of the continental monarchies avoided war in order to strengthen themselves against their internal enemies; after the Congress of Paris some of them sought war for exactly the same purpose. In domestic politics the ruling élites abandoned the policy of total resistance to change; this had united all their enemies against them and produced the crisis of 1848. They realized that survival and a secure future required a more flexible response to the problems they faced. In the 1850s and 1860s the conservative ruling groups attempted to divide their opponents: they were prepared to make limited concessions to some in order to concentrate on weakening and isolating their most dangerous enemies. This process took different forms in different countries. In Piedmont the liberal – monarchist Cavour worked with the conservatives to isolate the radical nationalists. In Prussia, and later in Germany, Bismarck, a conservative – monarchist, succeeded in separating the forces of liberalism and nationalism. He borrowed from the programmes of both, and gave to both movements a new character and new aspirations. In France Napoleon III was, in the 1860s, prepared to concede some power to his liberal opponents in an attempt to save his dynasty and contain the republican challenge to his regime. In the years between 1856 and 1871 both the Austrian and the Russian empires were forced to come to terms with fundamental problems: in Russia the social basis of the autocracy was modified by the abolition of serfdom, and in the Habsburg monarchy the political structure was changed by the compromise of 1867 with the Hungarians. It was defeat in war coupled with the determination to do better in the next war which produced both these changes. All these domestic realignments resulted in fundamental changes of foreign policy. The emphasis on peace and order and on the maintenance of the existing treaty structure in Europe which had characterized great-power relations before the revolutions of 1848 was abandoned. So too was the fear of a general European conflagration arising out of military conflict in one area. Both the upheavals of 1848 and the conflict in the Crimea had demonstrated that wars could be limited and localized. War therefore ceased to be regarded as a great danger to the social order and became instead the means by which political changes within states were consolidated and given the seal of popular and patriotic approval. The localized wars of the period from 1856 to 1870 were limited in their aims: the great powers did not fight to destroy each other, merely to redistribute territory among themselves. There was a conscious effort to make the wars as short as possible. The rulers of the great powers believed that if war was prolonged and caused great hardship to the civilian population then it could endanger the social order. The Paris Commune of 1871 proved them right in this respect. For the most part the politicians and the generals conducted their wars with a proper sense of restraint. Through the medium of the press governments were able to depict, to their civilian populations, war as a heroic spectacle which demanded respect and acclamation but not sacrifice.

The conduct of war in the mid nineteenth century was fundamentally affected by economic and technological change. The Crimean War was fought with 'the weapons and tactics of the Napoleonic era' yet contemporaries did not doubt that England and France won the war because they were modern states with industrialized economies and sound systems of public finance, whereas Russia was a backward and inefficient state with an almost purely

agrarian economy. The Russians themselves believed this to be true. By
1870 the armed forces of the great powers and the conduct of war itself
had been profoundly affected by new technology. Moreover, an
efficient system of public finance and competent military and civilian
administrations became acknowledged assets in the conduct of war.
Before 1848 the continental monarchies had feared that war would
impose an intolerable strain on their finances. Liberals in England and
France had claimed that war was a crime against civilization. In the
1850s and 1860s most of the governments of the great powers believed
that they could afford short wars without emptying their treasuries and
saddling themselves with enormous debts. At the same time many
intellectuals began to argue that war was an essential activity in the
onward march of civilization. These were profound changes. The
spread of daily newspapers made propaganda for a mass readership an
essential activity of government in wartime. Most governments
claimed at the outset of wars that they were the innocent victims of
aggression and urged the people to unite in defence of their fatherland.
Governments felt it necessary to conceal their very specific territorial
ambitions behind general and idealized value. In 1866 Bismarck asked
Germans to fight Germans not for Prussian expansion but for the sake
of the fatherland; in 1870 Napoleon III called upon the nation to recover
its glory on the battlefield, not to gain territory on the Rhine. There was
real truth in the cynical prophecy of Napoleon I that 'rulers who call
upon the people of Europe will be able to accomplish anything they
wish'.

The war in the Near East which began after the Russian rejection of
of the ultimatum of the western powers in March 1854 only became the
Crimean War after the British and the French decided to fight Russia in
the Crimea. This decision was not taken until some months after the
war had officially begun. Where to fight and what precisely to fight for
were questions to which the British and the French found it very
difficult to provide answers. In fact the Crimean War was more
dominated by diplomacy in Europe than it was by actual military
conflict in the Near East. The war nominally lasted for two years, but
there were only two short bouts of fighting in the Crimea, neither of
which lasted for more than three or four months and each of which was
preceded and followed by important diplomatic negotiations. For the
belligerent governments, if not for the soldiers in the Crimea, it was a
decorous war. In the first phase of the war both sides courted Austria,
the Russians to keep her out of the war, the western powers to bring her
in. The British and the French would have liked to have paid Austria to
fight a Balkan war against Russia, which would have enabled them to

fight a naval war in the Black Sea. This would have been the logical war because the Austrians wanted the Russians out of the principalities more than the western powers did. The emperor, Franz Joseph, and the generals were opposed to war on the grounds that Austria would bear the brunt of the fighting and that war would probably endanger the stability of the empire. They feared that the Hungarians would seize the opportunity to renew their struggle for independence. Austria's policy was therefore to keep out of the war, but at the same time to ensure that the western powers actually fought to protect her interests. This would combine the best of both worlds. One of the most urgent tasks of Austrian diplomacy was to provide for stability in central Europe now that the Holy Alliance had collapsed. Their anxiety on this score was shared by the Prussians. Five years after the great Austro-Prussian struggle in 1849 for the domination of Germany the two powers closed ranks to protect Germany against both war and revolution.

A weaker substitute for the Holy Alliance was secured in April 1854 when the Austrians responded to Prussian overtures and concluded a treaty of mutual defence. The two German powers would defend each other against revolution now that Russia had abandoned this task. It was a recognition of the fact that the two powers might face a common enemy. Fear, not friendship, drew them together. The Austrians insisted that the treaty should protect their interests in the Balkans as well as in central Europe. The Prussians agreed to this, first because there would have been no treaty had they refused, and second because they were convinced that Russia would not choose to fight Austria as well as the western powers. The treaty guaranteed Austria Prussia's support in the event of a Russian attack. In June the Austrians, with Prussian backing, demanded Russia's evacuation of the principalities. They then turned to the western powers to see what they would offer. In London and Paris these overtures were interpreted as an indication that Austria would join the war if the right terms could be secured. The British and the French thought that they could most easily secure Austria's entry into the war by defining the objectives for which the three powers would fight. In fact, however, the Austrians wanted to define the war aims of the western powers without joining the war. This was a Metternichian strategy: to claim the rights of a great power and at the same time to reject the responsibilities of one. Decades of dependence on outside support had induced this mentality at Vienna. In July these discussions resulted in the drafting of the Four Points. The first two points secured Austria's interests in the Lower Danube; the Russian protectorate over the principalities was replaced by an international guarantee, and the Danube was declared a free river for navigation. The third point stipulated that the Straits Convention of 1841 should be revived 'in the interests of the balance of power', and the last demanded the renunciation by Russia of her claim to protect the Christian subjects of Turkey. In August 1854 the two western powers accepted the Four Points and assumed that Austria would join the war. A few days later the Russian army evacuated the principalities. It was replaced by a small Austrian force which was to remain there until the war was over. Austrian diplomacy had triumphed; the Balkan issues at stake in the war were solved entirely to her satisfaction and without a single Austrian shot being fired. When it was clear that there was no chance of war in the Balkans, the war in the Crimea began. In September 1854 the British and the French landed an expeditionary force of 50,000 men in the Crimea. Two months of inconclusive fighting followed; the western allies failed to take the fortress of Sebastopol, and the Russians failed to drive their enemies out of the Crimea. When winter set in there was military deadlock. During the winter of 1854–55 the diplomats in Europe tried to do what the generals in the Near East had failed to do: end the war.

Once again the two western powers concentrated their diplomacy on attempting to bring the Austrians into the war. In December 1854 the Austrians signed an alliance with Great Britian and France to protect the principalities against Russia, and this was followed by a secret agreement with the French to maintain the *status quo* in Italy. Yet again Austria felt no need to join a war since she had secured the best protection possible for her interests in Europe and the Near East. The Piedmontese government, by contrast, anxiously entered a war in which it had no direct interest. The king, Victor Emmanuel, and his conservative advisers believed that Piedmont must at all costs retain the goodwill of England and France. Cavour, the prime minister, was more realistic; he believed that whatever attitude a small state like Piedmont adopted to the war in the Near East, she could count on French support in the future because without her grievances against Austria and her ambitions for territorial expansion Napoleon III could not begin to attack the 1815 settlement in Italy. Cavour yielded to the king rather than resign, and as a consequence Piedmont agreed in January 1855 to send 15,000 men to the Crimea. The months from December 1854 to February 1855 were, strictly speaking, 'the Italian phase' of the Crimean War.

By the spring of 1855 Anglo-French tension over the conduct of the war was a subject of public comment. In France the war was unpopular, and Napoleon III was anxious to placate public opinion either by spectacular military successes or by a negotiated settlement. In England the war itself was popular but the belief that it was being mismanaged by the government aroused immense indignation. The fall of Aberdeen's ministry in January 1855 and the formation of a new government led by Palmerston was generally regarded as a commitment to a more vigorous prosecution of the war. In fact the new ministry was almost immediately forced to begin peace negotiations. It was the Austrians who took the initiative in bringing the belligerents to a peace conference at Vienna. French war weariness, the death of the Emperor Nicholas on 2 March and the accession of Alexander II, whose personal prestige was not committed to the war, seemed to provide a possible basis for compromise, and now that their interests were secure the Austrians had no objection to a negotiated settlement of the third of the Four Points. At the outset of the Vienna conference, which lasted from late March to June 1855, the western powers demanded from Russia terms which implied her complete defeat: the neutralization of the Black Sea. The Russians refused to surrender at the conference because they had not been defeated in the Crimea. They suggested that their Black Sea fleet should be maintained at its pre-war level, and that the five great powers should guarantee the independence of Turkey. The Russian offer was accepted by Lord John Russell and Drouyn de Lhuys, the British and French representatives at the conference. To it they added a triple alliance with Austria for the containment of Russian expansion in the Near East. This was to revive the principles underlying the Treaty of Chaumont of 1814 – a limited peace and a guarantee of the territorial order combined with an alliance against future aggression – and to apply them to the Near East. In London and Paris these terms were rejected: the British government wanted to punish Russia and the French to humiliate her. Without a rude blow to Russian power and prestige the French feared that after the war was over in the Near East the 1815 order in Europe might remain stable and secure. The British feared that unless Russia was decisively defeated there would be no stability and security in the Near East. The western powers had no alternative but to resume hostilities in the Crimea. In June they began the siege of Sebastopol and in September it fell.

By the late autumn of 1855 the French government had had enough of war, and it suggested to Austria that she should communicate peace terms to Russia. The basis of the offer was the neutralization of the Black Sea and the cession of some territory to Moldavia. When Austria presented these terms to the Russians she demanded their unconditional acceptance. In January 1856, after a series of meetings of the Russian crown council, the decision was taken to accept the terms. One of the principal Russian fears was that disruption of the social order would be the consequence of further warfare. The campaigns in the Crimea were imposing immense strains on the Russian state. The new emperor had no wish to expose the weakness of his autocracy further. On 1 February preliminary peace terms were signed. The war in which both sides were reluctant to fight and equally reluctant to compromise was ended by the 'armed mediation' of Austria, who had offended the western powers by her refusal to join the war and the Russians by her refusal to remain neutral. The peace conference began its deliberations in Paris on 15 February, attended by Austria as well as the belligerents. After the peace conference was over, the Prussians arrived and the Congress of Paris began. Napoleon III attached great importance to the fact that it was a congress which had created the 1815 settlement. He hoped that a new congress system, presided over by the Second Empire, could begin to destroy it. He saw congresses as a means to accomplish change without war and to unite the powers under French leadership. These hopes were almost immediately dashed.

The British delegation arrived at the peace conference with a series of harsh demands, the object of which was to weaken and contain Russia in the Near East. They were based on two false assumptions: first, that Russia had been decisively defeated; and second, that France would readily co-operate in the containment of Russia. The French and the Russians soon made it clear that they intended to adhere strictly to the terms of the preliminary peace. It was therefore the British rather than the Russians who were isolated at the peace conference. The gulf between the British and the French was wide. The British had fought the war to establish a stable order in the Near East, the French to reshape the alignments of the European great powers. At the peace conference there was very little common ground between them. No firm decision was taken before the conference met on the future on the two principalities. Both the British and the French would have liked Austria to have exchanged them for Lombardy and Venetia, which Piedmont could then have acquired. This would have brought peace to Italy as well as to the Near East. Austria was the stumbling-block to this arrangement. She wanted to acquire the principalities and retain her Italian provinces. This was unacceptable to the western powers; they had already fought to defend Austria's interests, and they baulked at a peace which extended her empire. The peace treaty, signed on 30 March, was an elaboration of the Four Points of August 1854 combined with terms which Russia had rejected at the Vienna peace conference in 1855. The principalities were granted autonomy under Turkish suzerainty, and Russia ceded some territory to Moldavia. This was the first step towards the complete independence of Romania. The navigation of the Danube was placed under a European commission. Most important of all, the Black Sea was neutralized: closed to all warships, with naval arsenals and dockyards forbidden on its shores. Lastly, all the powers agreed to respect the independence of Turkey, and in return the Turks promised good treatment for their Christian subjects. This was mere window-dressing; because the Russians had claimed special rights over Turkey the other powers felt the need to deprive her of them. The only way they could do this was by asserting a general right for all the powers.

The major consequence of the Near Eastern settlement of 1856 was to change the priorities of Russian foreign policy. The Russians were deeply humiliated by the exclusion of their naval forces from the Black Sea. They regarded it as an affront to their status as a great power. After the Peace of Paris the principal objective of their foreign policy was to rid themselves of this humiliation. Under Nicholas I Russia had been the guardian of the *status quo* in Europe; French revisionism in the west and the eastward spread of revolutionary ideas had been identified as the great dangers to the stability of the existing order. After 1856 the maintenance of order in Europe was relegated to second place. This was a profound change which significantly altered Russia's relations with the other powers. French desire for the revision of 1815 in the west was now a force to be exploited to achieve Russian revision of the treaty of 1856 in the Near East. The Russians knew that they had only to wait a short time before the French would make overtures to them. Napoleon III in the late 1850s was, like Polignac in the late 1820s, anxious to link Russian dissatisfaction in the Near East with French dissatisfaction in Europe. In one important respect, however, he modified the legacy of Polignac: whereas the latter had wanted a Franco-Russian alliance directed against England and Austria, Napoleon strove to maintain good relations with England at the same time as he attempted to establish closer relations with Russia. This meant that he could not offer the Russians a direct and brutal bargain: French support for Russian revision in the Near East in return for Russian support for French revision in the west. The most he could offer was French support to rid Russia of the Black Sea clauses at another five-power congress. In fact, therefore, the two powers could not agree to work together; all they could do was to promise not to work against each other. This had important consequences for French diplomacy. If he had been able to offer a direct bargain to the Russians, Napoleon III, like Polignac, would have demanded Belgium. Denied this opportunity by fear of England, he was forced to pursue revision indirectly and encourage Piedmont to seek a new showdown with Austria. It was as much

French weakness as Austrian weakness that resulted in the revival of 'the Italian question' in the late 1850s. The change in Franco-Russian relations fundamentally affected Anglo-Russian relations. In the decade after 1841 they had worked together in Europe to contain the French threat to the 1815 settlement. On most issues the other powers had been forced to follow either a British or a Russian lead. In the fifteen years after the Crimean War the British and the Russians ceased either directly or indirectly to co-operate; consequently they ceased to dominate Europe.

The Austrians could have frustrated the emergence of a Franco-Russian *rapprochement* after the congress of Paris by offering to revive the Holy Alliance in return for supporting Russian claims for the revision of the Black Sea clauses at a future great-power conference. This would have been a good bargain for Austria: she would have strengthened herself in Europe without conceding anything in the Near East. Before the outbreak of the Crimean War she had not been in the least alarmed by the presence of a Russian fleet in the Black Sea. The fact was, however, that the Austrians wanted the best of both worlds: the maintenance of the 1815 treaties in Europe and the 1856 treaty in the Near East. This was indeed an ambitious policy. Between 1815 and 1822 Austria had relied on Great Britain to contain Russia; from 1823 to the mid 1850s she had depended on Russia to contain France and the revolution. After 1856 the Austrians were forced to rely on their own strength and their treaty rights to maintain their empire in its entirety. Austria's unwillingness to sacrifice any of her interests certainly strengthened her enemies. It is often argued that in the years from the collapse of the 1848 revolutions to the Peace of Frankfurt Europe was dominated by 'realist statesmen'. This is only partly true: in Vienna illusions prevailed. It was this that gave the realists their opportunities.

It was Napoleon III who decided to begin the work of territorial revision in Italy. His policy was secret and conspiratorial; at certain stages of the negotiations he was working behind the backs of his own ministers. He liked to think of himself as a bold and masterful strategist in diplomacy. In fact, French policy towards Italy in the years from 1858 to 1861 was characterized by great caution. The choice of Italy was in itself cautious. Napoleon III knew that the only satisfactory gains for France were in Belgium and on the Rhine. When Frenchmen talked about 'natural frontiers' it was to these areas that they were referring. Yet the emperor knew that if he attempted to incorporate part of Belgium into France, England would organize a coalition against him. If he began to work for a rectification of the frontier along the Rhine he would face the united opposition of the two German powers. In

Belgium and on the Rhine France would have openly to avow her ambitions and face a coalition of her enemies whereas in Italy Napoleon III could hide behind the ambitions of Piedmont and confront Austria alone. Moreover, France could appear as the liberator rather than the aggressor. A war in Italy was much less dangerous than a war in the north or the east. In northern Italy France would take the offensive on foreign soil and Austria would only fight to retain her Italian possessions. This meant that the war would be localized and limited. By contrast on the Rhine and in Belgium the powers opposed to French expansion would probably take the offensive and fight the war on French soil. This was a possibility Napoleon III did not wish to contemplate until Bismarck forced him to do so.

In January 1858 Orsini, an Italian conspirator, attempted to assassinate the French emperor. Before he was executed Napoleon III allowed him to publish an impassioned plea for Italian unification. Within six months Napoleon III reached an agreement with Cavour for a war against Austria in northern Italy. From the outset of the negotiations the French found Cavour a willing accomplice in their schemes. Cavour had two great enemies: Austria, which stood in the way of the expansion of Piedmont, and the Italian radical-nationalists, who threatened the existence of the monarchy which he governed. He saw in France an ally against both. With French help he could drive the Austrians out of Lombardy and Venetia and create a strong liberal and monarchical state which could dominate the rest of Italy. Piedmont would, in Cavour's vision of things, be to Italy in the future what Austria had been between 1815 and 1848: the power which controlled and regulated the politics of the central and southern states. The French, by contrast, believed that with Austria expelled from the north, the central Italian states would look to France to protect them against an enlarged Piedmont. Behind the Plombières agreement of 1858 there was an unspoken conflict of ambition between the two signatories. Cavour and Napoleon III met in July 1858 and agreed that in return for the cession of Nice and Savoy to France and a marriage between Victor Emmanuel's daughter and Napoleon's cousin, Prince Jerome, France would join Piedmont in a war against Austria to create a new kingdom of upper Italy from the Alps to the Adriatic. The rest of Italy was to form a new confederation under the presidency of the Pope. Piedmont would assume responsibility for provoking the war, and the task of France was to ensure that Austria was isolated. The Pact of Plombières initiated the first planned war of aggression since the days of the first Napoleon.

At any stage in the twelve months between the agreement of

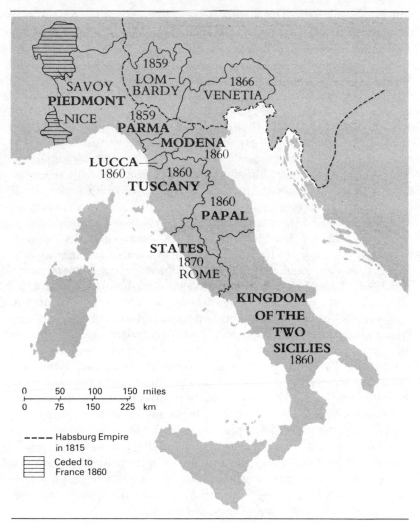

Map 3   Italy in 1815 and the expansion of Piedmont 1859–70

Plombières and the outbreak of war Austria could have prevented war by providing herself with an ally. In return for Austrian support for revision in the Near East the Russians would have defended the *status quo* policy in Europe. The Prussians were equally prepared to support Austria in northern Italy if she would recognize Prussian predominance in northern Germany. The Russians asked the least, but even so the Austrians would not modify their policy of defending the

91

empire in its entirety. The Austrians never placed their interests in any order of priority but put their faith in their treaty rights. Despite Austria's intransigence Napoleon III did not find it easy to isolate her. His difficulty was that he had very little to offer Russia in return for her neutrality. After a series of inconclusive negotiations, in which the Russians tried unsuccessfully to link war in Italy with the revision of the Black Sea clauses of 1856, they agreed in March 1859 that in the event of a Franco-Austrian war Russia would maintain an attitude of 'benevolent neutrality'. Russia did not sacrifice Austria for her disloyalty during the Crimean War, she merely placed her own interests above those of her erstwhile ally. This was prudence, not revenge. Cavour found it equally difficult to provoke a war with Austria. His first attempt failed completely. The second, which involved mobilizing the Piedmontese army, was foiled by the British government which offered mediation. In late March 1859 the Russians proposed a congress to discuss the affairs of Italy; they hoped that after the congress had settled Italian problems it could proceed to discuss Russia's grievances in the Near East. When the British government supported the Russian proposal of a congress, Cavour had no alternative but to agree to attend it. It was the Austrians who eventually provoked war. They demanded Piedmontese demobilization before the congress met, and in late April they sent this demand to Turin in the form of an ultimatum. By humiliating Piedmont before the congress the Austrians hoped to strengthen themselves at the congress. Cavour refused to comply with the ultimatum, and on 29 April Austrian troops invaded Piedmont. On 12 May the French entered the war. In the end, therefore, both sides wanted war: the Austrians hoped to repeat the short war of 1849 and confirm their position in northern Italy by military victory; the French wanted war to destroy the 1815 settlement in Italy, to gain Nice and Savoy, and enhance their prestige in Europe as a whole; and Cavour aimed to expand Piedmont from the Alps to the Adriatic. In fact, the war of 1859 achieved none of these desired results.

The war of 1859 was the first short war in modern history. It was over quickly not because the belligerents had perfected the art of fast mobilization, which the Prussians were later to do, but because it ground to a halt. In May and June the French and the Italians conquered most of Lombardy and won two battles at Magenta and Solferino, but they failed to drive the Austrians out of the Quadrilateral fortresses in northern Lombardy and their troops did not even enter the province of Venetia. A complete Franco-Italian victory would have required a long war in which Austria was isolated throughout. It was the Prussians who made this impossible. On 24 June the government in Berlin mobilized its army and announced that it proposed to offer 'armed mediation' to defend the treaties of 1815. Napoleon III realized that this could mean war on the Rhine as well as in Italy. He feared that defeat and humiliation would be the consequences for France. The only way to avoid this was to abandon Piedmont and begin peace negotiations with Austria. On 11 July the two powers concluded the Truce of Villafranca: Austria ceded most of Lombardy to France who in turn ceded it to Piedmont. The truce also provided for a congress to discuss final arrangements for the future of Italy. With the collapse of the Plombières agreement, Cavour resigned. Yet the inconclusive end to the war was a greater setback for Napoleon III than it was for Cavour. The Italians had after all gained something whereas the French had lost a good deal. By failing decisively to defeat Austria they had lost military prestige, by failing to fulfil the agreement of Plombières they had lost Nice and Savoy, and by his retreat at the prospect of a two-front war Napoleon III had been humiliated by the German powers. It was perfectly clear that if the three eastern powers could patch up their differences, they could contain France in the future as they had done in the past. The next phase of the Italian crisis proved, however, that no such reconciliation would be forthcoming. Prussia had voluntarily forced France to withdraw from northern Italy, but neither she nor Russia would assist Austria to maintain the 1815 settlement in central and southern Italy without concessions by Austria to Prussia in northern Germany and to Russia in the Near East. Once again the government at Vienna refused to consider bargains of this sort. In effect, the Austrians decided to abandon their client states in central Italy rather than compromise their interests in Germany or the Near East. The disagreements of the eastern powers, combined with the determination of France to retrieve something for herself after the fiasco of the war of 1859, resulted in a new Italian order made by the Italians themselves. Cavour's task on his return to office in January 1860 was to save the social and political order by isolating the republican–nationalists after they had destroyed the territorial order of 1815.

During the war in northern Italy the rulers of the central duchies of Parma, Modena and Tuscany had fled, and popular governments had been established. At Villafranca the French and the Austrians agreed that the exiled rulers, mostly cadet members of the Habsburg family, should be restored, although there was a verbal agreement that the Austrian army should not be used for this purpose. It proved impossible for them to recover their thrones unaided. In December 1859 a pamphlet, *The Pope and the Congress,* was published in Paris; it argued that the Papacy should lose its temporal dominions. The Austrians rightly regarded this as government-inspired propaganda, an attempt by the French to keep the question of territorial revision open. When Napoleon III declined to disavow the pamphlet, the Austrians retaliated by refusing to attend the congress. Once again they opened the way to territorial revision in Italy by a clumsy attempt to strengthen the 1815 order. Cavour was quick to exploit the free hand that the French had acquired with respect to central Italy after the cancellation of the congress. He proposed plebiscites in the duchies to see if the people wanted union with Piedmont. The plebiscites were to be held under the auspices of the Piedmontese army; after the confidently expected majority for union, annexation to Piedmont would follow. In return for French agreement to these measures, Cavour offered Nice and Savoy. This was an offer Napoleon III could not refuse; without war France would break out of the limits imposed upon her in 1815. She would, moreover, be compensated for the increase in Piedmontese power in Italy merely by sacrificing a few Habsburg client states. In any case Napoleon III could only prevent the union of the central Italian states with Piedmont by war. This would cast France in the role of upholder of the treaties of 1815, a part Napoleon III had no wish to play. An agreement was reached between France and Piedmont in March 1860. The other great powers were more shocked by the French acquisition of Nice and Savoy than by the Piedmontese absorption of the central duchies. They believed that it revealed the true nature of French foreign policy, and they feared that expansion at the expense of Belgium and on the Rhine would be next on the agenda. In the 1860s first the British and then the Russians, the two powers who traditionally regarded it as their responsibility to contain France, were extremely hostile to the prospect of French expansion. It was this more than anything else that affected fundamentally their attitudes towards the expansion of Prussia. Throughout the 1860s Bismarck never failed to remind the British and the Russians that Prussia was fulfilling the task imposed upon her by the peacemakers in 1814–15, of guarding the Rhine, at the same time as he was destroying the principal features of the Vienna settlement in central Europe.

The French assumed that the agreement of March 1860 was the last act of territorial revision in Italy. There is evidence to suggest that Cavour shared this view; he certainly did not plan nor completely control what followed. In May Garibaldi and his expedition set out from Genoa for Sicily. There it met with very little resistance, and when Garibaldi crossed the Straits of Messina into the kingdom of Naples itself Cavour was forced to act. On 11 September 1860 Victor Emmanuel and his army marched into the Papal states. Cavour acted on the assumption that the great powers would hesitate before they punished the aggression of Piedmont whereas they would certainly respond to a papal appeal for help against revolutionaries. In any case he was determined to prevent the emergence of a southern republic and a separate Sicily. The success of 'the revolution' in southern Italy was regarded with profound dismay at Vienna, Berlin and St Petersburg. Whereas in the pre-Crimean period the common fear of popular disturbances had resulted in punitive action, in the post-Crimean period intervention was not possible without a common accommodation of conflicts of interest in other areas – between Prussia and Austria in Germany and between Austria and Russia in the Near East. In fact Prussia and Russia in 1860, like France in 1859, sought to exploit the weakness of Austria to promote their own ambitions. In the last week of October 1860 the sovereigns and ministers of the three eastern powers met at Warsaw to discuss common problems but no common front was established on Italian questions. In the same week (26 October) Garibaldi met Victor Emmanuel outside Rome and paid homage to him as king of Italy. The new kingdom consisted of the whole of the peninsula except Venetia and Rome. England was the first great power to approve publicly of the new arrangements. Palmerston and Russell, the foreign secretary, did again in 1860 what they had done in 1848: they abandoned the precise form of the 1815 settlement in Italy in an attempt to uphold its basic principles, which were a stable order in the peninsula and freedom from French control. The Italians must provide in the future what the Austrians had since the 1820s demonstrably failed to secure. In their attitude towards the Vienna settlement the British distinguished between the settlement in the west and the settlement in the buffer zone beyond the French frontier. It was only in a limited sense that the British were revisionist in the 1860s; above all they tried to strengthen the states surrounding France. They were prepared to sacrifice the arrangements made at the Congress of Vienna in order to uphold the provisions of the first and second Peace of Paris.

Neither of Napoleon III's informal alignments, with England and Russia, emerged unscathed from the Italian crisis. In March 1860 the British and French governments signed the Cobden Free Trade Treaty which was supposed to inaugurate a new era in which ever-increasing commercial intercourse between the two countries was expected to render political differences less important. In fact, after the war in northern Italy and the French annexation of Nice and Savoy there was a marked deterioration in Anglo-French relations. The British government, however, moved cautiously: it did not want to provoke an open breach with France, first because it feared that this might drive the imperial government closer to Russia, and second because it wanted to keep a free hand in Europe in case Great Britain should become involved in the American Civil War. The basic problem of the Franco-Russian *entente* in the early 1860s was the same as it had been in the late 1850s: the two powers failed to find any important issues on which they could co-operate wholeheartedly. From 1861 to the beginning of 1863 the French and the Russians continued to exchange protestations of friendship and goodwill. After the Polish revolt these were abruptly withdrawn, and by the end of the year the *entente* was in ruins. It proved impossible for Napoleon III in 1863, as it had been for Louis Philippe in 1830, to appease liberal opinion in France and keep on good terms with Russia.

In January 1863 there was an insurrection in Warsaw which quickly spread to the rest of Russian Poland. The Russians were determined to treat it as a purely domestic matter. It was the Prussians, and then the French, who turned it into an international question. In February 1863 Bismarck, who had been appointed minister-president of Prussia in September 1862, sent Count Alvensleben to St Petersburg to reach an understanding with Russia on Polish problems. The two powers agreed that the Prussians should police their Polish frontier and apprehend and return any Polish rebels who attempted to cross the border. The French took great exception to this agreement. Drouyn de Lhuys began immediately to cultivate good relations with England in order to establish a common front on the Polish question. Bismarck was alarmed by French opposition to the Alvensleben Convention and he endeavoured to underplay its significance. In April, and again in June, the French presented strong protests to the Russians demanding lenient treatment for the rebels and a reform of the administration of Poland. After the Russians rejected the June protest the French government began to hint that Russia would not be allowed to continue the brutal suppression of the revolt. This was an empty threat. The French had long since lost the power to intervene effectively in eastern Europe (in fact in 1813 when Napoleon I had been forced out of eastern Europe by the army of Alexander I). The Russians easily and eagerly exposed the emptiness of this threat. In a last and desperate attempt to save his prestige and do something for the Poles, Napoleon III proposed in November 1863 a general congress of the powers to discuss outstanding problems. It was the British government which led the opposition to this proposal. It feared that a congress held under French auspices would discuss Belgium, the Rhine and the Black Sea clauses of the treaty of 1856 as well as Poland. This would merely have been a public discussion of differences which the powers knew to exist but on which they could not agree. The Russians supported British opposition to a congress, and the French were forced to drop the idea. The brief ascendancy which France had enjoyed since the Congress of Paris was over; the two powers on whose friendship she had relied had turned against her. The post-Crimean alignments had proved extremely fragile. The French found it impossible to remain on good terms with both England and Russia and satisfy their own ambitions. The British wanted the maintenance of the Treaty of 1856 in the Near East and the containment of France in western Europe; the Russians wanted revision of the Black Sea clauses of 1856 with as little revision of the peace settlement of 1815 as possible; the French wanted territorial gain without provoking coalitions against them. In the years from 1856 to 1863 the fundamental incompatibility of these policies was inexorably exposed. Bismarck, who played no direct part in the destruction of the post-Crimean system, certainly profited from its collapse.

Prussia's submission to Austria at Olmütz determined her foreign policy for the next fifteen years. A reversal of the submission and Austria's acceptance of Prussian dominance in northern Germany were the minimum limits of Prussian ambitions. Most of Bismarck's predecessors thought in terms of a political rather than a military humiliation of Austria. There was still a lingering fear amongst the old-style Prussian conservatives that war might yet again unleash the forces of revolution. In his attitude to foreign policy Bismarck differed from them in two important respects: he was prepared to carry the process of the revision of the 1815 settlement in Germany farther than they had ever contemplated, and he was also willing to exploit any opportunity to achieve his ends. Although the boldness and confidence of his policy owed much to his personality and to his unique vision of an expanded Prussia and conservative Germany, he was placed in a very favourable position. The Prussia over which he ruled was rich and powerful. By the 1850s the economy was expanding at a rapid rate, and Germany already had an economic identity under Prussian leadership which excluded Austria (the *Zollverein*) before Bismarck gave her a matching political identity. In the late 1850s and early 1860s military reforms, which included the application of the most modern technology to armaments production, made the army an efficient instrument of state policy. The expanding revenue of the Prussian government meant that it need not fear the financial strains of war; the campaign against Denmark in 1864 was paid for out of ordinary government revenues. The Austrian government could not contemplate war with the same financial equanimity. The fact was that by the

1860s dualism in Germany no longer accorded with economic or military reality. During the 1840s and 1850s Prussia had ceased to be the lesser of the two German powers.

At the outset of his ministerial career it was necessity rather than choice that led Bismarck to seek a striking success in foreign policy. Like Napoleon III he was forced into adventure by domestic pressures and fears. He was called to office by the king to defend the monarchy and the army against the liberal opposition in the Prussian parliament. The political conflict over the issue of army reform was fierce and prolonged. Moreover, it reflected an underlying social struggle: the middle-class liberals resented the monopoly of office in the state and the army enjoyed by the landed aristocracy (the Junkers). Bismarck's basic aim was to defend the privileges of his class and the alliance which existed between the aristocracy and the monarchy. This determination to defend and strengthen the conservative political order in Prussia combined with an equal determination to enhance the Prussian state provides the key to both his domestic and his foreign policy. At first Bismarck attempted to reach some sort of agreement with his liberal opponents. When this failed he defied them. For almost four years Bismarck's rule in Prussia was unconstitutional. This defiance was of more than purely Prussian significance. The liberals in the other German states were anxious for Bismarck's experiment to fail. They believed that failure would discredit the political ideals and the political system he represented. It was not only the Prussian and German liberals who were hostile to Bismarck. In the Confederation Austria and a majority of the other German princes were strongly opposed to Prussian aggrandizement, either political or territorial. This was the position in which Bismarck found himself between 1862 and 1866. One possible solution to this complex of Prussian and German conflicts was compromise. Although Bismarck did not rule it out, he was anxious to avoid it. There can be no doubt that in 1864 and in 1866 he saw conflicts first with Denmark and then with Austria as a means of avoiding compromise with the Prussian liberals.

In 1864 the Danes presented Bismarck with something he needed: a non-German enemy. In November 1863 Christian IX, a distant cousin of the former king, inherited the Danish throne. Three days after his accession he signed a document redefining the relationship between Denmark and the two duchies of Schleswig and Holstein. The actual incorporation of Schleswig into Denmark and the new arrangements for Holstein (a member of the German Confederation) constituted a breach of the Treaty of London of 1852 which had been signed by all the powers. The treaty explicitly stated that the two duchies must be ruled separately. It did, however, uphold the principle that Christian should succeed in the duchies even though there was another prince, the Duke of Augustenburg, with a better claim under German law to the succession. Bismarck at first opposed Danish action on the grounds that it infringed treaty rights. This gave Prussia a good cause; it united right with might. It made the military action which Prussia, a great power, took against the small state of Denmark more respectable than it would otherwise have been. Most important of all, Bismarck's insistence on treaty rights enabled him to separate Prussian policy from German nationalist policy which wanted to detach the duchies from Denmark and create a new and independent state under Augustenburg. It was the prospect of this solution to the question that alarmed Bismarck most: he did not want another small state in north Germany, jealous of its independence and therefore anti-Prussian. He would have preferred the duchies to remain with Denmark than for them to become another obstacle to Prussia's ambitions to dominate north Germany. Moreover, Bismarck feared that if Prussia did not take the initiative in opposing Denmark, the German nationalists would rush in and compound Danish treaty breaking with German treaty breaking. The Austrians could not allow Prussia to act alone on the duchies: dualism in Germany demanded that the two powers should be seen to act together in defence of German interests. The Austrians would have liked to work for a separate state under Augustenburg because this would have strengthened the anti-Prussian forces in northern Germany, but as they had made the defence of treaty rights the central principle of their foreign policy they could not abandon it when it did not suit their interests. In any case it would have resulted in an immediate and direct conflict with Prussia which the government at Vienna was anxious to avoid. In January 1864 the two powers concluded an agreement to defend the Treaty of London. A further clause stipulated that if the position proved impossible to uphold, the two powers would settle the future of the duchies by joint discussions. This vague clause suited both parties: for Bismarck it left open the possibility of the annexation of the duchies to Prussia, and it gave Austria time to mobilize support in the Confederation for the creation of a separate state.

In late January and early February 1864 Austrian and Prussian troops occupied the two duchies, and on 19 February they crossed into Denmark. The Austrians would have liked the two armies to have acted in the name of the German Confederation. Bismarck refused. He was determined that there should be no 'German policy' until such time as he could call Prussian policy German policy. After the invasion of Denmark the British government hastily attempted to make the future of the duchies a matter for the five powers. Palmerston hoped to force the Austrians and the Prussians to retreat, and then to negotiate a new settlement favourable to Denmark. This was an ambitious policy, since Great Britain had no means with which to threaten the two German powers. Russia and France were the only powers that could co-operate with Great Britain against Austria and Prussia, and neither was well disposed towards her, the Russians because the British had gone too far in criticizing their suppression of the Polish revolt, the French because the British had not gone far enough in supporting them over the same question. These recent differences could have been set aside if the British had been prepared to offer the Russians revision in the Near East and the French some concessions in western Europe in return for their active support over the duchies. In fact, however, the maintenance of existing treaties in these areas were higher priorities in British policy than the maintenance of Danish rule in the duchies. Palmerston did on the Schleswig–Holstein question what he had never done so obviously before: he adopted a position which in the last resort he could not defend and staked British prestige on an issue of secondary importance. The logic of the situation was for the British government to retreat and allow the two German powers to settle the issue. Palmerston and Russell attempted to avoid this by suggesting a conference of the five powers at London. This suited all parties to the dispute. It would enable the two powers in possession of the duchies to repudiate the Treaty of London and thus jointly to decide the future of the duchies. The Danes also wanted to be released from the treaty which no longer served their interests, and they hoped to gain the support of the three non-German powers for their unitary proposals. The London Conference of 1864 had no real purpose other than the repudiation of the Treaty of 1852. Between April and June a series of conflicting proposals for the future of the duchies was made by the Prussians, Austrians, Danes and French. They were all rejected. It was impossible to reconcile the Danes, who were determined to keep the duchies, with the Austrians and the Prussians, who were equally determined not to return them to Denmark. On 25 June the conference broke down. On the same day the British cabinet decided by a small majority to take no action to defend Danish rights in the duchies. This was a clear admission by the British that without allies they could not shape decisively events in central Europe. The other powers had realized this before the British government did. In the Schleswig–Holstein question Palmerston and Russell played a bad hand badly.

The Austrians and the Prussians renewed the war after the collapse of the London Conference, and within three weeks they defeated

Denmark. On 1 August 1864 a preliminary peace was signed by which Denmark ceded the duchies to Austria and Prussia. The first phase of the crisis was over. It was more of an Anglo-German than a truly European crisis. The Russians had worked on the same assumption in 1864 as they had in 1848: that no vital Russian interest was at stake. And Napoleon III had also concluded that French interests in Europe were unaffected by the fate of the duchies. The British retreat in June 1864 left the two German powers masters of the situation. Bismarck owed his success in the first phase of the Schleswig-Holstein question to the fact that the three non-German powers decided at various stages in the conflict that they would not fight to maintain Danish control of the duchies. The Danes made the fundamental mistake of defying the two great powers without first ensuring that other great powers would support them wholeheartedly.

The second phase began in August 1864 when the Austrians and the Prussians met at Schönbrunn to determine the future of the duchies. This meeting produced no solution to the problem. Bismarck was determined upon the annexation of the duchies to Prussia. This was not part of a long-term plan for the reorganization of Germany. He was motivated by more local ambitions and fears. Bismarck wanted Prussian conservatism, which he increasingly identified with himself and his policies, to have the credit for expanding the Prussian state. This would be an achievement which his liberal critics within Prussia would find it difficult to denigrate. Also he feared the intentions of Prussia's opponents within the German Confederation. He knew that Austria and most of the other German states wanted to create a new state in northern Germany which, jealous of its independence, would be anti-Prussian. The aim of his opponents was to strengthen the federal structure in order to contain Prussia. Annexation was the only policy which could satisfy his ambition and destroy his fears. In 1865 Bismarck did not consciously set out to use the question of the duchies as a means with which to destroy the authority of Austria in Germany and the position of the Confederation in German political life. But gradually he came to realize that he could not separate the three issues; the Austrians and the other German states would not allow him to do so. Bismarck's solution was to enlarge the issues at stake. He linked these three German problems with other issues in European diplomacy. First, he suggested to Napoleon III that an attempt by Prussia to solve her German problems could be associated with revision of the 1815 settlement in the west. Then he proposed to the Italian government that if it worked with Prussia it could solve the Venetian problem. Finally, he was able to exploit Russia's fears in the Near East to secure her neutrality in Europe.

Because Austria had a majority of states behind her in the Confederation, Bismarck sought to isolate her amongst the great powers. In the months from October 1864 to the outbreak of war in June 1866 Austria and Prussia were engaged in two separate struggles, one purely German which was conducted within the Federal Diet and which Austria easily won, the other in the councils of the great powers which Austria lost. It was the first which from Bismarck's point of view made the war necessary; it was the second which made it possible.

The Austrians were not prepared to make substantial concessions to Prussia in Germany. The policy makers at Vienna were convinced that if Austria was to remain a great power she must retain her position in Germany. Moreover they did not believe that a stalwart defence of their German interests was incompatible with the maintenance of their inflexible policy towards Italian questions. The imperial government adamantly refused to recognize the new kingdom of Italy and still believed that their retention of Venetia placed them in a good position to recover what they had lost at Villafranca and enforce the terms of the Treaty of Zurich, thus restoring the deposed rulers of the central Italian states and creating a new Italian Confederation. At the same time as he held on to these illusory ambitions, Mensdorff, who became foreign minister in 1865, realized that in a war with Prussia Venetia was no more than an exposed southern flank. This uncomfortable fact did not lead him to modify his Italian policy, largely because he attached extreme importance to the honour of the emperor and the prestige of the empire. He regarded the abandonment of Venetia before a war with Prussia as an act of weakness. By adopting this intransigent position Mensdorff ruled out any possibility of agreement with either Italy or France.

In February 1865 the Austrians proposed that Prussia should annex Schleswig and Holstein, and that Austria should receive from Prussia the county of Glatz in compensation. This Bismarck refused. He then suggested conditions under which the two duchies could become an independent state which amounted to almost complete Prussian control. This was unacceptable to the Austrians because if they had accepted they would have lost face with the other German states. On 29 May the Prussian crown council discussed the possibility of war with Austria. This meeting was an important turning-point in the evolution of Prussian policy. In the past the crown council had ruled out the possibility of war on the grounds that it would divide Germany, provide radical elements with a good opportunity to strike a blow at the monarchical order, and probably result in French intervention and demands for compensation on the Rhine. This time it did not.

Bismarck's response was twofold: he concluded a temporary agreement with Austria at Gastein on the administration of the duchies which relieved the pressure on Prussia in the Confederation, and then seriously set about the isolation of Austria. The principal provision of the Gastein agreement of August 1865 was that Austria should administer the duchy of Holstein and Prussia that of Schleswig. It was, of course, no more than a further postponement of the problem.

In his anti-Austrian diplomacy from August 1865 to the summer of 1866 Bismarck decided that France and Italy were the only two powers who would affect decisively a struggle between the two German powers. He was convinced that England and Russia would do all they could by fair words and good intentions to preserve peace, but that they would take no action to prevent war. This was an accurate assessment of the situation. British policy was determined by two considerations. It was generally held that a strong state in central Europe was the best means to contain France and Russia. Secondly, the British government was acutely conscious of the lesson to be drawn from the failure of its intervention in the question of the duchies in 1864. Derby, who became prime minister in 1866, publicly stated that the British should 'abstain from menace if they do not intend to follow that menace by action'. The Russians were convinced that the empire needed peace to consolidate the programme of domestic reform which the emperor had inaugurated in the early 1860s, and that a strong conservative Germany under Prussian leadership would be a bulwark against the expansion of France in the west and against the eastward spread of western revolutionary ideas. Thus neither Great Britain nor Russia was wholeheartedly committed to the *status quo* in Germany, and certainly neither would go to war to defend it.

Bismarck was able to concentrate his diplomacy on linking Prussia's revisionist ambitions in Germany with those of France in the west and Italy in Venetia. In October Bismarck met Napoleon III at the French resort of Biarritz. This was the 'German Plombières', the isolation of Austria to make war against her. Unlike Plombières, however, there was no hard and fast agreement between the two predatory powers about the division of the spoils. Neither wanted one, Bismarck because he did not wish to give away territory on the Rhine, Napoleon III because he thought that he could gain more by waiting. The French calculated that the two German powers were evenly matched and that a war between them would be long, exhausting and inconclusive. They believed that they could intervene to end the war and thus earn a substantial reward, much greater than Bismarck was prepared to offer. By 1866 the French government had abandoned the pretence of altruism as the guiding principle of their diplomacy. They no longer spoke of the liberation of the oppressed peoples of Europe; their new maxim was 'if others gain, we must'. The understanding reached at Biarritz was all that Bismarck really needed; the alliance with Italy was more of an optional extra than a necessity. On 28 February 1866 the Prussian crown council decided that if the struggle with Austria over the duchies degenerated into war, Prussia must not shirk her duty. On 8 April Bismarck concluded an alliance with Italy which stipulated that in the event of war within three months between the German powers Italy would attack Venetia, and that Venetia would be her reward.

From May 1866 onwards both the Austrians and the Prussians accepted that war between them was inevitable. The Austrians did not know how to avoid it and the Prussians did not wish to avoid it. The Austrians were in the difficult position that mobilization of their forces would take several weeks longer than in Prussia; in order to be ready for war they had to take the first step to prepare for it. This suited Bismarck because it strengthened the motive of the king for war, and it would enable Prussia to claim that her own mobilization was a response to that of Austria. In 1866, as in 1870, Bismarck was anxious to shift the burden of war guilt on to his opponents. Whilst both sides prepared for war, Bismarck offered through secret envoys roughly the same terms to Austria as he intended to impose on her after her defeat. This was not so much a bid for peace as a willingness to accept victory without war. On 12 June Austria broke off diplomatic relations with Prussia, and two days later carried a motion through the Diet for federal mobilization against her. A majority of the German states voted with Austria. The Berlin government then declared the Confederation at an end; on 15 June the Prussian army invaded Saxony and a week later crossed the Austrian frontier. At this late stage the Austrians tried to break out of their isolation in Europe. In the second week of June they agreed to cede Venetia to the French who in turn transferred it to Italy. This belated recognition of the realities of the plight which faced Austria brought little in the way of consolation; the Italians still entered the war to fulfil their alliance obligations to Prussia and the French made no positive offers of support. From the outset the war was disastrous for Austria and on 3 July the imperial army was decisively defeated at Sadowa. Two weeks later Bismarck announced his peace terms: the Confederation of 1815 was to be dissolved, and Austria was to relinquish completely her position as a German power. With the old dualist structure destroyed, the other German states were at the mercy of Prussia. Their losses were considerable. Hesse, Hanover, the city of Frankfurt, Schleswig, Holstein and a large part of Hesse-Darmstadt were annexed to Prussia. The Austrians had no choice but to accept these terms; the road to Vienna was open to the Prussian army, and Austria was forced to abandon her position in Germany and her allies within the Confederation in order to survive as a great power. Austrian acceptance of Bismarck's terms was followed by the preliminary Peace of Nikolsburg which was signed on 26 July. By this stage both sides wanted to end the war quickly, the Prussians in order to forestall French intervention and the Austrians to prevent the collapse of the empire. The final peace treaty was signed at Prague on 23 August. Although more German rulers had fought against Prussia than with her, it was in the course of the war that Bismarck forged the new alliance between the Prussian monarchy and German nationalism which was to dominate central Europe for the next half century. The old connection between German nationalism and German liberalism was severed; henceforward nationalism was the junior partner of Prussian conservatism. During the war Bismarck announced that the parliamentary institutions of the new German state would be based on universal manhood suffrage. This proved to be no more than a facade behind which the real power of dynastic and aristocratic conservatism was strengthened. Bismarck had in truth fought a war for the mind of Germany.

The territorial and political settlement of 1866–67 in central Europe was the single most important and extensive revision of the treaties of 1815. The Prussian annexations in Germany made her larger, more populous and richer than all the other German states combined. Austria ceased at one blow to be an Italian and German power, relinquishing Venetia to France (who transferred it to Italy) at the same time as she was expelled from Germany. The loose Confederation of 1815 was replaced by the new centrally-controlled and Prussian-dominated Confederation of 1867. All this was accomplished within a few weeks by a single power after victory on the battlefield. Short localized wars between two powers had, as one British diplomat observed, replaced conference diplomacy of all the powers as the principal means of treaty revision. The 1815 settlement in central Europe was totally destroyed. Austrian power, which the peacemakers of 1815 had overstretched, was reduced to new and narrow limits. This changed the balance of forces within the empire, and the agreement of 1867 between the emperor and the Hungarians (the *Ausgleich*), which gave to the latter a real measure of equality in government, was a clear recognition of the diminished empire. The only area in which Austria remained a great power was the Balkans. The other great powers were determined to sustain Austria as a great power because they could not face the calamities which her destruction would entail. Neither the British nor the Russians were unduly alarmed by these great changes. Although both governments, largely for dynastic reasons, disapproved of Prussia's annexations in 1866, they nevertheless regarded a strengthened Prussia as a bulwark of order in central Europe. Both governments regarded the central principle of the 1815 settlement as the containment of France. This was still intact. From their point of view Prussia's victory in 1866 involved the transfer of the joint responsibility of Austria and Prussia to protect Germany to Prussia alone. The British hoped that this would consolidate the existing order in the west, and the Russians believed that it strengthened their position in Poland. The borders imposed upon France by the second Peace of Paris and the congress kingdom of Poland were in 1866 the two principal features of the Vienna settlement which remained undisturbed. This was why the British and the Russians were willing calmly to accept so vast an increase in Prussian power.

Austria's humiliation in 1866 was obvious; that of France was concealed but was no less real. At Biarritz Napoleon III had gravely miscalculated: there was no long war of attrition which France could end by intervention and thus take her reward. After the Prussian victory at Sadowa the French government hastily made demands for compensation on the Rhine which Bismarck curtly refused. He warned that if France pressed her claims, war would be inevitable and he would unleash on France the fury of German nationalism. This was bluff: if the French had accepted the challenge he would have conceded something to avoid war. Napoleon III was not familiar with tactics of this sort; he was accustomed to devious deals, not to hard and brutal bargains. In the aftermath of the Peace of Prague Napoleon III abandoned the policy of compensation on the Rhine at the expense of Germany for the pursuit of gain elsewhere with the support of the new Confederation. In November 1866 the French government intimated that its pride would be satisfied with the acquisition of Luxembourg. During the next four months the two governments discussed various ways in which the French might annex the duchy. The legal position was complicated: the king of Holland was the ruler of Luxembourg, but it was garrisoned by Prussian troops because the duchy had been a member of the Confederation of 1815. Napoleon III expected Bismarck to work actively with him on Luxembourg to pave the way for its negotiated transfer to France. Bismarck's position was that he could not give away what belonged to another, and that France must follow Prussia's example and take what she wanted. England would certainly protest, but without allies she would not fight to deny France Luxembourg. The

French shrank from such a course. Napoleon III, like his predecessors, was held back by the fear of coalitions against him. After the failure of their plan to secure the duchy by agreement with Berlin, the French tried to purchase it from the king of Holland. His position was that he would sell it only if the French first secured the support of Prussia for the sale. When these negotiations were leaked to the press there was an immediate outcry in Germany and England. The British, alarmed by the prospect of France breaking out of the frontiers of 1815, suggested a conference of the great powers to settle the future of Luxembourg. When the other powers agreed to this, the French had no alternative but to accept. This was the end of their hopes: for the British the only purpose of a conference was to keep Luxembourg out of French hands. This was the last time the British used the Coalition of Chaumont to contain France in the west. Thereafter there was no need to do so. At the London Conference of 1867 the powers agreed to the withdrawal of Prussian troops from Luxembourg and to confer upon it neutral status.

In late 1867 and 1868 the alignments of the great powers were as much affected by events in the Near East as they were by the multitude of outstanding problems in Europe. What were in effect minor crises over Crete and Romania produced diplomatic results out of all proportion to their significance. Since the Crimean War there had been a tendency amongst all the powers to exaggerate the importance of Near Eastern questions. This was particularly true of the Russians who hoped to improve their position in the area, and of the Austrians who feared their position might deteriorate. Near Eastern developments had a direct impact on Austro-French and Russo-Prussian relations. The French and the Austrians began alliance negotiations which were intended to provide both powers with security, for Austria against Russia in the Near East, and for France with an ally in Europe. It was also assumed in Paris that Austria was as anti-Prussian as France. Beust, who was appointed foreign minister in 1867, was generally regarded as Austria's man of revenge. In fact the Austrians were much more cautious than the French imagined. They were prepared to fight to defend the independence of the south German states but they would not join a war in which France fought for the principle of territorial compensation. In the event of a French victory Beust was prepared to join the winning side to revise the settlement of 1866, but he was determined to avoid another defeat for Austria. In his negotiations with the French Beust wanted friendship without binding commitments. The French government wrongly assumed that it could, when necessary, convert these paper assurances of goodwill into the hard currency of a military alliance. At one stage they tried to include the

Italians by negotiating a withdrawal from Rome. This would have created a triple alliance in which Austria would support France and the Italians would guarantee not to attack Austria. These negotiations, although immensely protracted, resulted in no definite agreement.

In 1868 Russo-Prussian relations were, by contrast, marked by an increasingly precise definition of obligations. It was the fear of being isolated in the Near East which led the Russians to seek close relations with Prussia. What the Russians feared was another Crimean coalition against them. In March 1868 the two powers exchanged verbal assurances that if either were threatened by two powers, the other would come to her assistance. This was more valuable to the Prussians than to the Russians. There was little likelihood of an outbreak of great-power hostilities in the Near East, whereas the European situation was very volatile. Bismarck in fact secured Russian neutrality in the event of a war between Prussia and France without having to ask for it and in return for very little. Moreover, the agreement of March 1868 weakened Austria because if she joined France in a war against Prussia she would have to face the prospect of war with Russia as well. Bismarck had in fact succeeded in isolating France. Russia's fear of the revival of a coalition against her in the Near East enabled Bismarck to contemplate a solution to the south German problem. Like the Schleswig-Holstein question in 1864, this was a problem which his opponents within Germany would not allow him to ignore. While the south German states remained outside the new Confederation, the remnants of the German liberal party still had an issue with which they could attack Prussian conservatism and claim with justice that Prussia had failed to unite the German people. Moreover, Bismarck was well aware that if the four southern states freely negotiated their entry into the new Confederation, they would certainly demand terms which he would be reluctant to concede. A war against France had the obvious advantage that in the heat of the conflict and in the full flush of patriotic enthusiasm it would be extremely difficult for the southern states to reject whatever terms the Prussians offered. In addition to this domestic consideration, Bismarck saw a war with France as the means of consolidating the Peace of Prague as the permanent basis of Austro-Prussian relations; only after the defeat of France would Austria accept her expulsion from Germany in 1866 as final.

It was not to provoke France into war but to humiliate her and to complete her encirclement that Bismarck took up the question of the Hohenzollern candidature to the Spanish throne. Despite his subsequent denials, he was deeply involved in the question from the start. On 19 June 1870 Prince Leopold of Hohenzollern-Sigmaringen, a member of the Catholic branch of the family and a cousin of the king of Prussia, accepted the Spanish throne which had become vacant after the deposition of Queen Isabella II. By early July news of this reached Paris, and there was an immediate outcry in the French press. Gramont, the recently appointed foreign minister who was strongly anti-Prussian, and Ollivier, the prime minister, were deeply offended by the interference of Prussia in Spanish affairs; they immediately sent a protest to Berlin. The strength of the French reaction alarmed the Catholic Hohenzollerns, and on 12 July Prince Leopold withdrew his acceptance. The French refused to be satisfied with this and demanded assurances that the candidature would not be renewed. Like Bismarck, the French government was determined to use the Spanish question to determine the future of the Rhine. If France could humiliate Prussia publicly, the union of the four south German states with the Prussian Confederation could perhaps be delayed, or, better still, France would be well placed to demand territorial compensation when it did take place. Bismarck was delighted that the French had shifted the challenge to the Rhine. If the diplomatic conflict were to degenerate into war, Prussia could fight for her prestige and for the sacred soil of Germany, whereas she could not have easily fought for the dubious claims of an obscure German prince to the Spanish throne. The French demand that the candidature of Prince Leopold would never be renewed was made by the French ambassador to the king of Prussia who was staying at the resort of Ems. His polite but evasive reply to the French, which he communicated to Bismarck by telegraph, was transformed in the abbreviated version which Bismarck published into a rude rebuff. This was to turn the tables on the French: they had sought to humiliate Prussia and Bismarck had succeeded in humiliating France. On 19 July, after several meetings of the French cabinet, France declared war. The imperial government was confident, despite the hurried reorganization and re-equipment of the army in the 1860s, that France was ready for war and assured of victory. After more than fifty years of containment the French were determined to destroy the limits imposed upon them by the second Peace of Paris.

For decades after 1815 the four allies of Chaumont had feared that war on the Rhine would be the first step in the destruction of the Vienna settlement. In fact, it proved to be the last. It took place in circumstances entirely different from those which the powers had expected. France fought for the principle of territorial compensation, a legacy of eighteenth-century dynasticism, Prussia for the ideal of the nation state, a legacy of the French Revolution. This was a dramatic reversal of roles. From the outbreak of war, Bismarck in his anti-French propaganda played on the old fears of an ambitious and aggressive France. This was designed to appeal especially to the British and the Russians. He leaked to the English press the draft treaty which the French had drawn up in July 1866 which provided for the incorporation of Luxembourg and part of Belgium. This confirmed traditional British fears about the nature of French foreign policy. In late July the British government quickly negotiated treaties with France and Prussia in which the belligerents pledged themselves to respect the neutrality of Belgium. Within a few weeks of the outbreak of war, the diplomatic and military calculations of the French had proved entirely groundless. The Austrians refused to join the war until the French had shown that they could win it. The French had also expected the goodwill of Russia; this too was denied them. The devastating defeat of the French army at· Sedan on 2 September 1870 shattered the aspirations which the French had entertained since 1815 for the recovery of their dominance in Europe. For the French, defeat at Sedan changed the purpose of the war. Until then they had fought to expand the borders of 1815; thereafter they fought to defend them. In Paris a republic was declared; although the new government had no illusions that it could find allies, it had at least expected to find friends who would intercede with the Prussians to preserve for France the borders of 1815. This too was an illusion.

While the Prussians fought to revise the settlement of 1866 in Germany, and France to defend the borders of 1815, the Russians took the opportunity to destroy the treaty of 1856 in the Near East. On 31 October 1870 the Russians denounced the Black Sea clauses of the Treaty of Paris. They expected 'a war of words' in Europe as a consequence of their action, but they were confident that there would be no armed conflict in the Near East. The British demanded a conference to discuss the matter. They could no longer uphold the treaty, but their prestige as a great power required that they should give formal assent to its destruction. This was done at a conference held in London in January 1871. The French defeat at Sedan also enabled the Italians to fulfil their revisionist objective by completing the overthrow of the old order in the peninsula. The French garrison in Rome was withdrawn and on 1 September 1870 the Italians took possession of Rome. Austria was equally affected by the French defeat; it confirmed her expulsion from Germany. The government at Vienna had to abandon all hope of reversing the Treaty of Prague.

In January 1871 the provisional government in France acknowledged defeat. The only centre of resistance to the German advance was Paris where a revolutionary committee (the Commune) refused to accept defeat. Bismarck completed the reorganization of Germany before the war was over. The Confederation of 1867 and the four south German states united to form the German empire, with the king of Prussia as German emperor. This new state was brought into existence in the Hall of Mirrors in the Palace of Versailles which for two centuries had been a great symbol of French power and of her leadership of European civilization. In 1871 it was the power of France, and not just the aspiration of a particular government, that was destroyed. A preliminary peace was signed on 26 February 1871, which did not become a formal peace treaty until 10 May. The terms of the treaty, the cession of Alsace and Lorraine and the payment of a huge indemnity, were an appalling blow for the provisional government and shocked the rest of Europe. Bismarck claimed that they were a necessity: France would never be reconciled to defeat; it was therefore essential to destroy her ability to take revenge. In 1815 the four allies had believed that their common resolve and their combined strength could hold France in check; they had seen no need to dismember her. In 1871 Bismarck had no allies, and the only way to strengthen the new Germany was to weaken France. In 1815 the anti-French alliance was already in existence before the peace settlement. Bismarck had to create an anti-French network of alliances in the years after the Treaty of Frankfurt. It was the search for these alliances that linked the destruction of the old order in international relations with the evolution of the new.

European statesmen and diplomats of the early 1870s were astonished by the revolutionary changes which had taken place in great-power relations since the Crimean War. Many of them had for decades regarded 'the arrangements made at the Congress of Vienna as if they were the final forms into which Europe was to be moulded'. Few of them acknowledged that the old order between states had now been sacrificed to maintain the old order within states. Yet there can be no doubt that both Cavour and Bismarck intended the revolutionary characters of their foreign policies to conceal the conservative nature of their domestic policies. The triumph of monarchical conservatism over the forces of liberalism and its compromise with nationalism enabled it to survive into the late nineteenth century, when it was confronted with a new challenge from socialism and socialist internationalism. The response of the ruling elites to their new opponents profoundly affected great-power relations in the half century between the Treaty of Frankfurt and the outbreak of the First World War.

CHAPTER FIVE
A decade of loose alignments 1871–1879

Essentially, the European states system between 1871 and 1914 was of a piece with that which had prevailed for the previous two hundred years. Policy-making was still in the hands of small élites. And as for most of the period between the end of the religious wars in the seventeenth century and the rise of totalitarian régimes in the twentieth the élites had shared a common culture, the European states between 1871 and 1914, too, can be regarded as members of a 'system' in an ideological sense. The very prevalence of such concepts as the Yellow Peril, the Pan-Islam menace, and the 'dying' pagan empires testifies to the continuance of some notion of a comity of Christian Powers, both among worried conservatives and confident Social Darwinists; and viewed in a world perspective, this common European culture outweighed any differences discernible between the parliamentary, constitutional and autocratic régimes that constituted the European states system. With regard to inter-state relations, too, the unspoken assumptions of the governments of the period testify to a generally accepted code of conduct: the distinction was always recognized between adjustable interests, which could be bargained over, and vital interests, for which a state must fight. So long as the decision-makers managed to avoid posing threats to vital interests, peace was assured. Indeed, the whole pattern of inter-state relationships in this period, whether it took the form of alliances, loose alignments, or simply *ad hoc* bouts of co-operation, bears witness to a sense of belonging to some sort of international community or 'states system'.

Moreover, as in the previous two hundred years, the states system of 1871 to 1914 was still very much a European one – albeit with extra-European ramifications – rather than a 'world' system. Extra-European developments could certainly affect the tone of relations between states, or even, if they seemed to imply threats to vital interests of the powers in Europe, have far-reaching effects on the alignments of the powers within the system. But extra-European questions, like economic rivalries, could generally be handled peacefully; they were only indirectly a factor in the final crisis of 1914. That was a crisis of the European states system itself: several powers found themselves suddenly confronted with a choice between ceasing to exist as independent great powers and fighting to maintain (and once the war had started, to improve and reinforce) their positions within the system – even, eventually, to attempt to establish a hegemony and transform beyond recognition the system of independent but interrelated units. For the most part, however, between 1871 and 1914 the system functioned effectively enough in enabling its members to adjust their divergent interests by diplomatic means, and to cope with even quite major upheavals.

The creation of the German Empire in 1871 had repercussions throughout the whole European states system. The old German Confederation, for all its faults and its proven inability to satisfy or contain the demands of German nationalism, had been a stabilizing element in international terms. It had been strong enough, in defensive terms, to check the ambitions of the restless powers, France and Russia; but its complex and cumbersome federal structure prevented its organization into a state that might pose an offensive threat to its neighbours. Like the Ottoman Empire later, the *Bund* of 1815 was a passive element, a shock-absorber, in the international system. The new German Empire was very different. Already, in terms of population, military capacity, and industrial development, the strongest power on the continent, it was now inspired, controlled, and, above all organized by a Prussian élite that had just proved its determination and efficiency in three successful wars within seven years. From being a constitutionally inert buffer, Germany had become a dynamic element in the system, with a potential for exerting pressure outwards on its neighbours that was bound to alarm them. Bismarck himself had acquired an alarming reputation; and Russian fears as to where 'the Minotaur in Berlin' might strike next were widely shared in Europe. Even so, the long peace from 1871 to 1914 showed that the problem was not unmanageable: the war of 1914 to 1918 showed that it had not been solved.

At first sight the problem was eased by the fact that German policy was eminently conservative and pacific. True, Germany maintained the largest army on the continent; but the Treaty of Frankfurt had institutionalized not war, as Marx declared, but armed peace. Bismarck

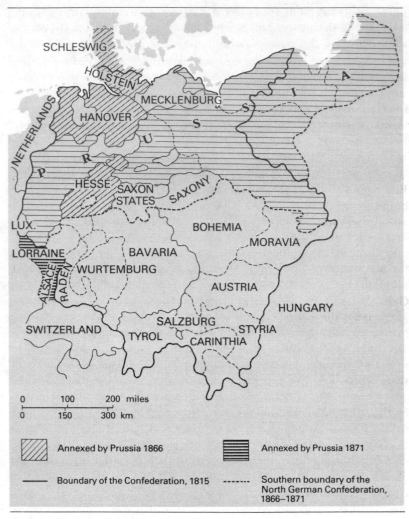

Map 4   Germany 1866–71

had now achieved his ideal German Empire, and a small group of Prussian, conservative, protestant Junkers controlled the most powerful state on the continent. Bismarck's aim after 1871 was simply to perpetuate this state of affairs. Any change must be for the worse: hence his opposition to Pan-German dreams of Great Germany, involving the incorporation of ten million Austrian Germans, potentially a rival element who might combine with the south Germans to wrest control of the empire from Prussia; hence his hatred of internationally minded Social Democrats and of 'doctrinaire' Liberals, who sought to make the *Reichstag* an effective force in German political life and rejected a constitutional system that simply glorified the Prussian national monarchy and left the imperial chancellor largely independent of *Reichstag* control. Hence too his ruthless persecution of 'alien' elements – Danes, Alsace-Lorrainers, Hanoverian patriots, with their almost treasonable links with foreign powers, Poles, and even ultramontane Catholics: none of these people really ever had any place in Bismarck's Germany. Bismarck's career after 1871 was one long, conservative rearguard action in defence of the agrarian Junker élite – and later of their allies in industry – against this host of 'enemies of the Empire'. Yet although his intentions may have been conservative at home, he used methods which led ultimately to Germany's ceasing to be a conservative and conciliatory power abroad: his support of Junker economic interests, for example, was eventually to damage Germany's relations with Russia beyond repair; and the tradition he established of resorting to war scares and foreign adventures to escape from mounting difficulties at home was in the long run to prove disastrous both for Germany and for Europe. In the 1870s, however, Bismarck still appreciated the need for caution and conciliation if he was to avoid provoking the formation of hostile coalitions, and to secure the acceptance of the German Empire into the European states system.

Equally, in the 1870s almost all of the other powers were prepared to accept the new order of things, or at least to reserve judgement on the new Empire. Only France was irreconcilable and vengeful: no French politician could accept the Treaty of Frankfurt as the last word. But at the same time the French fully realized that, even when they recovered from the war, they would never be able to reverse the verdict of 1871 without the assistance of an ally; and an alliance was hard to find. In France itself the proponents of alliances with Austria, Russia, and Britain were all at odds with each other; and the monarchist government's quixotic and emotional attachment to the Papal campaign against the Kingdom of Italy made the task of French diplomacy no easier. Altogether, the political system of the Third Republic, with its kaleidoscopic parliamentary alignments and its lack of any experienced directing hand in foreign affairs put France at a disadvantage in competing with the military-aristocratic empires of the east, where policy remained firmly in the hands of the monarch and a few expert advisers. Even when the *Intérêts* – the financial and commercial circles who controlled the politics of France behind the scenes – ousted the monarchists and established the *République des Affaires* in 1877, their utter opportunism produced only one unstable coalition government after another – sometimes with disastrous consequences for the position of France as a great power: the sudden fall of Gambetta in January 1882 was to bring her twenty years of trouble over Egypt. In short, the isolation and impotence of France in the 1870s was due as much to conditions at home as to the machinations of Bismarck.

The other powers were more ready to accept the new Germany into the international community, but always with one proviso: that she did not seek to expand any further. Italy, for example, had welcomed Prussia's victories over Austria and France, which had brought her a rich province and a capital city; but she still had reservations about the even more astronomical rise of Prussia herself. The right-wing northern professionals who dominated the Italian foreign office, and whose ideas largely determined the character of Italian foreign policy whatever government was in power at Rome, were firm believers in the Piedmontese tradition: that Piedmont had risen to greatness not by virtue of her own strength – indeed, in their eyes Italy, with fewer material resources than Belgium, could never be a great power in her own right – but by skilfully exploiting the rivalries of others. Obviously, if one power ever dominated the continent, Italy would lose her freedom of manoeuvre; so although Germany might be useful,. France and Austria must also remain in play. Of the last two, Austria was the less dangerous, so on the whole Italy inclined towards the Central Powers – who as the stronger side offered better chances of pickings in any case; and the demands of the left for an irredentist policy at Austria's expense were given short shrift. This trend was particularly marked under Crispi, after 1887. As a southerner, Crispi was more interested than the traditional Piedmontese politicians in expansion in North Africa to relieve the surplus population problems of the south; and he also hoped to make his name as the founder of a new Roman Empire straddling the Mediterranean. He was always totally indifferent to irredentist claims, except possibly at the expense of France, Italy's Mediterranean rival; and he was more rigidly committed than any other Italian politician to a close alignment with Britain and the Central Powers. But even his predecessors since 1871 had had no reason to regret or disapprove of the creation of the German Empire

If any power might have been expected to resent it, it was Austria-Hungary, who had been striving since 1866 to prevent it. But in the event the prevailing uncertainty about Prussian intentions, and in particular the fear of another *Blitzkrieg* and the loss of Austria's German territories, determined Vienna to prefer discretion to valour and to seek to conciliate the new Empire. After all, Austria's expulsion from Germany and Italy in the 1860s was now clearly irreversible; and

Austria-Hungary now had other preoccupations: the avoidance of a third defeat, in the south, at the hands of embryonic South Slav and Romanian nationalist movements which had already taken on a disturbingly anti-Habsburg tinge and which might, especially if they secured Russian backing, eventually threaten the existence of what was left of the Monarchy. Rather than tolerate a repetition of 1859 and 1866 in the Balkans, Austria-Hungary would fight to the death. In this sense, in terms of the peace and stability of the European states system, south-east Europe already harboured explosive material. True, left to itself, the Monarchy was a distinctly conservative power. It had no territorial ambitions, and would be content if the Ottoman Empire and any national states that emerged from it remained open to Austro-Hungarian trade and cultural and political influence. Necessity, as much as choice, dictated a passive policy. The monarchy was still essentially a military-aristocratic state, relatively backward in terms of economic development, and hamstrung by a complex constitutional structure that both technically and psychologically worked against an active foreign policy. In the early 1870s it lacked confidence and needed support; and although Andrássy remained firmly opposed, like the rest of Europe, to any further increase of German power at the expense of France, he did in fact hope to enlist the support of the new empire against Russia.

In fact the Russian government was less concerned with stirring up Balkan nationalism than the Austrians imagined, and usually managed to ignore Pan-Slav pressures at home. Since the Crimean War, the tsar was convinced that he was facing a British offensive on a world-wide scale. Russia's efforts to establish her position in the Caucasus and in Central Asia in the 1860s were certainly in part an attempt to prepare for a renewed British onslaught; and even the 'threat to India' that the British perceived therein was partly a defensive move, calculated to deter a British attack on Russia in an area where she was still painfully vulnerable – at the Straits. There, certainly, Russia's chief opponent seemed to be Britain. Despite the revision of the Treaty of Paris in 1871, it was almost twenty years before the Russians managed to build a fleet capable of defending their southern coast against a British incursion into the Black Sea – hence their obsessive insistence on the strictest interpretation of the rule of the Straits. But even if Britain remained Russia's main preoccupation, other problems were already beginning to appear in Europe. Admittedly, the traditional Hohenzollern-Romanov friendship had held good in the 1860s; Bismarck was keenly aware of his debt of gratitude to Russia – hence his rejection of Andrássy's schemes; and Russia and Germany still had a common interest in suppressing Polish nationalism – where 'liberal' Austria had again broken ranks. But despite all this the Russians were concerned at the exceedingly independent behaviour of their erstwhile Prussian protégés in 1871, particularly at their ignoring Russia's interest in a German balance of power based on the independence of the southern German states. The decisive role Russia had played in German affairs for more than a century had clearly come to an end; the Treaties of Teschen, Vienna and Olmütz had been replaced by the Treaty of Frankfurt. The shock was enough to make Alexander II at last implement the military reforms that had been under discussion since the Crimean War; and to convince him that Germany must certainly not be allowed to shift the European balance any further in her favour.

The preoccupations of the other world power, Britain, were more exclusively extra-European. The balance of power, anchored in a strong, conservative Central Europe, had allowed Britain to concentrate her attention on her territorial Empire, especially India, and on her informal, commercial empire. Certainly, Britain would never shrink from involvement in Europe if the maintenance of the balance of power or the security of the Empire demanded it: she had been quick to react to even the most tentative efforts of France and Russia to challenge the 1815 settlement; and she had allied with France, Austria and Piedmont, and fought a war against Russia to prevent Russian control of the Ottoman Empire, a vital link in Britain's communications with India. But by the early 1870s, Britain seemed almost on the periphery of the European states system. True, there was no pressing need for intervention: despite Russia's advance in Central Asia, India seemed relatively secure; and the Royal Navy had proved well able to assert British commercial interests against non-European Powers such as China. But Britain's reserve was also a result of her unpleasant experiences with the continental powers in the 1860s, when Austria and Prussia, the great stabilizers of the 1815 system, had joined France and Russia as disruptive elements, inflicting a particularly galling diplomatic defeat on Britain in the Danish war. A general revulsion of feeling in Britain against involvement with the selfish and immoral diplomacy of the continental powers was certainly one element in the isolationism of British governments until well into the 1870s. In any case, the Russian threat, such as it was, lay outside Europe; with the fall of the ambitious schemer Napoleon III, France had ceased to be a threat at all; and there was no reason to fear the new German Empire, protestant, apparently liberal, and with no extra-European ambitions, provided it did not strike out on a path of continental domination.

In sum, therefore, provided the new German Empire did not have designs to expand any further, it could be accommodated easily enough within the European states system. The 1870s proved to be a period of relatively low tension, when no two powers felt threatened or aggrieved enough to form binding alliances committing them to support each other to the death. In these years of loose alignments, almost of anarchy, in the best sense of the word, there was little risk of local disputes producing general wars. True, Franco–German hostility was an immovable obstacle to real harmony; but it was not a threat to peace. France in isolation was too weak to attempt to overthrow the 1871 settlement; and no other power had any desire to do so. Equally when Bismarck created a war scare in 1875 and talked of weakening France further, he found the rest of Europe combined against him in an overwhelming show of unity: if the British and the Russians called Germany to order publicly, the Austrians and the Italians made it perfectly clear through private channels that they were of the same mind. In preventing any further weakening of France by Germany, all the powers had a common interest; and so, as Bismarck's hasty retreat demonstrated, on the German side too Franco–German hostility presented no serious threat to the peace and stability of the European states system. The same could not be said, however, of the other potential area of friction, the Eastern question which, as the powers themselves had conflicting interests in it, presented a more intractable problem.

The Eastern question concerned the future of the Ottoman Empire, a future which appeared increasingly problematical as nationalist feeling developed among the empire's subject peoples in the Balkans. These subject peoples constantly sought to drag in the great powers, seeking support not only for their complaints against the Ottoman government, but for their own mutually incompatible territorial claims against each other. The powers, for their part, had interests of their own at stake, and were usually concerned to preserve the integrity of the empire. After all, so long as the Ottoman Empire existed, it provided for the interests of all the great powers a safeguard, not ideal for any, but tolerable for all. Within the confines of that inert and labyrinthine power structure there was room for all the powers to manoeuvre, and for all to maintain a measure of influence. So long as the empire continued to exist as an independent state, it offered each of the powers a measure of security and served to postpone a clash of great-power interests which were in the last resort incompatible. Thus, the empire gave the British some security against a Russian advance towards the east Mediterranean and overland route to India; for Austria-Hungary, it prevented the establishment in the Balkans of national states with territorial claims against the Monarchy and potential allies of Russia; and Russia saw in the empire, as guardian of the closure of the Straits to foreign warships, an obstacle to a British incursion into the Black Sea. Yet the attempts the powers made to prolong the existence of the empire – by ordering the sultan to institute reforms to make life tolerable for his Christian subjects, or even by themselves assuming responsibility for the administration of certain areas, such as Lebanon or Crete, were largely self-defeating. They not only weakened the sultan's authority, but by encouraging the Christians to hope for even greater privileges, they made them less willing to seek an accommodation with the Ottoman government. The disintegration of the empire thus remained a real possibility; while the efforts of the powers to defend their conflicting interests within it led ultimately to dangerous divisions within the European states system.

Even so, for most of the 1870s, the international situation remained fairly fluid, and a confrontation over the Near East was avoided. Andrássy's plans for a great bloc of powers to oppose Russia's supposed Balkan designs met with no response from Britain or Germany; and he himself changed his mind when he discovered, during a meeting of the three eastern monarchs in Berlin in September 1872, that the Russians were not in fact planning to disturb the *status quo* in the Near East. With both Vienna and St Petersburg alive to the dangers inherent in any attempt to change the *status quo*, and with no immediate crisis to revive their mutual suspicions, the way was clear for a return to the spirit of Münchengrätz. By the Schönbrunn Convention of 6 June 1873 the two powers sought to guard against surprises and to avoid drifting into positions from which they could not retreat. They agreed to keep in touch about Near Eastern developments and, above all, to reach agreement before taking any action. But although the Schönbrunn Convention was to become the basis of a Three Emperors' League – Bismarck saw in its emphasis on monarchical solidarity a further guarantee of the isolation of the French Republic – this was hardly the original intention of its architects, Gorchakov and Andrássy. On the contrary, both of them were more suspicious of Germany than of France in 1873: Article I of the Convention, providing for common action 'to enforce the maintenance of European peace against all disturbances from any quarter whatever' was obviously directed, not against impotent France or isolationist Britain, but against incalculable Germany. Even with the accession, in October, of Germany – still after all, the power least interested in the Eastern question – the Three Emperors' League was essentially an Austro-Russian arrangement, and in no sense part of any Bismarckian 'system' of alliances.

Not that the arrangement did not suit Bismarck. Germany might as yet have virtually no interests in the Eastern question as such; but she was extremely interested in the state of Austro-Russian relations. An Austro-Russian war would be a disaster for Germany. In the first place, France would find an ally; in the second, if Austria-Hungary were destroyed, ten million unwanted Austrian Germans would gravitate into the German Empire and change its character completely. The existence of the Habsburg Monarchy was a prerequisite for a protestant, Prussian, Junker-controlled Germany. (Bismarck admitted as much when he told Andrássy in 1872 that Germany could never allow Austria-Hungary to be destroyed by Russia: in this respect, the alliance of 1879 said nothing new.) On the other hand, Bismarck was genuinely appalled at the prospect of war with Tsarist Russia, a conservative neighbour who had served Prussia well in the past, with whom Germany still had great common ideological interests, and whom Bismarck regarded as ultimately invincible. The dilemma was too much for Bismarck to face. Far from pushing himself forward in the thankless role of honest broker, he in fact simply retired from the scene, hoping that, left to themselves, Austria-Hungary and Russia might somehow be able to reconcile their interests in the Near East without obliging Germany to choose between them. In this respect the Schönbrunn Convention was most welcome to him. But, at the same time, Austro-Russian co-operation should not go so far as to suggest an exclusive *entente* against Germany – and there were overtones of this in Article I. German participation coped with this problem, but for the rest, as the great Eastern crisis of 1875 to 1878 showed, the League remained to all practical purposes an Austro-Russian instrument.

The crisis that started in 1875 was typical of the Eastern question – the crisis of 1854 was exceptional – in that it was not so much provoked by the ambitions of the great powers as forced on them by unstable conditions in the Ottoman Empire. A revolt in Bosnia in 1875 was followed in 1876 by a revolt in Bulgaria, a series of palace revolutions at Constantinople, and Serbian and Montenegrin declarations of war that seemed to portend the collapse of the Ottoman Empire in Europe. Yet until the beginning of 1878 the Three Emperors' League coped with these upheavals, and proved itself to be far more than the fair-weather system some historians have alleged it to have been. Russia and Austria-Hungary, acting in the spirit of the League, collaborated successfully, if not to solve the problems of the Ottoman Empire, at least to prevent a confrontation between the great powers. In local terms the results of their co-operation were meagre: the Andrássy Note of December 1875 completely failed to satisfy the rebels; the Berlin

Memorandum of May 1876, with its implications of pressure on Constantinople, failed to overcome British opposition to anything that might strengthen Russian influence in Turkey. But the community of interest between Russia and Austria-Hungary in avoiding a clash between themselves was so strong that they even managed to agree, at Reichstadt in July 1876, about possible alterations to the *status quo* in the event of the collapse of the Ottoman Empire: the Balkan Christians would receive a measure of independence; and the Austrians would allow Russia to advance in Bessarabia and the Caucasus in return for security in Bosnia.

Throughout 1877 the Austro-Russian combination dominated the international scene. A British attempt to use the Concert of Europe to

Map 5   The Balkans 1878–1914

save Turkey's face failed when the Turks themselves rejected an astonishingly mild set of reform proposals from a six-power conference at Constantinople. A Russo-Turkish war now loomed. Yet as St Petersburg was reluctant to be pushed forward by Slav opinion at the risk of war with Austria-Hungary; and as Vienna was reluctant to fight in defence of the Turk at the risk of driving all Slav opinion, at home and abroad, into the arms of Russia, the two governments agreed to limit the scope of the impending war. The Budapest Convention (January/March 1877) endorsed the Reichstadt arrangements as far as the collapse of Turkey was concerned; Russia would not allow the war to become a Pan-Slav crusade, and would create no big Slav state in the Balkans; and Austria-Hungary would frustrate any British attempt to invoke the Triple Treaty of 1856 and make the war European. Hence, once the war started, in April, the Austrians steadily ignored British soundings; and the British, faced with this combination of the two most interested powers, were helpless. It was not the first or last time that British statesmen had reason to fear 'the Alliance of the Three Northern Courts'. So long as this alliance operated, the Concert was paralysed: but the Eastern crisis was contained.

Everything was changed in 1878 when the Russians, in the elation of victory, imposed on Turkey the Pan-Slav Treaty of San Stefano. In local terms, the Treaty was by no means indefensible: it might have prevented the bloodshed that ultimately resulted from the decisions of the Congress of Berlin to reduce the Big Bulgaria of San Stefano and hand Macedonia back to the Turks. Nor need undue weight be given to the chorus of protests from disappointed religious and national groups: the racial and religious structure of the Balkans was so hopelessly confused that no treaty could ever have been devised that would have met with general approval. In the Balkans only force could determine frontiers – as was shown in 1913, 1919 and 1945. In terms of the European states system, however, San Stefano was totally unrealistic. The British were bound to see in the clauses about Bulgaria and Asia Minor a Russian bid to control the Ottoman Empire; and they would never admit the implied Russian claim to settle single-handed a question which the Treaty of Paris had formally declared to be the concern of the Concert of Europe. The Austrians were equally outraged, and suddenly rediscovered their responsibilities to the Concert – although their indignation really sprang from Russia's flagrant violation of the spirit of bilateral agreements made outside the Concert. At any rate, Russia had destroyed the Three Emperors' League, and it remained for the Concert of Europe to attempt a solution, under Bismarck's reluctant leadership, at the Congress of Berlin.

The Congress of Berlin was a success, in so far as the main business was settled within a month, thanks largely to a series of bilateral agreements reached beforehand. Like the Congress of Aix-la-Chapelle, it demonstrated the usefulness of congress diplomacy when the broad lines of a settlement had already been agreed. Certainly, in European terms, the Treaty of Berlin was an improvement on San Stefano. Russia's exorbitant pretensions were checked; and Britain and Austria-Hungary strengthened their position as counterbalancing powers in the Near East, posing as the patrons of not only Turkey, but of the non-Bulgarian Balkan states. The principle that the Eastern question was a matter for the Concert of Europe had been triumphantly vindicated. Nevertheless, some unsettled business – notably the exact frontiers of Greece and Montenegro – remained to plague the powers; and no agreement was possible about the rule of the Straits, the directly opposed views of Britain and Russia being simply recorded in the protocols of the Congress. More serious was the fact that, in local terms, Berlin was less realistic than San Stefano. Superficially Turkey's geographical position in Europe had improved; but the fundamental problem of her weakness was still there; and the Ottoman government itself was by no means inclined to wholehearted co-operation with its self-appointed defenders, Austria-Hungary and Britain – the former having appropriated occupation rights in Bosnia and Herzegovina and garrison rights in the Sanjak of Novibazar, the latter occupying Cyprus and pressing for reforms in Asia Minor. Worst of all, by handing Macedonia back to the Turks, while at the same time – albeit unwittingly – fostering the belief in the Balkan states that violence brought rewards of Ottoman territory, the Congress of Berlin created a serious Macedonian problem for the future.

More immediately the Congress had far-reaching consequences for the European states system. The Three Emperors' League, which had localized the Eastern question and allowed Bismarck to stay in the wings, had disappeared; and the alarming state of Austro-Russian relations was to force him to come forward on to the centre of the stage. Although, at the Congress, the honest broker had in fact supported the Russians throughout, he now found that they took British and Austrian opposition for granted and blamed Germany for their diplomatic defeat. Moreover, Russia began to take measures to protect her infant industries against competition from the west, introducing a high protective tariff in 1878. Bismarck made things worse by raising German tariffs against Russian grain exports, exports on which Russia's whole economy, modernization programme, and ultimately, great-power status depended. This was only partly a retaliatory measure against the Russian tariff. At home, Bismarck was preparing to abandon his uncongenial liberal allies and free trade – discredited by the depression that had prevailed since 1873 – and align himself with the agrarian right. Herein lay the roots of a grave conflict of interest between Germany and Russia. Bismarck was in turn irritated by Russia's incessant armaments, and by the tsar's gloomy letter of 15 August to the German emperor, hinting at the possibility of war. The last straw was the news of Andrássy's impending resignation, which might be the signal for a realignment of Austro-Hungarian policy in a pro-Slav and anti-German direction.

Bismarck's answer was the Dual Alliance of 1879 – in the short term a device to gain control of Austro-Hungarian policy and to bring the Russians to their senses, but in the long term a manoeuvre to reconcile Austria-Hungary and Russia and control them both within a Three Emperors' Alliance. The old Three Emperors' League had been, essentially, an Austro-Russian affair: the new Three Emperors' Alliance was to be very much a Bismarckian instrument. The crisis of 1878–79 had shown that the loose diplomatic arrangements characteristic of the 1870s could not give Germany adequate security. Now Bismarck would have to come forward himself, take a view on the Eastern question, and, eventually, try to take diplomatic control of the European states system. A new era was dawning, of formal alliances binding most of the continental powers to Germany. Not that this in itself threatened the peace of Europe. On the contrary, revanchists in France would be more helplessly isolated than ever. Nevertheless, the years 1879 to 1882 mark a decisive change, when the European states system moved from the loose, almost anarchical arrangements of the 1870s to a system in which one power and its satellites were clearly preponderant, a system that lasted until the mid 1890s.

CHAPTER SIX

The conservative powers dominate the states system 1879–1895

It was by no means apparent in 1879 that the Dual Alliance would give Bismarck the control he wanted. In the first place, the alliance was of a very limited nature. This was partly Bismarck's own doing: his ultimate aim, after all, was to create a Three Emperors' Alliance by forcing Austria-Hungary to make concessions to Russia. Thus he told the Austrians point blank that the Dual Alliance was not designed to give them any support whatever in the Balkans. The strictly defensive Article I promising assistance against a Russian attack was no more than Bismarck had given the Austrians verbally in 1872; and even this was vitiated by the lack of any military agreements to back it up – until 1882 the Austro-Hungarian and German general staffs did not even exchange information about each other's contingency plans. In economic terms, too, Bismarck gave nothing away, and his new protectionist tariff hit Austro-Hungarian agricultural exports very hard. Whether Bismarck really believed, as he always insisted, that economic policy and diplomatic policy moved on completely different and unrelated planes, or whether he simply could not face up to the diplomatic consequences of his dependence on the agrarian right, by 1881 the two allies were on the verge of a tariff war. It was hardly surprising, therefore, that in return for so little, the Austrians were reluctant to give very much. They refused to undertake any commitments whatever in the west; and they regarded the alliance as the precursor, not of a revived Three Emperors' Alliance, but of a great diplomatic and military bloc, designed to oppose Russia, enforce the Treaty of Berlin, and strengthen Austria-Hungary's position in the Balkans. The mere conclusion of the Dual Alliance, therefore, still left Bismarck very far from his ultimate objective.

Events played into Bismarck's hands, as Austrian and British attempts to establish themselves as the guardians of the Ottoman Empire made no headway against Turkish resentment of their behaviour at the Congress of Berlin. When in 1881 Gladstone's Liberal cabinet switched to an openly anti-Ottoman policy over the Greek and Montenegrin frontier questions, the Austrians at last despaired of Britain and yielded to Bismarck's demands for negotiations with Russia. But if they were expecting German backing in the tripartite negotiations that followed, they were to be disappointed. The Three Emperors' Alliance of 18 June 1881 was very much a German treaty – Bismarck's attempt to solve the Eastern question by forcing Austria-Hungary to make concessions to Russia. Thus the main articles of the Treaty stipulated that the Central Powers pledged themselves to support an eventual union of Bulgaria and the autonomous Ottoman province of Eastern Roumelia should Russia desire it; and to support the Russian, not the British, interpretation of the rule of the Straits. Austria-Hungary's gains, by contrast, were relegated to an annexe of the Treaty. And although the Russians recognized Austria-Hungary's right to annex the occupied provinces of Bosnia and the Herzegovina, they refused to extend this to the Sanjak of Novibazar, a strategically important wedge between Serbia and Montenegro, and a vital link between Bosnia and the rest of the Ottoman Empire. Bismarck, for his part, stubbornly rejected Austrian requests for a guarantee of Romania against Russia. Superficially the negotiations gave substance to Bismarck's doctrine of Balkan spheres of influence, which consigned the western Balkans to Austria-Hungary's sphere and Bulgaria and Romania to Russia's. Certainly Bismarck was well pleased with the treaty. For him the Dual Alliance was a mere tactical manoeuvre: the Three Emperors' Alliance was his diplomatic masterpiece. It could influence the whole functioning of the European states system: as a demonstration of monarchical solidarity it confirmed the isolation of republican France; by the Straits article it isolated Britain; it demonstrated Bismarck's control of Austria-Hungary; and it established Russo-German relations on a really sound basis.

All this was, of course, too good to be true. In the first place, the Russian government was by no means entirely satisfied. The Dual Alliance had not been abolished, and its existence continued to rankle in St Petersburg: the means Bismarck had employed to achieve the reconciliation between Russia and Austria-Hungary prevented his ever achieving his ultimate objective, the establishment of lasting and cordial relations between Russia and Germany. As for the Three Emperors' Alliance itself, its success was limited in practical terms. It could not give Russia control of Bulgaria, where she was at loggerheads with a princc and a nationalist liberal bourgeoisie who looked to Austria–Hungary for assistance, especially in economic questions. In fact, neither Russia nor Austria–Hungary could ever bring themselves to accept Bismarck's doctrine of spheres of influence. As in 1879, however, Russia's frustration found expression in charges of insufficient German support. And the Russians were taking an increasingly serious view of the tariff question as their growing commitment to military and industrial development made them increasingly anxious about their sources of income. But perhaps the worst flaw in the system was the ingrained and loudly expressed hostility of educated opinion in Russia towards the Central Powers. 'The road to Constantinople lies through Vienna', General Fadeyev had proclaimed in 1867; and a veritable hysteria seized the Russian press at the end of 1881, when the Austrians suppressed by force a rising against new conscription laws in Bosnia. The fiery General Skobelev toured Europe, crusading for a Franco–Russian alliance against the German powers. True, the Russian government demonstrated its loyalty to the alliance, and strove manfully to restrain the press. But it was all too obviously awed by the Pan-Slav campaign, and did not dare call Skobelev to order for several months. The Skobelev affair in fact forced even Bismarck to recognize that the Three Emperors' Alliance provided no absolute guarantee of security. The immediate consequence was the conclusion of the Triple Alliance of 20 May 1882 between Germany, Austria–Hungary, and Italy.

Italy had been seeking closer relations with the Central Powers for some years. But despite the protestations of successive Italian governments, Austrian suspicion of irredentism and of supposed Italian designs across the Adriatic, together with the Roman question, had been formidable obstacles to an Austro-Italian *rapprochement*. When, after 1879, the Austrians had become interested in Italy, as a potential member of a big anti-Russian bloc, they had come up against Bismarck, set on a course of reconciliation with Russia. Once this reconciliation was a fact, the idea of an Italian alliance naturally lost much of its appeal. Indeed, it began to seem positively unattractive when Italy became embroiled in a quarrel with France in North Africa. Until 1881, Italy's purely economic interest in Tunis, a possible outlet for the surplus population of the south, had not alarmed anybody, even the French in neighbouring Algeria. And the French, for their part, were in no hurry to follow Bismarck's advice and annex Tunis. It was only foolish talk of Italian politicians, leading the French to suspect Italy of planning to establish exclusive control of Tunis, that precipitated the declaration of a French protectorate over Tunis in May 1881. Yet whereas the enraged

Italians now became more desperate than ever for an alliance with the Central Powers, the latter became less willing than ever to listen. Bismarck had no reason to object if the French busied themselves more with North Africa and perhaps less with Alsace-Lorraine; and if the Austrians had always refused to commit themselves against France for Germany's sake, they would certainly not do so to please Italy. It was only when the Skobelev crisis suddenly revealed the fragility of the Three Emperors' Alliance that the Central Powers concluded the alliance with Italy. Even then, although Italy and Germany promised to support each other against an unprovoked attack by France, the Austrians were content with a mere assurance of Italian neutrality in the event of a war with Russia – a promise of assistance might have entailed granting Italy a voice in Balkan affairs.

Like the Three Emperors' Alliance, the Triple Alliance had certain general political implications: it was a demonstration of monarchical solidarity with the express aim, stated in the preamble, of maintaining the existing social order. Both Vienna and Berlin were concerned lest republicanism gain a hold in Italy, spread to Spain and Portugal, and produce a confederation of Latin republics grouped round France. But, even here, the allies were not quite in line: the Germans, expecting positive military assistance from Italy, wished to see her as strong as possible, and indeed played a major role in building up her economy in the 1890s; whereas the Austrians, for whom the alliance simply neutralized a potential enemy, preferred to see Italy in a weak and chaotic condition. For the rest, the Triple Alliance resembled the extremely limited Dual Alliance of 1879; it had no military infrastructure, and its obligations were very strictly circumscribed. The Austrians, as in 1879, still refused to undertake any obligations whatever in the event of a French attack on Germany; and although the allies promised to help Italy in the – extremely unlikely – event of an unprovoked French attack, they had no wish to provoke a quarrel with France, and promised no assistance whatever for Italian ambitions in the Mediterranean. Equally, Italy undertook no commitments whatever to help Austria-Hungary against Russia (except perhaps in the case of a general European war). The common view that in 1882 Italy 'joined the Dual Alliance, making it Triple' is a gross error. The most that can be said is that by freeing Austria-Hungary from the incubus of an Italian attack in the rear, the Triple Alliance had enhanced her capacity to defend herself against Russia; and in this sense, the Triple Alliance was complementary to the Dual Alliance. And it is true that it was part of the same 'system' of alliances as the Dual Alliance and the Austro-German alliance with Romania of 1883. But none of these alliances was really central to the Bismarckian states system as the Three Emperors' Alliance was. They were all *ad hoc* responses to temporary scares that a war party might be about to seize control of Russian policy, that the Three Emperors' Alliance was about to fail. They were simply Bismarck's reinsurance treaties.

Indeed, as the Russian war scares all proved transitory, as the eminently pacific Alexander III in fact retained control of Russian policy, and as Bismarck remained as stubbornly determined as ever to cultivate Russian friendship, the European states system continued to revolve round the Three Emperors' Alliance. It was renewed in 1884; and the three emperors' meeting at Skiernewice again demonstrated their solidarity to the world. These years mark the zenith of Bismarck's power in Europe. Whereas the Three Emperors' League, in which Germany had been only peripherally concerned, had allowed for her humiliation in 1875, Germany's central role in the Three Emperors' Alliance put her in a really commanding position. Russia, despite her frustrations, was beholden to Germany for forcing the Austrians into line. Austria-Hungary was her helpless, if disgruntled, prisoner; for the Three Emperors' Alliance had succeeded, where the Dual Alliance had failed, in 'digging a ditch between Austria and the Western Powers'. As for those western powers, the Triple Alliance had aligned Italy firmly with Germany, if not with Austria-Hungary; and Britain and France, who had proved so tiresome in 1875, were now harmless, being firmly excluded from Bismarck's system and on bad terms with each other. This last happy circumstance, however, was less a consequence of Bismarck's diplomatic ingenuity than of extra-European developments beyond his control that had led to a sharp deterioration of Britain's relations with both France and Russia.

If the British had been able to check Russia in Europe by the Crimean War, they seemed fairly helpless in the face of her steady advance through the Central Asian khanates towards Persia and Afghanistan in the 1860s and 1870s. Certainly they were worried: they discerned a conscious Russian plan, if not actually to invade India, at least to acquire a position on the frontier from which to inspire or assist anti-British rebellions; and they failed to appreciate that Russia's advance was motivated largely by domestic factors – the desire for commercial gain, or simply for stable frontiers. In their search for a response, the British wavered between two policies, neither of which proved satisfactory: the 'forward policy' of anticipating Russia by advancing British influence beyond the frontiers of India produced two Afghan wars but failed to give the British any effective control; and the policy of direct agreement with St Petersburg. This latter policy might produce good results on paper – the Anglo–Russian agreement of 1873, for example – but as Russian commanders on the spot often refused to be bound by such agreements, and advanced even in defiance of orders from St Petersburg, it proved equally ineffective in practice. Russia's startling advance towards the frontiers of Afghanistan in the early 1880s, which reached Penjdeh in March 1885, made even the Gladstone cabinet consider the use of force against her. But this remedy too proved impractical: the Three Emperors' Alliance, supported by Italy and France, forbade the Turks to admit the British fleet into the Black Sea, and this effectively deprived Britain of any means of coercing Russia. The eventual Russian retreat that settled the crisis was a calculated one: the tsar decided that provoking the British in Asia only made them more obstreperous in the Near East, and that Russia's security in Europe must not be jeopardized for the sake of gains in Asia that were never worth a war. After all, in European terms, the Penjdeh crisis was reassuring for Russia. It demonstrated not only Britain's impotence when confronted with an alignment of the three Eastern powers, but her total isolation within the European states sytem. Gladstone had succeeded, as Salisbury pointed out, in uniting the Concert of Europe – against Britain.

The hostile attitude of France in the Penjdeh affair was certainly a result of Gladstone's ineptitude. In the 1870s Anglo–French relations had been cordial enough. Although France had been interested in Egypt since the eighteenth century, she had been prepared to make room for Britain. The French had not objected to Disraeli's purchase of Suez Canal shares in 1875; and they went on to co-operate with the British in establishing a dual control over the Egyptian finances and in resisting the efforts of native nationalists to expel the foreigner. Indeed, by 1881 the two powers had been ready for even military co-operation in defence of their bondholders and of their own nationals in Egypt. As Gladstone always made it clear that he would have preferred to act together with France and Italy in the name of Europe, the French did not suspect anything particularly sinister in an almost accidental British military intervention which was single-handed only because they themselves and the Italians had decided at the last moment to abstain. British intervention would in fact have been perfectly acceptable if only Gladstone had gone on to restore the dual control and to remove the British occupying forces. But Gladstone did neither. Instead of restoring Anglo–French control, he demonstrated his devotion to the Concert of Europe by establishing as the ultimate effective authority in Egypt the *Caisse de la dette,* on which all the powers were equally represented: and although it was his sincere intention to withdraw

British forces – an intention formally restated forty-four times by successive British governments in the next twenty-two years – he was unwilling to do so before an orderly and sound system of government had been established. And if, under Gladstone, temporary local conditions, such as the rebellion in the Sudan, made immediate withdrawal impossible, general considerations, above all the strategic importance of Suez on the route to India, made his successors deliberately dilatory. The upshot was that France was alienated beyond all measure; and Anglo-French hostility became a fixed point in international relations for the next twenty years. Moreover, as Gladstone had chained Britain to the Concert, France and the other powers had plenty of opportunities to exploit the situation.

Bismarck, certainly, included the 'Egyptian lever' in his diplomatic armoury as he cast around for a solution to his growing domestic problems. The conservative and protectionist 'Alliance of Rye and Steel' of 1879 had not only failed to relieve the depression but had failed to give him control of the *Reichstag*. If the anti-socialist law had intensified the opposition of the extreme left, the new tariffs, which made themselves felt in terms of 'dear bread', resulted in the defeat of the right in the elections of 1881. Now although the chancellor could never be overthrown by a vote in the *Reichstag,* he needed a working majority there if he was to carry positive legislation, such as the social legislation on which Bismarck was now counting to win the workers for the monarchy. The 'Alliance of Rye and Steel' was clearly inadequate in itself; but it might be possible to add to it the small but vocal colonial lobby, and to focus opinion generally on imperialist expansion. At first Bismarck shrank from this expedient: colonies might be expensive, and make the government even more dependent on the *Reichstag*. But by 1884 he seems to have been convinced by ardent colonialists in the foreign office that colonies could be made to finance themselves. Moreover, there seemed to be positive danger in delay. Whereas so far an 'informal empire' of free trade had suited the Germans well enough, the spread of protectionism in Europe – and no one knew in 1884 that Britain would continue free trading for another half century – might well mean a radical restriction of the opportunities for German commerce, with disastrous consequences on the German parliamentary scene: *Torschlusspanik* was certainly one strand in German colonial expansion.

At first Bismarck was undoubtedly a reluctant imperialist. He tried for years to persuade the British to take on the task of protecting German traders, such as Lüderitz in South West Africa; and it was only when the British were simply too bemused and incompetent to answer his enquiries, and when the Cape authorities began to harass Lüderitz, that he assumed direct responsibility for South West Africa as a German colony in 1884. It was genuine anger at the behaviour of the British, and perhaps also his obsessive desire to embarrass the hated Gladstone, that determined him to apply brutal diplomatic pressure, including the Egyptian lever. Hence his notorious 'colonial *entente*' with France in 1884–85: his support for France in frustrating Britain's financial proposals for Egypt at the London conference of 1884 (where Germany's allies also obediently fell into line); and in refusing recognition to the Anglo-Portuguese Congo Treaty in 1884, insisting instead on putting the whole affair before the Concert of Europe at the Berlin West Africa conference of 1884–85. Yet when Bismarck discovered at this conference that Germany's interests in Africa would be better served by co-operation, not with protectionist France but with free-trading Britain, he was quick to switch to seeking agreement with the latter. This brought dividends to both parties: the 1885 London conference on Egypt endorsed the British programme; and as the British, still feeling their isolation, were prepared to be generous to Germany in East Africa, Germany at last acquired a significant colonial empire.

It should be emphasized that Bismarck's colonial *ententes* were colonial devices used for colonial, and ultimately domestic, purposes. The view that they were essentially 'European' in origin, that Bismarck was interested in a French *entente* largely for its European implications, as enhancing his control of the European states system, is unconvincing. As for his famous remark 'my map of Africa lies in Europe, there is France and there is Russia . . .', this must be considered in its context. Bismarck was seeking to dampen the enthusiasm of the explorer Nachtigall for further acquisitions in 1887 – by which time, having secured control of the *Reichstag,* and having discovered that colonies were by no means self-financing, he had reverted to his earlier anti-colonialist stance. He had never in fact believed that French policy in Europe would be determined by extra-European considerations. If France could be distracted in Africa, well and good; but as the hostility of the growing nationalist movement in France to colonial adventures in the Far East showed, France would never forget Alsace-Lorraine. 'Ferry Tonkin' was hounded from office; and Déroulède castigated the insolence of Germany who, having taken two children, offered France twenty domestic servants in exchange. Bismarck certainly went too far in assuming that colonial questions, like economic questions, were on a completely different plane from high policy and could not affect it in any way. That might have been true for Germany, but it was certainly not true for Britain; and Bismarck, perhaps misled by his experiences with an incompetent and isolated Gladstone government, had set a dangerous example for his successors who would be faced with more determined British governments of whose help Germany would be in sore need. But as far as Bismarck was concerned, his colonial *ententes* were in fact on a completely different plane from his European policy. His colonial *entente* with Britain in 1885 did not imply any closer co-operation with her in the crisis that broke out almost simultaneously in the Near East.

Although the eventual union of Bulgaria and Eastern Roumelia had been provided for, at Russia's insistence, in the Three Emperors' Alliance treaty, its promulgation without warning by an insubordinate Prince Alexander in September 1885 amounted to a Bulgarian act of defiance of Russia. By the same token the British, who in 1878 had insisted on an Ottoman administration for Eastern Roumelia, now on reflection welcomed the union, calculating that strong and independent-minded Balkan states might yet provide the best barrier to the extension of Russian control. Britain and Russia were again at loggerheads; and like the Three Emperors' League, the Three Emperors' Alliance had more vitality than might have been expected. Throughout the crisis the Central Powers stood loyally by Russia in demanding the rescinding of the union. All three powers had every reason to dread the opening up of the whole Eastern question that would result if Bulgaria's neighbours demanded compensation in terms of the Balkan balance of power. As it was, the Alliance was severely tested when Serbia, the ally of Austria–Hungary since 1881, suddenly resorted to arms to enforce her claims against Bulgaria, and was in turn invaded by Russia's – albeit erring – protégé Bulgaria. But Bulgaria's victory in fact resolved the crisis, putting an end to all talk of restoring the *status quo ante*; and by February 1886 the union had been recognized by all the powers. The British were well content: the Three Emperors' Alliance had suffered a defeat, at least on the local issue. But in terms of the European states system, the significance of the Bulgarian crisis of 1885–86 was that the British remained isolated, and that as an Austro-Russian communiqué announced to the world in August 1886, the Three Emperors' Alliance had survived the test.

The Bulgarian crisis of 1886–87 was a very different matter, and it destroyed the Three Emperors' Alliance. The collapse of the alliance, like that of the League before it, was precipitated by a Russian attempt to break out of the agreed framework of Austro-Russian relations. Neither Russia nor Austria–Hungary was capable of the degree of self-denial implied in Bismarck's doctrine of spheres of influence. The

Austrians would never concede untrammelled control of Bulgaria to Russia: that would not only allow Russia to threaten the Ottoman capital by land, and to hold Romania in a pincer: it would threaten the security of the Habsburg Monarchy directly, encircling it in the south and east. Not surprisingly, therefore, Russia's exasperated attempt to establish such control, with the kidnapping and forced abdication of Prince Alexander and successive attempts to bully the Bulgarians into accepting a Russian nominee as his successor, resulted by November 1886 in open threats of war from Vienna. These in turn only stiffened Bulgarian resistance to Russian demands, and by the spring of 1887 the infuriated Russians were refusing to renew the alliance with Austria-Hungary and, as usual, complaining to Germany about insufficient support. As these same months saw the meteoric rise of General Boulanger in France, and such a great upsurge of nationalism there that even a trivial frontier incident like the Schnaebelé affair could fill the press with talk of a Franco-German war, Bismarck was naturally alarmed.

His immediate reaction – as in 1882 when he had been worried about Russia's intentions – was to tighten the defences. He was even able to exploit his embarrassments abroad to solve his problems with the *Reichstag,* threatening France with annihilation, demanding more money for the army, and holding a timely election which produced the '*Kartell-Reichstag*', in which the 'patriotic' parties – alias the 'Alliance of Rye and Steel' – held control. The Triple Alliance was renewed in February 1887, although this time the Central Powers, owing to the deterioration of their diplomatic position since 1882, had to pay more for the same return: Germany now had to give some diplomatic support to Italy's Mediterranean ambitions. Austria-Hungary had to concede to Italy, at least indirectly, a voice in Balkan affairs: the famous Article VII granted to one power the right to compensation if the other should advance at the expense of the Ottoman Empire. At the same time an Anglo-Italian agreement to co-operate and consult (to which Austria-Hungary and Spain had acceded by May) was designed ostensibly to maintain the *status quo* in the western Mediterranean, but really to complete the isolation of Russia. Russia certainly suffered a resounding defeat in June, with the election to the Bulgarian throne of Ferdinand of Saxe-Coburg-Koháry – as a Catholic Austrian army officer and a relative of Queen Victoria, the most anti-Russian candidate imaginable. But the Mediterranean *Entente* powers were having to struggle hard. They were unable to persuade the sultan to sanction Ferdinand's election, even if Russia, backed by France and, as always in Bulgarian questions, by Bismarck, could not secure his actual removal from Bulgaria either. And when Russia and France succeeded in frightening the sultan into abandoning the Drummond–Wolff Convention (by which Britain had arranged to evacuate Egypt on terms very favourable to herself) the Mediterranean world appeared to be divided into two fairly evenly balanced camps.

Between these two camps Bismarckian Germany took up an intermediate position. The old system, based on the Three Emperors' Alliance, had ended, but Bismarck was working towards a new one, designed to prolong German control of the European states system by establishing a foothold in both camps. Even if Austria–Hungary and Russia were no longer on speaking terms, Bismarck was determined to maintain the wire between Berlin and St Petersburg. And while he took care to build up Germany's military and diplomatic defences in 1887, he was at the same time untiring in his efforts to reassure Russia and restrain Austria–Hungary: witness his open declaration in the *Reichstag* that Germany would not support Austria–Hungary in Bulgaria; his publication of the terms of the Dual Alliance, emphasizing their strictly defensive character; his stubborn refusal to sanction Austro–German staff talks; witness, finally, the Reinsurance Treaty, committing Russia and Germany to abjure any aggressive designs that France or Austria–Hungary might be harbouring, and committing Germany to support Russia diplomatically in Bulgaria and at Constantinople. There a struggle was beginning to rage between Russia who, having built up a sizeable Black Sea fleet, was pressing the Turks to allow her warships through the Straits, and the Mediterranean *Entente* Powers who had adopted the strict interpretation of the rule of the Straits formerly propounded by Russia at the Congress of Berlin. At the same time, however, unbeknown to the Russians, Bismarck gave his blessing to the conclusion in December 1887 of a further, very specific agreement between Britain, Austria–Hungary and Italy, pledging the three powers to diplomatic co-operation to frustrate Russian plans in Bulgaria and at the Straits. He was in fact trying to keep Russia out of the arms of France and dependent on Germany by supporting her diplomatically in the Near East, while behind the scenes he encouraged the formation of a counter-bloc to prevent Russia from advancing so far as to precipitate an Austro–Russian war. This second Bismarckian system was thus a network of fundamentally contradictory policies. It has nevertheless been regarded as Bismarck's crowning achievement.

Yet it was already apparent that Bismarck's diplomatic superstructure had no foundation in reality, particularly in economic reality. The root of the problem lay ultimately in the structure of imperial Germany, and in Bismarck's determination to maintain the alliance between the imperial government and landowners, industrialists, and colonialists. This was bound to have an effect on Germany's position in the European states system. For example, pressure from East Prussian landowners for protection against imports of Russian grain had pushed up German tariffs to unprecedented heights by the mid 1880s. And there was widespread resentment in Germany at Russia's parallel efforts to protect her own developing industries by tariffs against industrial imports from the west, and at an *ukaz* of May 1887 forbidding foreigners to hold land in Russia's western provinces. Indeed, the famous *Lombardverbot* of November 1887, closing the Berlin stock market to Russian bonds, was issued partly in retaliation against this measure. But other factors were involved. Many Germans felt it wrong that money that could be used to subsidize German agriculture should be going into Russian loans which were then spent on armaments and on railways to facilitate the transport of Russian grain, if not troops, into East Prussia. Bismarck could not ignore this pressure despite the appalling risk for Russo–German relations. His insistence that economic issues had no bearing on the political relations between states was only a measure of his desperation. True, there were illusions in the Wilhelmstrasse that Russia would be unable to find alternative sources of capital – 'France is no market for Russian paper', Herbert Bismarck confidently declared – and would humbly return to the German fold. But if 'reconciliation through intimidation' had succeeded in 1879 it failed in 1887. By then the Tsarist government, with its industrialization programme entering on the critical 'take-off' phase, was absolutely desperate for money; and it would not be restrained by any ideological scruples about republican gold. January 1888 saw the conclusion of the first of a long series of French loans to Russia. As the Germanophiles in Russia dolefully admitted in later years, the roots of the Franco-Russian alliance lay in the financial policies of Bismarck.

In terms of ensuring German security through control of the European states system, the second Bismarckian system was even less adequate than the first. Bismarck had failed; and he left to his successors a *damnosa hereditas*. Just as his crude attempt to win popular support for Prussia by seizing the trophy of Alsace-Lorraine in 1871 had left a legacy of undying enmity between France and Germany, so his own enslavement to the traditional ruling élite in Prussia had by the end of the 1880s sown the seeds of a Franco-Russian alliance. One might add that his rough handling of the British in colonial matters had set yet another fatal precedent, and that he bequeathed to his successors all the elements of encirclement by a triple *entente*. But that lay in the future. At the end of the 1880s Britain had been drawn by the Near Eastern crisis into undertaking far-reaching commitments, if not to Germany, at least to her allies. True, even this favourable development had been partially vitiated by Bismarck, whose continued support for Russia in Bulgaria and at the Straits confused the sultan, disheartened the Mediterranean *Entente* powers and was, according to the Austrians 'the worst feature of the situation'. Not the least deficiency of the second Bismarckian system was its utterly debilitating effect on Germany's alliances. But there were others in Berlin who recognized its inadequacy, and who were anxious to strike out on a new course; to look facts in the face, accepting the hostility of Russia and even the likelihood of a Franco-Russian alliance, and seeking a remedy in wholehearted support for Germany's friends and allies. If Britain, Austria-Hungary, Italy, and their associates could be welded into an efficient diplomatic and military bloc, Germany might still achieve that security through predominance that had eluded the over-subtle Bismarck.

These ideas began to make headway in Berlin even before the fall of Bismarck. The chancellor's control of policy was clearly disintegrating by 1889, when the new emperor William II gave the Austrians the first of his many assurances of full German support in the Near East. Austrian hopes rose further when Bismarck himself was dismissed – he had always been regarded in Vienna as incorrigibly Russian in his sympathies. With the appointment of the able and straightforward General Caprivi to the chancellorship, the *Neue Kurs* policy went into operation. The Reinsurance Treaty was dropped – largely because any leakage of its existence might do irreparable damage to Germany's relations with her allies, with Britain and with Turkey; and Germany swung firmly into line behind the Mediterranean *Entente* in the interminable diplomatic battle over Bulgaria at Constantinople. Caprivi's determination to establish closer relations with Britain was demonstrated by the speedy conclusion, after years of haggling by Bismarck, of the Heligoland–Zanzibar ageeement of July 1890. This agreement was a deliberate attempt by Caprivi to bring Germany's colonial and European policies into line, by making concessions to Britain in Africa in order to win her support in Europe. Here Caprivi, with his integrated view of the interrelationship between political, economic and colonial issues, saw more clearly than the sometimes almost schizophrenic Bismarck. For example, he made a determined effort to bring Germany's economic policies into line with her diplomatic position. It is true that a start had been made by Bismarck, who in 1887 had bought up Italian bonds when France had resorted to the tactics of a *Lombardverbot* and a tariff war in an effort to oust Crispi. But Caprivi's aims were altogether broader, ultimately to reinforce

Germany's alliances with something approaching a central European customs union. In a whole series of commercial treaties in 1892 and 1893 Germany lowered her tariffs to facilitate the import of agrarian produce from her allies, in return for more favourable terms for her own industrial exports. Russia paid the price, in a commercial war that lasted until 1894. But for a couple of years in the early 1890s the *Neue Kurs* seemed to have given Germany more security than she had enjoyed since 1871.

It was nevertheless the object of violent criticism from the start. The Heligoland-Zanzibar Treaty had outraged colonialist opinion and precipitated the formation of the Pan-German League, the first of several extra-parliamentary pressure groups to bedevil German political life, and one that was later to exercise a most baleful influence on Anglo-German relations. Caprivi's commercial treaties and cheap bread might have done more to reconcile the masses to the régime than any of Bismarck's diversionary manoeuvres, but they also led to a fall of 50 per cent in home grain prices. A Farmers' League was duly formed and its violent propaganda campaign in defence of landowners' interests contributed to the ousting of Caprivi as minister-president of Prussia in 1893. Equally forceful criticism focussed on the external consequences of the *Neue Kurs*. Bismarck might have sown the seeds of a Franco-Russian Alliance, but their germination was not inevitable: Alexander III was as distrustful of French republicanism as Jewish financiers in Paris were of him; and the French, with their heavy financial stake in the Ottoman Empire, were always somewhat apprehensive as to Russia's intentions there. After all, if France's principal enemy was Germany, Russia's was Austria-Hungary: only in Britain did France and Russia have a common opponent. Now it was certainly undeniable that the tightening of the links between France and Russia, from Kronstadt to Toulon, seemed to be directly related to the behaviour of Germany and her allies, and particularly to their relations with Britain. The rather flamboyant renewal of the Triple Alliance was bad enough, but tactless references in the Italian parliament to Britain's association with it alarmed Paris and St Petersburg even more; and Caprivi's army bill, passed by the *Reichstag* in 1893 after an orgy of anti-Russian speeches, was that last straw. The conclusion of a Franco-Russian military convention at the end of 1893 demonstrated, Caprivi's critics argued, that his methods of guarding against a Franco–Russian threat had only intensified it.

And if Germany could no longer feel entirely secure in the centre of Europe, her allies and associates were facing increasing difficulties on the periphery. In the Balkans, for example, although Bulgaria remained firmly in the Anglo-Austrian camp, a tariff war between Austria-Hungary and Romania and the abdication of the Austrophile King Milan of Serbia had lessened Austria-Hungary's chances of controlling her two potentially irredentist neighbours, thereby weakening the whole southern flank of the alliance. Moreover, throughout the whole Mediterranean and Near East the Franco-Russian alliance was proving a formidable combination. The British made a brave effort to counteract a big French naval building programme by adopting a two-power standard in 1889 despite the horrendous cost. But Russia's simultaneous creation of a big Black Sea fleet was exceedingly worrying – especially as the sultan was proving alarmingly yielding to Franco-Russian pressure to allow Russian warships to pass through the Straits at will; and as he was concentrating his fortifications at the Dardanelles and not at the Bosporus. Indeed the Mediterranean *Entente* powers had ruefully to admit that the sultan was completely overawed by France and Russia; and the British Admiralty concluded in 1892 that the Royal Navy was simply no longer in a position to defend the Straits against France and Russia. All this was grist to the mill of the opponents of the *Neue Kurs* in Berlin. Their nightmare was that Britain might some day embroil Germany in a Near Eastern war against France and Russia, and then herself withdraw behind her maritime defences. Indeed, this distrust of Britain was so ingrained that in the spring of 1894 Germany turned down an Anglo-Austrian request for a pledge to keep France neutral in the event of an Anglo-Russian war. The *Neue Kurs* policy had not solved the problems facing Germany's friends in the Near East, but perhaps largely because Caprivi was not strong enough at home to apply it effectively.

In 1894 the *Neue Kurs* system finally disintegrated, partly owing to Caprivi's loss of control, partly owing to a general loss of coherence in German policy altogether. Not only did Germany shrink from accepting the logical consequences of the *Neue Kurs* in the Mediterranean, she reverted to a thoroughly Bismarckian attitude towards the whole Eastern question, informing Vienna that, as far as Germany was concerned, Russia could have the eastern Balkans, and even Constantinople. In African questions, too, Bismarckian tactics were in vogue, and in the summer of 1894 Germany joined France in forcing the British to abandon a treaty they had just concluded with the King of the Belgians. This treaty had been designed primarily to reinforce Britain's position on the upper Nile against French encroachment; but it is true that the cession to Britain of a slice of territory in the Congo to complete the 'Cape to Cairo' route was somewhat offensive to Germany. Indeed, Salisbury had turned down a similar project in 1890 for that very reason. But the German move was ill timed nevertheless. Rosebery was not Gladstone; and since the middle 1880s a powerful imperialist feeling – commercial, religious, humanitarian, or sheer jingoistic – had grown up in Britain which no government could ignore. At any rate Rosebery, hitherto the most pro-German prime minister the British had ever had, reacted exceedingly sharply, giving the lie to complacent Bismarckian theories about separate planes by threatening to cease supporting Germany's allies in Europe if Germany continued her unfriendly attitude in African questions. This was the end of the *Neue Kurs*.

The confusion that marked the decline of the *Neue Kurs* was not merely the result of blunders and Bismarckian misconceptions, but was itself a sign that German policy was going through a transitional stage. The creation of the Franco-Russian alliance had undoubtedly given many people in Berlin a real fright; and to some of them the costs of the *Neue Kurs* policy were simply too high to bear. True, realities had to be faced; and the adoption in 1892 of a strategic plan to cope with a two-front war by concentrating first on eliminating France, show that they were faced. But Caprivi's critics still believed that such a dreadful catastrophe as a two-front war might yet be staved off indefinitely – perhaps by restoring the traditional ties with Tsarist Russia. This was the aim of Caprivi's successor, Prince Hohenlohe, a very conservative liberal whose wife had vast estates in Russia. The death of the embittered Alexander III in November 1894 seemed to offer the chance of a fresh start; and in 1895 German policy gradually moved into the era of the *Freie Hand*. The dogma behind this policy was that international relations must be seen in a world context, essentially as a struggle between the world empires of Britain on the one hand and France and Russia on the other. If Germany were skilful she could exploit this, committing herself to neither side irrevocably and extracting concessions from both. The period when Germany had sought security through preponderance within an enclosed European states system – whether by co-operation with Russia, as under Bismarck, or by a combination with Britain against her, as under Caprivi – was ending. International relations were entering on a period of unstable equilibrium, between Triple Alliance, Franco-Russian Alliance, and British Empire, within a world context. As far as the peace of the European states system was concerned, this would be no more at risk under the unstable equilibrium of the next fifteen years than it had been under the system of the preponderance of one power that had prevailed for the previous fifteen years.

CHAPTER SEVEN

Unstable equilibrium
1895–1911

There were two factors making for peace within the European states system in the decade after the middle 1890s. In the first place the attention of almost all the powers was being drawn increasingly on to extra-European questions. Indeed, Austria-Hungary, the power with the most narrowly European interests, was somewhat at a loss: the United States and Britain, an Austrian diplomat complained, regarded the continental countries as

Beasts shut up in a menagerie fighting over scraps of meat, while they themselves graze the broad pastures of the earth in freedom. At present, the poor animals are looking out through the bars on to the wide ocean. There is nothing going on in the Balkan cockpit.

This was, of course, a short-sighted view: it was in fact almost entirely conducive to peace that there was 'nothing going on' in the Balkans, and that the other powers were preoccupied with extra-European questions. For these questions could never cause a general war. People stationed out on the frontiers of empire, Curzon in India, Russian officers in the Pamirs, might be full of sound and fury; but they were never able to convince their governments. So long as there was no clear threat to the vital interests of a great power, that is, to its existence as an independent power within the European states system – and no extra-European question ever presented such a threat – there was no danger of general war.

If the preoccupations of the powers outside Europe made for peace in these years, so did the constellation of the powers within Europe. In the European states system general war was probable if there was a preponderance of an insatiable power, such as Napoleonic France; or if there were two evenly balanced groups of powers in confrontation, each so desperately nervous about the intentions of the other as to regard any local crisis as a threat to its very existence – as in the middle of the eighteenth century or in the couple of years preceding the First World War. General war was not likely if the European powers were in a state of anarchy or only very loosely aligned, as in the 1870s (although this situation admitted of local wars, as in the 1860s); or if a clear preponderance lay with a conservative power, such as Germany after 1879, strong enough to overawe troublemakers without threatening their existence as independent states; or, finally, if blocs of powers existed, but sufficient in number and complexity to allow both for a variety of links between the blocs and for limited agreements to settle disputes between the powers immediately concerned without involving others. Such a fluid situation prevailed in the heyday of imperialism after the middle 1890s, years of kaleidoscopic alignments which, as they usually resulted from extra-European interests, could cut across existing groupings that reflected an infinitely more dangerous clash of interests within Europe. True, the extra-European activities of the powers were sometimes contributory factors in modifying their alignments within Europe – as in the case of the Anglo-German estrangement in the early twentieth century. But even after the system began to degenerate into two opposing blocs after 1905 the fronts were by no means solid in either the Moroccan or the Bosnian crises. Warning signs were there: the most dangerous aspect of Germany's Moroccan and naval policies lay, not in German activities themselves, but in the threats they seemed to present to France and Britain respectively as independent powers within the European states system. Even so, it was only after Germany largely lost interest in *Weltpolitik* after 1911 and turned, with the other powers, to concentrate on the galloping crisis in south-east and central Europe, that the 'two-blocs' mentality finally came to prevail and a really explosive situation developed.

The growing emphasis on extra-European issues in the 1890s did not, of course, necessitate any reordering of priorities on the part of Britain, already primarily an imperial power. But her problems would increase, as she would be called on to defend in an age of competition what she had acquired in an age of monopoly. Not that she was without resources, naval, strategic or diplomatic. The Royal Navy was obviously of prime importance, given the far-flung nature of the empire; and the naval programmes of 1889 and 1893 showed that both Unionist and Liberal governments were determined to trust first and foremost in Britain's own strength. They were both equally determined to control – by armed force if necessary – strategically important areas on the routes of empire: as the British gradually lost ground at Constantinople, Egypt replaced Turkey as the key point on the Mediterranean route to India; and by the middle 1890s the securing of Egypt had led to an extension of British control in the Sudan and East Africa. In this limited area, the diplomatic support of the Triple Alliance against France and Russia had been quite useful. But the general nature of Britain's relations with the continental powers was still a matter of debate. Some imperialists, like Chamberlain, alarmed at Britain's apparent isolation, and inspired with fashionable Social Darwinist ideas, were demanding an all-out alliance with the 'Anglo-Saxon' Germany and United States in preparation for the impending great struggle of nations. But they could not overcome Salisbury's constitutional and moral scruples about undertaking binding commitments to fight when the final decision in fact lay not with the Cabinet but with an unpredictable parliament. Salisbury was in any case thoroughly sceptical about Chamberlain's whole analysis. He simply did not believe that the continental powers would ever be able to unite in one bloc against the British Empire; and the fluid situation that continued even throughout the Boer War confirmed his unperturbability. Diplomacy had its uses: it was important to keep in touch with the Triple Alliance powers, not least as a precaution against a revived *Dreikaiserbund;* and like Lansdowne later, Salisbury was always prepared for limited and practical agreements about extra-European questions with Britain's principal rivals, France and Russia. But neither Salisbury nor Lansdowne saw any need to commit Britain to either of the great continental alliance blocs. For a decade after the middle 1890s Britain did her share towards maintaining the healthy fluidity of the European states system.

The other Eurasian world power, Russia, had perforce to concentrate her attention primarily in Europe, where lay the chief potential threat to her existence as a great power. At the end of the nineteenth century, when technological and scientific developments in warfare had deprived her of the supremacy her vast manpower resources had given her in 1815, she was also a relatively weak power in military terms. War against a European great power, therefore, could have no attractions for her; and she was generally disposed to seek settlements by negotiation with her rivals, both European and non-European: the cost of disregarding realities was seen in 1905. Moreover, the very range and variety of Russia's world commitments had a distracting and even debilitating effect on her policy. It is not true that Russia 'abandoned the Balkans for the Far East' after her rebuff over Bulgaria in the late 1880s, only to 'return to Europe' with a vengeance after 1905. Even at the height of the diplomatic battle over

China in the late 1890s, Russia had still felt unable to reduce her forces in Europe by a single man; and even after the war with Japan and the agreement with Britain she still had to devote a good deal of attention to events in China, Mongolia, and Persia. The very complexity of Russia's interests, therefore, contributed to the flexibility of the European states system in these years. Of course, Russia was obliged to pay more attention to the Far East once she had started to build the Trans-Siberian railway, and once she was drawn into the struggle to control China. But the European repercussions of all this were only indirect. In the Far East itself Russia enjoyed the support of both France and Germany in the political demonstration against Japan in 1895; but in the ensuing struggle for economic concessions Germany tended to support Britain and the open door against the protectionist Franco-Russian bloc – none of which precluded a separate agreement between Britain and Russia over spheres of predominant interest in 1899. Russia's extra-European activities did not threaten the peace of Europe.

Nor did the African ambitions of France and Italy do any lasting damage. True, the struggle between France and Britain intensified in the 1890s. French colonialism, which in the early 1880s had been largely a manoeuvre by which the *Intérêts* sought to rally opinion to the régime with the offer of quick profits, assumed a more fiercely ideological character as the intellectuals of the *parti colonial* began to influence French policy. The aim was no longer primarily economic but strategic – the construction of a North African empire and French supremacy in the western Mediterranean. The conclusion of the Franco-Russian alliance brought the prospect of Franco-Russian domination of the eastern Mediterranean too, and the expulsion of the British from Egypt. This last was almost an obsession with Delcassé, later the architect of the *Entente Cordiale,* but in the 1890s an ardent opponent of the British, from Siam to Morocco, the Congo, and the Sudan. But in the last resort these dreams were never worth a war with the British Empire, as even Delcassé was responsible enough to realize. The Italians, by contrast, had all the recklessness of the weak. Crispi's ambition to make Italy a real imperial power with the help of Germany and possibly of Britain had reduced Franco-Italian relations to a state bordering on enmity by 1890. But Italy's allies were always insistent that the Triple Alliance was an insurance company, not a joint-stock venture; and Salisbury was always suspicious of the restless Crispi: although Britain might prefer Italy to France or Russia on the Red Sea coast, she frowned on Italy's efforts to expand inland, uncomfortably close to the Sudan; and she had no relish for a confrontation with the Franco-Russian alliance on Italy's behalf. Thus, Italy was virtually isolated as she plunged on to disaster at

Adua. And the indirect consequences – the fall of Crispi and a great revulsion of feeling in Italy against imperialist ventures – were generally beneficial. Henceforth, until the revival of national feeling in the Tripoli war, Italian governments were obliged to confine their imperialist schemes to secret negotiations with the other European powers, outside and even contrary to her alliances – all of which only enhanced the flexibility of the European states system.

Perhaps the most far-reaching change in the behaviour of a European power in the 1890s was the shift in German policy from Bismarck's and Caprivi's concentration on the defence of Germany's continental position to an attempt to establish Germany in the ranks of the real world powers: *Weltpolitik*. Bismarck's tentative efforts in the colonial field had been critized even in his lifetime as the merest half-measures; and Caprivi had been decried as almost a traitor by the Pan-German League. By the 1890s a sizeable and extremely voluble body of opinion had grown up in Germany demanding the 'crowning' of Bismarck's uncompleted edifice by the acquisition of world-power status. Social Darwinist doctrines were rife amongst German intellectuals: the great struggle of the nations was beginning, in which the inferior – Portugal and Belgium certainly, perhaps in the long run Britain too – would go to the wall and Germany would acquire her world empire from the spoils. Mahan's teachings on the importance of sea-power as a prerequisite of empire had made a tremendous impression in Europe, particularly on the German emperor himself. Clearly Bismarck's fleet, designed for the coastal defence of a European state, was pathetically inadequate: Germany must have an ocean-going battle fleet capable of inspiring respect in the fleets of the established imperial powers. Yet the fact that such ideas were widespread in German society in the 1890s does not explain why they were suddenly adopted as the official policy of the imperial government.

The answer lies – as in the case of Bismarckian colonialism – in the domestic crisis in Germany: and the more desperate the problem, the more spectacular and elaborate the remedy. The élites were facing a growing challenge from the mass forces that were the inevitable product of Germany's becoming the leading industrial state in Europe. Bismarckian repression had failed; and Caprivi's conciliatory policies had made things even worse, threatening the landed classes with ruin while failing to stem the advance of the Social Democrats – now the largest party in the *Reichstag*. As the right still shrank from the risks involved in a *coup d'état*, some means would clearly have to be found of 'rallying' the masses behind the régime – another '*Sammlung*', with a broader appeal than Bismarck's colonialism. In 1897 the emperor and his intimate advisers embarked on a deliberate attempt both to establish their 'personal rule' and to bolster the position of the propertied elements by cultivating a popular mass movement for *Weltpolitik* and naval expansion. The élites would stand to gain from this in a direct material sense: naval expansion would mean profits for industrialists; and if East Prussian landowners instinctively jibbed at spending on what they termed 'the hideous fleet' instead of on subsidies to agriculture, they would vote for it in return for a new protective tariff (duly introduced on the expiry of Caprivi's treaties in 1902). Any popular opposition must be drowned in a wave of patriotic fervour. Altogether, the new policies constituted a conscious attack on the pretensions of the *Reichstag* to an effective role in governing Germany: Bülow avowedly determined to bring the matter of imperial expansion before the *Reichstag* in order to distract its attention from domestic grievances; and just as Bismarck had freed the army, the instrument of Germany's rise to continental greatness, from the effective control of the *Reichstag,* so Tirpitz aimed ultimately to deprive the *Reichstag* of control over spending on the navy, the designated instrument of Germany's rise to world power status. The express purpose of the Navy League – indeed, in Tirpitz's view the chief purpose – was to create a patriotic mass movement to halt the alarming progress of social democracy.

Not that the new policies were thought out solely in domestic terms. After all, the hearts of the masses would only be won if the new fleet actually succeeded in hauling Germany into the ranks of the world powers. But Tirpitz was confident of success, and even without an actual war. That was the essence of the 'risk theory': Germany must acquire a fleet of such a size that none of the existing world powers could challenge it without putting at risk its own position *vis à vis* other rivals; and then Germany would be in a position to exploit the rivalries of the established powers, extracting concessions from them by diplomatic pressure. Yet although the 'risk theory' was designed to give Germany an empire by peaceful means, that means was after all pretty close to blackmail, and Tirpitz's plan could hardly have been regarded by the established powers – especially by Britain, whose sole defence lay in the supremacy of the Royal Navy – as other than hostile in intention. Indeed, Admiral Fisher even advocated preventive war as preferable to creeping paralysis. Tirpitz himself was alive to this possible reaction, and developed his 'danger zone theory' to avert it: while the German fleet was still in its infancy, in a 'danger zone' where it was vulnerable to a preventive strike, it was essential to maintain good relations with the established powers, especially with Britain. This calculation at least was realistic; and the new policy was certainly compatible with, indeed a welcome addition to, the policy of the *Freie Hand* which Germany had been pursuing since 1895.

Even in its early years, the *Freie Hand* policy had not been without drawbacks. True, it had put an end to the confrontation of the early 1890s. After the Sino-Japanese war Germany joined with France and Russia in the 'Far Eastern Triplice' to force Japan to disgorge some of her gains, including Port Arthur. Russia's interest in the affair was primarily Far Eastern: she hoped some day to acquire Port Arthur herself. But for Germany the Far Eastern Triplice was very much an aspect of her European policy. She was competing with France for Russia's friendship, both in order to repair the damage done in the years of the *Neue Kurs* and to weaken the Franco-Russian alliance. Her direct interests in the Far East were almost exclusively economic, and here Germany, as an advanced industrial power well able to cope with competition, generally found herself aligned with Britain against France and Russia with their protectionist, monopolistic ambitions. In the Far East, therefore, the *Freie Hand* policy tended to blur the lines of division that had emerged from the conflict of interests in Europe, and if anything contributed to a reduction of tension. In other areas the results were less fortunate. The Kruger telegram affair, for example, was of a piece with German co-operation with France and Russia in China: Germany had no real interests at stake in the question; and she accompanied her dramatic gesture against Britain, significantly enough, with a proposal to Paris for the formation of a continental league. This perversion of Caprivi's doctrine of the interrelationship of European and extra-European affairs was disastrous: the *Freie Hand* could never wash out the stain of the Treaty of Frankfurt, and the French not only rejected the German proposal, but transmitted it to London. The affair was an early example of the dangers both of taking the *Freie Hand* too far and of assuming – and this was later to be all too characteristic of *Weltpolitik* – that other powers had no right to handle any question, anywhere in the world, without the permission of Germany. It did irreparable damage to Germany's reputation in London.

Germany's allies, certainly, thought her behaviour little short of lunacy, especially at a time when the future· of the Mediterranean *Entente* hung in the balance. The Ottoman Empire had been convulsed with crises since 1894, when the Armenians had staged a rebellion with the usual intention of provoking massacres to force the great powers to intervene and liberate the Christians after the manner of the 1870s. This time, however, the Armenians came up against a very negative Concert of Europe. None of the powers could face the task of attempting a final solution of the Eastern question. True, the British government, under pressure from humanitarian opinion, tried to help the Armenians; but when they started to discuss possible reforms with France and Russia, they found their partners merely obstructive – this was one Christian rebellion the Russians, with restless Armenian subjects of their own, did not favour. By the end of 1895, however, the disorders in Armenia, and even in Constantinople itself, reached such proportions that the Ottoman Empire seemed to be on the point of dissolution. Salisbury talked gloomily of having 'backed the wrong horse' in 1878; he hinted to the Germans about a possible partition, and to the Russians about their eventual acquisition of Constantinople – which the Germans, anxious to miss no chance to improve their own relations with Russia, readily endorsed. But this gloomy talk caused a great crisis of confidence in Vienna: Austro-Russian relations were still exceedingly bad, and offered no prospect whatever of an agreement in the event of the disappearance of the Ottoman Empire. For the time being, the Austro-Hungarian foreign minister, Goluchowski, maintained his anti-Russian posture: even though Salisbury refused for constitutional reasons to extend the Mediterranean Agreements to include a British promise to fight if Russia ever attempted to seize Constantinople, he still hoped that if Russia actually moved, parliament might yet spring to the sultan's defence. But when in January 1897 Salisbury confessed that further rounds of Armenian massacres had deprived him of even this hope, Goluchowski concluded that it would be too dangerous to continue, without any definite assurance of British support, a policy that might lead to confrontation with Russia. He decided in turn to assume a free hand.

Austria-Hungary's abandonment of the Mediterranean agreements left her in a more parlous position than ever if the Ottoman Empire in fact dissolved. At home, the wranglings of Czech and German nationalists paralysed parliamentary life in Vienna and Prague; and a determined campaign for greater independence by Budapest convinced many observers at the turn of the century that the Dual Monarchy itself was on the point of breaking up. Abroad, Russia, despite her increased preoccupation with the Far East, had started to re-establish her influence in the Balkans, especially in Bulgaria; and the Austro–Serbian alliance had expired in 1895. But the whole situation was suddenly transformed in the summer of 1897 when the Turks spectacularly demonstrated that they were not after all on the point of collapse. The Ottoman-Greek War was a veritable *deus ex machina*. The ultimate incompatibility of Austro-Hungarian and Russian interests had precluded any agreement about what might replace the Ottoman Empire in Europe; but agreement might well be possible on the basis of preserving the *status quo*. With the Ottoman victory over the Greeks, this now appeared to be a practical possibility. In St Petersburg in May the Austrians and Russians in fact agreed to refrain from disturbing the political *status quo* in the Near East, to keep the Balkan states in hand, and themselves not only to determine but to impose on the rest of Europe a territorial settlement when the Ottoman Empire disappeared. On this last point little progress was made, even on such elementary matters as the future of Bosnia and of the Straits. But the agreement was of considerable significance in European terms. The fundamental concept of 'dual control' of the Near East by Russia and Austria-Hungary, with the other powers very much in the second line, was certainly a moral betrayal of the existing alliances of both partners, and it set the seal on the end of the Mediterranean *Entente:* if the agreement gave the greatest offence at Rome, it was – like that of 1873 – hardly welcomed by Berlin, whose services as honest broker were clearly no longer required. But in a sense it was only another example of the health and flexibility of the European states system in the later 1890s.

If Russia and Austria-Hungary could reach agreement on a central issue vital to their existence as great powers, it was hardly surprising that agreements proved possible about peripheral issues in the Far East and Africa. The situation in the Far East was particularly fluid, and the interests of the powers involved so at variance that no power was tempted to cast in its lot with another to the extent of risking a confrontation. When the inauguration of *Weltpolitik* with the German seizure of Kiao-Chow in November 1897 provoked Russia to establish herself at Port Arthur a whole series of British attempts to enlist the support of another power for a confrontation over the issue all came to nothing. The Americans were fully occupied with their own confrontation with Spain in the Caribbean; the Japanese were themselves negotiating about a *modus vivendi* with Russia and were prepared to concede her a preponderance in Manchuria in return for Japanese preponderance in Korea. Chamberlain's attempt to take advantage of Salisbury's absence abroad by concluding an alliance with Germany fell completely flat: for Germany, an alignment with Britain in the Far East would mean an irreparable breach with Russia, with disastrous consequences for Germany's position in Europe. This was always the insurmountable obstacle to any Anglo-German agreement, in 1897 and later. As a single-handed confrontation with Russia was unthinkable, the British fell back on a simple counterbalancing policy, and accepted a Chinese offer of the lease of Wei-hai-wei. The same confusion of conflicting interests conspiring to localize a crisis was apparent in the 'scramble for concessions' at the end of the century. Britain, Germany, and the United States were generally aligned in defence of the open door against Russia and France; but Salisbury was still able to reach agreement with St Petersburg on the basis of spheres of predominant interest (as opposed to exclusive spheres of influence, the prelude to partition) in 1899; and when the Boxer Rising broke out against the foreigners in 1900, all the powers combined to organize an international expedition, under a German commander-in-chief, to suppress it.

The complexity of alignments in the late 1890s made for the localization of crises in Africa too. The French expedition to the Sudan, for example, was from the start a triangular affair: the assumption of German diplomatic support against Britain was central to French calculations. As it happened, Marchand arrived at Fashoda at the worst possible time. The *Freie Hand* policy was moving from a pro-Russian into a pro-British phase: the Germans had just congratulated Wolseley on his victory at Omdurman, and were engaged in very promising negotiations with the British over the future of Portugal's possessions in Africa. In these circumstances, French hopes of German diplomatic support vanished into thin air. Russia was plainly uninterested in the whole business; and as France was no more prepared to confront Britain alone in North Africa than Britain had been prepared to confront Russia alone in China, the upshot was a French withdrawal. When, despite this rebuff, the French persisted in their machinations to oust the British from Egypt, attempting in March 1900 to capitalize on Britain's almost universal unpopularity in the Boer War to organize a continental league against her, the divergent interests of two of the parties again ensured the security of the third. No French government could pay the price the Germans demanded for their participation – the endorsement of the Treaty of Frankfurt. The wound so gratuitously inflicted by Bismarck had not healed; and this being the case, Germany, with her fleet still in the 'danger zone', would not consider incurring the hostility of Britain over a peripheral issue in Africa any more than she would cut the wire to St Petersburg for the sake of a quarrel in Manchuria.

It was ominous for the future, however, that the failure of his approach to Germany in March 1900 led Delcassé to the dangerous conclusion that there was no point in trying to reach even a limited agreement with Germany about anything – a step towards the ossification of the European states system into rigidly opposed blocs. And his disillusionment with Germany coincided with a strengthening of the Franco-Russian alliance. Already in 1899 it had been amended to take account of the possible dissolution of Austria-Hungary: it was, therefore, no longer limited to the lifetime of the Triple Alliance; and its purpose was redefined as the preservation of the balance of power – to cope with any German attempt to acquire too great a share of the Habsburg heritage. Not that all this gloom about German intentions led the French to seek closer relations with Britain. On the contrary, the Franco-Russian alliance was supplemented by military agreements at the turn of the century, providing for indirect support in the event of war between either of the allies and Britain: France would move 100,000 men to the Channel coast, Russia the same number to the frontiers of India; and to facilitate this last manoeuvre Russia was given another huge loan to advance the construction of the Orenburg-Tashkent railway.

But if as yet there was no prospect of an alignment of the Franco-Russian Alliance with either Britain or Germany, these two powers could not make an alliance either. True, in October 1900 they reached an agreement to defend their commercial interests and preserve the open door in China; but when in March 1901 the British tried to argue that this obliged Germany to support them in pressing for an end to the Russian military presence in Manchuria – technically not even a part of China at all – the Germans rather brutally reminded them that they were not prepared to jeopardize their relations with St Petersburg for the sake of British interests at the other end of the world. They were not necessarily averse to an alliance with Britain on principle; but it must be worth the price of a breach with St Petersburg – Britain must assist in the defence of Austria-Hungary and Italy. Indeed, on the false assumption that Britain's difficulties with France and Russia must inevitably grow, the Germans placidly decided that if they simply waited, Britain would eventually have to beg them for an alliance on these very terms. Lansdowne was in fact prepared to consider it in May 1901, but Salisbury's arguments won the day: experience had shown that the continental powers were far too divided ever to combine effectively against Britain; and this being so Britain had no reason gratuitously to assume the burden of defending tottery Austria or erratic Italy. Even later, Lansdowne was still prepared to offer Germany limited agreements about local issues. But part of the difficulty was that whereas there were plenty of disputes between France and Russia that might – and later did – form the basis of such agreements, there were virtually none between Britain and Germany. As the Germans, not unnaturally, insisted that before they could abandon the *Freie Hand* Britain must join the Triple Alliance, the negotiations faded away. The

British found an alternative, outside Europe, in the Anglo-Japanese alliance of January 1902. This was partly a last-minute emergency measure to stave off the danger of a combination of Russian and Japanese naval power against Britain; but it had the great advantage over a German alliance of checking Russia in the Far East while allowing Britain to remain free from commitment to a continental bloc.

If the *Freie Hand* policy entailed the renunciation by Germany of advantages that might have accrued from a definite commitment to either Britain or to France and Russia, it also had a debilitating effect on her alliances. When Germany refused either to oppose Russia in the Balkans or to support Britain in the Mediterranean, Austria-Hungary and Italy began to look elsewhere. The Italians, for example, worried by Austria-Hungary's secretive co-operation with Russia across the Adriatic, and with their colonial policy in ruins, began to consider an accommodation with France, both to end the wearisome tariff war and to get French recognition for their ambitions in Tripoli. In 1899 and 1900 the able veteran Visconti-Venosta had secured both these objectives, the only restriction being that French recognition of eventual Italian control of Tripoli was dependent on France's getting control of Morocco. By 1902 Britain and Austria-Hungary had also agreed not to oppose Italy's eventual acquisition of Tripoli. Even so the Italians were not in any hurry to move in Tripoli; and Visconti's inexperienced successor, Prinetti – a former bicycle manufacturer – displayed a crass lack of perspective when, in return for a completely free hand in Tripoli and the promise of financial assistance, he gave the French a promise of Italian neutrality in any Franco-German war provoked by Germany. Taken together with his exceedingly sweeping verbal definition of provocation, the Prinetti-Barrère agreement of 1902 came close to a moral denunciation of the Triple Alliance. It is true that such behaviour was nothing exceptional within the Triple Alliance, as Germany had shown in 1887 and Austria-Hungary in 1897. And it is often forgotten that Prinetti's successors, more conservative by temperament and more mindful of Italy's dependence on German, not French, capital, regarded Prinetti's rash action as a grave blunder. For the next ten years they all strove to mitigate its effects and prove themselves loyal allies. But what Prinetti had done was never undone; and Italy's *extra tour* had certainly undermined the effectiveness of the Triple Alliance.

The Austrians, who had no interest in fighting the French and in fact welcomed the Franco-Italian *détente*, did even more damage. True, they had made an effort to reassure the Italians about the St Petersburg agreements: an Austro-Italian agreement of 1899 provided for the establishment of an autonomous Albania in the event of the collapse of the Ottoman Empire, for both parties recognized that neither could allow the other to control the Albanian coastline, key to the Adriatic. But the Austrians soon embarked on a further round of exclusive negotiations with St Petersburg, in an effort to control the violence that had broken out between Turks and Christian guerillas in Macedonia at the end of 1902. The aim of the Austro–Russian Mürzsteg agreement of October 1903 was not the liberation the terrorists had been hoping to provoke, but the conservation of the Ottoman Empire by the introduction of reforms to reconcile the Christians of Macedonia to the sultan's rule. Although all the powers were invited to supply personnel to supervise the reforms, the whole scheme was to remain firmly under Austro–Russian control. This reassertion of 'dual control' naturally angered Rome; but British and Italian efforts to mobilize the Concert came to nothing when the French refused to embarass their Russian allies. The culmination of Austro–Russian collaboration came in the Russo–Japanese war, when an Austro–Russian neutrality agreement of October 1904 spoke boldly in terms of benevolent neutrality in the event of war with 'a third power'. In so far as this was an allusion to a possible Austro–Italian war, it was a far more devastating comment on the state of relations within the Triple Alliance than anything Prinetti had done.

Indeed, in so far as it pledged Austria–Hungary to benevolent neutrality in the event not only of a Russo–British but even a Russo–German war, it was an equally damning comment on the state of the Dual Alliance. This had naturally been at a discount ever since the Germans had abandoned the *Neue Kurs* for the *Freie Hand;* and if the Austrians resented Pan-German meddling in the Czech-German conflict at home, they were equally exasperated by the conflict of Austro–German interests that was beginning to develop throughout the Near East. As the Kaiser's visit to Constantinople and the Baghdad Railway project demonstrated, Germany was beginning to develop her own interests in the Ottoman Empire, and these by no means coincided with those of her ally. The Germans had no relish for the prospect of an exclusive Austro–Russian *entente* laying down the law to the Turks. They disliked the Mürzsteg agreement, not merely as the product of the Austro–Russian *entente*, but as a provocation to the sultan, the patron of German economic interests in Asia Minor. In fact, in their efforts to promote these interests, the Germans did not shrink from encouraging the sultan to defy Austro–Russian pressure for reforms. In the Balkan states too German trade was making great inroads into what had formerly been a largely Austrian preserve. German traders were quick to take advantage of tariff wars provoked by protectionists in Hungary, to gain a firm foothold in Romania in the 1890s and in Serbia after 1906. This naturally undermined Austria-Hungary's prestige amongst the Balkan states, as did the Germans' infuriating habit of negotiating commercial treaties with Balkan states without waiting for the Austrians. The years that saw the zenith of the Austro-Russian *entente* marked the nadir of the Dual and Triple Alliances.

The French, meanwhile, were pressing ahead. Ever since Fashoda the *parti colonial* had been urging Delcassé to forget about Egypt and concentrate on Morocco – in their eyes not so much a potential *colonie d'exploitation* as 'a future part of a Greater France built round the shores of the Mediterranean'. By mid 1902 Delcassé had in fact squared Italy and was negotiating with Spain. But he stubbornly refused to attempt negotiations with Britain or Germany: he would neither abandon Egypt nor reaffirm the Treaty of Frankfurt. He was planning simply to confront Britain and Germany with French control of Morocco as a *fait accompli*. This was a dangerous policy: the Madrid Convention of 1880 had proclaimed the right of all the powers to a voice in the Moroccan question; and by virtue of its strategic position at the entrance to the Mediterranean, Morocco had a special significance for Britain. But events forced Delcassé's hand: at the end of 1902 Morocco fell into anarchy and civil war; Spain broke off negotiations, apparently out of respect for Britain; and the German colonial lobby declared its interest and formed a Morocco Association in February 1903. All this made Delcassé at least consider negotiations with Britain as advocated by the *parti colonial*. The British, for their part, were in a mood to listen: the disorder now prevailing in Morocco had made them sceptical as to its chances of survival as an independent state; and from February 1903 Cromer in Cairo had been recommending negotiations to secure French support for his latest scheme of financial and administrative reforms in Egypt. It was only after Edward VII's famous state visit to Paris in May that Anglo-French relations really became more cordial; but by October negotiations had started and in the agreements of 8 April 1904 the French and British settled a whole complex of longstanding extra-European differences and promised each other diplomatic support in Egypt and Morocco respectively.

It is true that France was not yet in possession of Morocco, whereas Britain was already established in Egypt. But French opponents of the agreements, who complained that France had made a cash payment in return for a mere promissory note, were short-sighted. After all, no one was seriously challenging the British in Egypt; whereas the British were to find themselves involved in far-reaching diplomatic, and even military complications, when France eventually made a forward move in Morocco and was challenged by Germany. Lansdowne himself had certainly not foreseen the European implications of the agreement. For him, it was in no sense intended as a challenge to Germany, but was, like the Anglo-Japanese alliance, and like his attempt in 1903 to safeguard British interests in the Persian Gulf by negotiating with Germany for British participation in the Baghdad Railway, simply one aspect of a policy of securing British imperial interests by limited bilateral agreements, while remaining aloof from continental alignments. Not that the agreement had no wider implications whatever, even for Lansdowne. He certainly hoped that it might pave the way to a similar settlement of differences with Russia. The outbreak of war between the allies of Britain and France in February had made the British doubly sensitive to the risks of an open breach with St Petersburg – hence their haste to disavow Younghusband's expedition to Tibet in September. They much appreciated Delcassé's conciliatory efforts during the Dogger Bank crisis in October, a welcome contrast to Germany's gloating; and they in turn pressed Spain to negotiate with France over Morocco despite German advice. Limited though the original Anglo-French agreement had been, the patent desire of both parties to maintain it was already beginning to create something of an '*entente cordiale*'.

If the Far Eastern crisis had been peripheral to the making of the Anglo-French agreements, and even to their development in 1904, the results of the Russo-Japanese War were of a very different order, and helped to transform the whole European states system. By 1905 the Tsarist monarchy, defeated on land and sea, was paralysed by revolution. The European states system had in effect lost one of its members; and such a profound disturbance of the balance of power was bound to cause the others to reconsider their alignments. One consequence was to be the transformation of the 'extra-European' agreements of 8 April 1904 into an Anglo-French *entente* operating in Europe.

But even here a European catalyst was needed, and this was provided by Germany's wildly opportunistic attempt to take advantage of Russia's embarrassment to re-order the European states system: a continental league was to be created, centring on a Russo-German alliance, neutralizing the Franco-Russian alliance and isolating Britain. Thus, in October, the Germans proposed to the Russians a general alliance against attack 'by another power', to which France might later accede. This project, which made nonsense of both the Franco-Russian and Austro-German alliances, was both totally unrealistic and a gross blunder. At any rate, the French protested to St Petersburg, the Russians refused to proceed, Franco-German relations deteriorated sharply, and, worst of all, the French confided in the British. Now, one consequence of the demonstratively anti-British gestures that characterized the *Freie Hand* policy had been to build up a body of anti-German opinion in Britain. This was growing – witness the hostile' reaction to co-operation with Germany in a debt-collecting expedition to Venezuela in 1902; and the hysterical outburst a year later that actually brought the government's Baghdad Railway negotiations to a halt. Nor was this feeling confined to the half-educated public. It was marked amongst the cohort of young Germanophobe diplomats of the stamp of Hardinge and Nicolson who were fast rising, with the help of Edward VII, to influential positions in the foreign office. The admiralty had started to draw the cabinet's attention to the menace of the German fleet already in 1903; and the cabinet decided to build a new naval base at Rosyth, in Scotland. Thus, even before the elimination of the Russian fleet concentrated British minds even further on the German threat, influential circles in Britain were already beginning to incline more to the French than to the German side.

The decisive turning-point came with the second German attempt to exploit the collapse of Russia in the spring of 1905, which plunged Europe into the first Moroccan crisis. True, the Germans had a case against the French. It was only under duress that the Sultan of Morocco had accepted the St René Taillandier reform mission; and it undoubtedly threatened the independence of Morocco, of which Germany was a guardian as a signatory of the Madrid Convention of 1880. To this extent the Kaiser's visit to Tangier, to demonstrate that in German eyes Morocco was still an independent state, was perfectly justified. But German motives went beyond respect for the Madrid Convention. The fact that Delcassé had taken the trouble to square Italy, Britain, and even Spain, while ostentatiously ignoring Germany, convinced the Wilhelmstrasse that something had to be done, not so much for the sake of Morocco as for the sake of German prestige in Europe. The demand for a conference was designed to punish and humiliate France. More than this, however: as Britain would probably have to join the rest of Europe in condemning the wrongfulness of France's proceedings, the conference would destroy the Anglo-French *entente*. As the German plans developed, they became more ambitious. In May they began to include the dismissal of Delcassé among their demands. This was partly a panic reaction to the news that Delcassé was about to make his position impregnable by mediating peace in the Russo-Japanese War. But it also reflected a long-term plan whereby

France, once Delcassé had gone, was to be reconciled to Germany by means of concessions in the preliminary negotiations for the conference: and the whole diplomatic edifice was to be crowned by a revival of the 1904 plan for a continental league.

In the summer of 1905 the German plan seemed to be succeeding. In June the French cabinet, afraid that Delcassé was leading France, now without an effective ally, into a war with Germany that would only serve British naval and commercial interests, sacrificed Delcassé and embarked on negotiations with Germany for a conference. When, in an emotional meeting at Björkö in July the Kaiser prevailed on the Tsar to sign a Russo–German alliance, even the much-coveted continental league seemed within Germany's grasp. But in November the whole house of cards collapsed, when the Russian foreign office rejected the Treaty of Björkö as incompatible with Russia's obligations to France. This left the forthcoming conference as the Germans' only hope of salvaging some prestige. The prospects were poor: already in the summer, while the continental league had seemed a real possibility, the Germans had themselves given a good deal away in their preliminary negotiations with the French; it was now clear that France would have Russia's support; and German behaviour since the spring had pushed even Lansdowne into taking a diplomatic stand in support of France against Germany. The new Liberal administration in London (December) brought the Germans no hope of relief: its foreign secretary, Sir Edward Grey, a former parliamentary secretary in Rosebery's cabinet, was from experience suspicious of German methods; and although he was somewhat out of touch, he had plenty of advisers in the foreign office to confirm his natural inclinations to support the French.

The conference was a resounding diplomatic defeat for Germany. Although the final Act of Algeçiras formally – indeed, 'in the name of Almighty God' – proclaimed the independence and integrity of Morocco, the reality was very different. On the crucial issue Germany was supported only by Austria-Hungary and Morocco: control of the Moroccan police was handed over to France and Spain, with only a token supervisory role for the consular corps at Tangier. That the Germans fared better on other issues, such as the internationalization of the Moroccan bank, was cold comfort to them. They regarded the conference as a disaster; and their own irrational and clumsy reactions made their position still worse. The Italians, for example, had been committed to France on this particular issue since 1900: and they were not disloyal to the Triple Alliance (which did not cover Morocco anyway). Nevertheless, the Kaiser raged: 'This romance cat's meat betrays us right and left'; and even talked of war against Italy. Ungrateful Russia, the Germans decided, would certainly not be granted a German loan – whereupon the French provided further huge sums to speed up her reconstruction after the 1905 Revolution. The Germans even managed with their condescending 'brilliant second' telegram, to offend the loyal Austrians. If the events of 1905–6 marked a distinct worsening of Germany's international position, it must be said that the Germans were to a great extent isolating themselves.

Certainly the effect of Germany's behaviour on Britain's attitude towards her can hardly be exaggerated. Grey's experiences in his first weeks of office confirmed his initial prejudices: and whereas Lansdowne had supported France primarily as a matter of honouring the pledges he had given in 1904, Grey was determined to support her at all costs against a power that was threatening to overturn the European equilibrium. For the same reason he was 'impatient to see Russia re-established as a factor in European politics'. 'An *entente* between Russia, France, and ourselves would be absolutely secure. If it is necessary to check Germany, it could then be done.' Here was the difference between Grey's attitude towards an agreement with Russia and Lansdowne's. Lansdowne merely wanted a limited extra-European agreement with a power whom it would be difficult to resist by force. Of course, this motive still held good in 1907 too: the Liberal cabinet was convinced that India was not in fact defensible against Russia. Convalescent and enfeebled Russia was at this moment also willing to consider an armistice in the Asian 'Great Game'. In form, the Anglo–Russian agreement of 31 August 1907 was, like the Anglo–French agreements of 1904, concerned entirely with extra-European matters. But already in the negotiations Grey had hinted that Britain might some day agree to an alteration of the rule of the Straits in Russia's favour (to give her Black Sea fleet access to the Mediterranean); and he was beginning to find the Russians – in contrast to the Austrians – receptive to British amendments to the Macedonian reform programme. Indeed, he speculated that 'ten years hence, a combination of Britain, Russia, and France may be able to dominate Near Eastern policy'. For Grey, the Russian agreement was a weapon against the domination of the European states system by Germany and her allies.

Izvolsky's view of the agreement was different. In his concern to wind up Russia's disastrous Far Eastern policy and restore her position as a great power, he was obviously not interested in new alignments that would inevitably carry with them the risk of new conflicts. He wanted to make as many limited agreements as possible without committing Russia against anybody. There were compelling domestic reasons for this: for the Stolypin government it was axiomatic that Russia needed twenty years of peace if the embers of revolution were to be stamped out; and the old principles of monarchical solidarity, of keeping the wire open to Berlin, and co-operating with Austria-Hungary in the Near East, were still entrenched at court. The agreement of 31 August might be a notable landmark in British diplomacy, but for Russia it was balanced by an agreement with Japan which took the sting out of the Anglo-Japanese Alliance; by a Russo-German agreement to maintain the *status quo* in the Baltic; and by proposals to the Austrians to extend the *entente* of 1897. Izvolsky disliked Britain's hankering after disarmament in the 1907 Hague Peace Conference, especially as he suspected it was a move to isolate Germany; nor did he welcome an Anglo-Franco-Spanish agreement of May 1907 to maintain the *status quo* in the Western Mediterranean, and intended to prevent Spain ceding her interests in Morocco to Germany. Altogether it seemed to Izvolsky that Britain was far too set on 'weaving webs and forming rings round Germany'. The first Moroccan crisis might have produced something of a 'two-camps' mentality in London and Paris; but viewed from St Petersburg the European states system was still by no means one of two opposing blocs.

But if Izvolsky sincerely desired to secure Russian state interests through limited agreements with several powers, this was difficult to achieve in practice. In the first place, Russia's collapse in 1905 aroused widespread fears in St Petersburg that a continuance to the *entente à deux* with Austria-Hungary would lead to the domination of the latter in the Balkans. But his attempt to broaden the dual control in Macedonia into something resembling control by the Concert put a strain on Austro-Russian relations. Aehrenthal in Vienna feared that Britain's radical suggestions could only precipitate the collapse of the sultan's authority and cause chaos on Austria-Hungary's borders; and his ideal political combination was, after all, not the Concert, but a restored *Dreikaiserbund* to fight the proletarian revolution. In the second place, there was the continuing Pig War between Austria-Hungary and Serbia – a tariff war initiated by Goluchowski in an effort to re-establish Austro-Hungarian control of Serbia, where since 1903 the government had been in the hands of Pan-Serbian nationalists who openly avowed their designs on the South Slav provinces of the Monarchy. This not only embarrassed the government in St Petersburg, but inflamed public opinion against the Austro-Russian *entente;* and public opinion was increasingly a force to be reckoned with in Russia, since the 1905 revolution had established the Duma and a free press. Izvolsky, certainly, was inordinately sensitive to public criticism. Even so, despite growing public demands for the abandonment of the *entente* in favour of an alignment with the western powers in pursuit of Russia's Slav mission, he stubbornly persisted with schemes to secure Russian state interests by secret diplomacy. In Vienna, in September 1907, he tentatively suggested developing the 1897 *entente* to deal with the eventual collapse of the Ottoman Empire: Russia might then secure control of the Straits, and Austria-Hungary some compensation to suit herself. But when in January 1908 Aehrenthal suddenly announced his plans for a series of railways, in the Sanjak of Novibazar and elsewhere, all designed to increase Austria-Hungary's commercial and political influence in the Balkans, the indignation of the Russian public was so great as to give even Izvolsky pause.

Yet the Sanjak railway crisis was less important in terms of Austro-Russian than of British policy. Although the British suspected Aehrenthal of a deal with the sultan, to secure the railways at the expense of Macedonian reform, their indignation contained a strong admixture of fear of Germany: after threatening France in Morocco and Britain at sea, Germany was now grasping for control of the Balkans. In fact, the notion that the Germans were behind the railway projects was quite false: as the exasperated Aehrenthal pointed out, 'England had Germany on the brain'. But it showed how ready the foreign office was to assume – and this was an ominous comment on the deterioration of the international situation since the middle 1890s – that Austria-Hungary had virtually ceased to function as an independent power in the European states system. The British, for the first time since the 1820s, sided with Russia against Austria in the Balkans; and this time they were not out to restrain the Russians. On the contrary, the uproar in St Petersburg marked 'a very important development of the Anglo-French and Anglo-Russian agreement policy: Russia is now asking for our co-operation in the Near East'. The British press duly joined in the Franco-Russian hue and cry, and Grey sharply criticized Aehrenthal in parliament. Whether the Austrians had in fact betrayed the Concert or not was for the British less important than the fact that, as Hardinge observed, 'the struggle between Austria and Russia in the Balkans is evidently now beginning, and we shall not be bothered by Russia in Asia'. Within a few years, the British were to pay a high price for their peace in Asia. For the present, they seized on the Austro-Russian quarrel to substitute for the Mürzsteg scheme an Anglo-Russian scheme of reforms for Macedonia, finalized during Edward VII's meeting with the tsar at Reval in June. As far as the British were concerned, the Anglo-Russian *entente* had come to Europe.

Izvolsky still had other ideas. He was already negotiating secretly with Vienna, and on 2 July offered Aehrenthal a deal whereby Russia and Austria-Hungary might alter the rule of the Straits and the status of Bosnia to their own advantage. Aehrenthal was initially suspicious of Izvolsky, but he ceased to hesitate when the Young Turks seized power in Constantinople, restoring the constitution of 1876 for the whole Empire, and talking of subjecting Bosnia and the Herzegovina to the new régime. It was largely as a demonstration against any Young Turkish (and Serbian) aspirations in Bosnia that the Austrians decided in August to annex the occupied provinces outright, grant them a constitution of their own, and abandon Austria-Hungary's occupation rights in the Sanjak of Novibazar – which might only draw her into a maelstrom should the Young Turk Revolution degenerate into chaos. The annexation was, thus, essentially a conservative move to clear up a dangerously ambiguous situation by setting clear limits to what was Austrian and what was Turkish. Indeed, Izvolsky himself accepted it as such when he met Aehrenthal at Buchlau in September. He promised to adopt a benevolent attitude towards it: whereupon Aehrenthal endorsed his plans concerning the Straits and for a Bulgarian declaration of independence which Izvolsky was hoping to bring about under Russian auspices. But Izvolsky had not forgotten the state of feeling in Russia – hence his secret plans for summoning a conference, at which Austria-Hungary would appear as the accused, and Russia as the patron of outraged Slav and Turkish feeling.

His plans miscarried badly. Bulgaria declared independence without waiting for Russia; Austria-Hungary announced the annexation before Izvolsky had secured British and French approval for the Russian *quid pro quo*; and the Russian government tried to calm public opinion by disavowing Izvolsky's negotiations with Vienna and declaring for a conference and the creation of a Balkan League to oppose Austria-Hungary's supposed expansionist designs. A six-month diplomatic wrangle followed, in which Britain was Russia's chief supporter. But Britain was unwilling, and Russia unable, to go to war on the issue; and they were faced with the prospect of an Austro-Hungarian punitive expedition against Serbia – an expedition which the Germans warned Russia in their notorious 'ultimatum' they would do nothing to prevent. So Britain and Russia had to drop their demands for a conference, and even compel protesting Serbia not only to recognize the annexation without compensation but to promise to live henceforth on good neighbourly terms with Austria-Hungary.

The Bosnian crisis certainly marked a deterioration in the international situation. It was regarded in the *Entente* capitals as a victory for brutal diplomacy backed by superior force, and resulted directly in an increase in the tempo of the armaments race. The next three years saw Anglo–German tension over the naval issue reach its peak as the cry went up in England of 'we want eight and we won't wait'; and Nicolson in St Petersburg began to press Grey to turn the Anglo–Russian *entente* into a formal alliance. The Austro–German alliance certainly seemed more united and impressive than ever: in February 1909 Berlin had given the Austrians a most un-Bismarckian promise of support against Russia if they started a war in the Balkans. And with the total breakdown of Austro–Russian relations the European states system had moved a stage nearer to polarization into two armed camps. But this view should not be taken too far. The German promise of support for Austria–Hungary was vitiated by the news that Germany intended to concentrate so many troops in the west in any future war that Austria–Hungary would have to fend for herself at the start; and the blank cheque itself was cancelled eighteen months later at Potsdam. There, in November 1910, the Germans and Russians reached agreement over extra–European issues such as Persia and the Baghdad Railway; the Germans promised that they would have no truck with any aggressive moves by Austria–Hungary in the Balkans, the Russians giving the Germans a similar promise with regard to British designs. Extra–European issues could still provide links across the alliances to reduce the risk of a confrontation between two armed camps. The French, at the very height of the Bosnian crisis, in February 1909, had concluded an agreement with Berlin providing for the reciprocal recognition of French political and German commercial interests in Morocco – which had made war for Serbia even more unthinkable for the Russians. The British, too, after their experiences in the Bosnian crisis, had lost much of their enthusiasm for the intricacies of Balkan diplomacy, especially as they came to appreciate the essentially conservative nature of Aehrenthal's aims. Never again were they to take the lead in supporting Russia in the Near East. The fronts that had appeared in 1909 had dissolved by 1910 to leave the European states system in that unstable equilibrium that had served to mitigate conflicts since the middle 1890s.

CHAPTER EIGHT
Confrontation and the resort to violence 1911–1914

The unstable equilibrium that had prevailed since the middle 1890s, and had survived even the Bosnian crisis, was nevertheless destined to degenerate within the course of a couple of years into a confrontation between two armed camps and a cataclysmic war. Austro-Russian hostility was certainly a factor in this disastrous development; but it cannot of itself explain why the Eastern question, which had been contained peacefully within the European states system for over a century, should now prove unmanageable. After all, there had been a whole series of Austro-Russian *ententes* and arrangements in the past century; and when one had broken down, it had not been long before another had appeared. It would seem that part of the explanation lies in the changed character of the Eastern question itself after 1911, when it became one of the final liquidation of the Ottoman Empire in Europe, with that in Asia Minor soon to follow. Not only did the threats to the vital interests of Russia and Austria-Hungary thereupon assume an infinitely more acute form; the question affected the vital interests of the other powers – including, for the first time directly, those of Germany, who about 1911 abandoned *Weltpolitik* to concentrate on the Near East; and it involved not only their direct interests, but their interest in supporting either Russia or Austria-Hungary as allied or friendly powers within the European states system. But that the problem assumed such proportions was the result not only of the failure of the Young Turks to keep the Ottoman Empire on its feet, but also of the policies pursued in these years by the great powers themselves.

The Habsburg Monarchy was forbidden by its domestic weakness to adopt an adventurous policy abroad. Until 1912 Magyar opposition prevented any increase in the size of the army beyond the 1888 level; and although the quarrel between the Austrian and Hungarian ruling élites

164

that had threatened at the turn of the century to destroy the Monarchy had been patched up, this had only been done at the price of a tougher line against the subject nationalities, whose grievances continued to increase. True, none of these nationalities was as yet demanding actual independence; and the multinational Imperial and Royal Army was still loyal and capable of dealing with any domestic fracas. But there was the problem of the existence of the Monarchy's southern borders of irredentist states – most notably, Serbia, but also the allied Romania – where nationalist elements looked fixedly to the liberation of their brothers groaning under the Habsburg yoke. Even here the Monarchy could cope alone for the present: but hardly if the Balkan states ever absorbed the European territories of the Ottoman Empire and combined their forces in a Balkan League; and certainly not if ever such a league secured the backing of the tsar's armies. One Austrian guarantee against this danger in the past – a monarchical alliance with Russia – was unthinkable in the immediate aftermath of the Bosnian crisis; as was the alternative, the construction of a big diplomatic bloc to restrain Russia – the British would be at best neutral, certainly they would never oppose Russia at the risk of diverting her back to Asia; and after Potsdam, even German support was problematical. The Austrians in fact simply hoped against hope that the Ottoman Empire would somehow survive, and that they would be able to restrain or establish their influence in at least some of the Balkan states in order to keep them from uniting in a league. This was becoming increasingly difficult: Austro-Hungarian influence in the Balkan states, already undermined by the protectionist and Magyarization policies of Budapest, was increasingly threatened by British, and especially German, commercial competition; and since the disappearance of the united Austro-Russian front that had overawed them in the 1880s and since 1897, the Balkan states were notably unresponsive to orders from either Vienna or St Petersburg. In this situation, as the point approached beyond which Vienna would not be pushed without resort to battle, as in 1859 and 1866, the Habsburg Monarchy was undoubtedly a conservative power, but a desperate, even dangerous, one.

The Russian government – let alone the Russian public – regarded Austria-Hungary's attempts to retain influence in the Balkans in a completely different light. In Russia the annexation of Bosnia was seen as a forward, expansionist move, probably the first of several: Sazonov warned the Greeks to look to their armaments, or '*Vous verrez l'Autriche à Salonique*'. Moreover, it was – rightly – regarded as axiomatic in St Petersburg that if the Balkans and the Straits ever fell under Austrian or Austro-German control, Russia, with her lifeline at the mercy of her neighbours, would cease to exist as an independent power. In the last resort Russia would fight to prevent any other power replacing the Turk as guardian of the Straits. But meanwhile Russia could use diplomatic means to safeguard her interests; and if Russian public opinion ruled out an arrangement with the Central Powers, a defensive bloc of Balkan states, possibly including Turkey herself, would be both popular and effective. Hence Russia's untiring efforts after 1908 to construct such a league, even at the risk, as it turned out, of hastening the collapse of the Ottoman Empire and precipitating the very dangers the league was designed to ward off. The difficulty in terms of European peace was that what Russia saw as a defensive policy seemed to the Austrians exceedingly offensive. Both Russia and Austria-Hungary were primarily seeking security; but the solutions each devised inevitably appeared to threaten the security of the other. So long as the Ottoman Empire survived as a buffer, refusing to commit itself to either side, the problem was manageable. But after 1912 the European states system was presented with that most dangerous kind of clash of interests, a clash of two defensive strategies. It was to fail the test.

Events in the Near East obviously concerned Italy too, but on the whole they simply confirmed her alignment with the Central Powers, whose performance in the Bosnian crisis had made an awesome impression at Rome. True, Italy's increasing involvement, through traders and missionaries, in Albania had been ill-received in Vienna; and the Austro-Hungarian decision to build Dreadnoughts after 1909 had sharpened the rivalry between the two allies for control of the Adriatic. But if, at Racconigi in October 1909, the Italians made a *status quo* agreement with the Russians to guard against future surprises in the Balkans, they took care to balance it by an almost identical agreement with Austria-Hungary two months later; and Aehrenthal was for his part particularly anxious to improve Austro–Italian relations if only to offset the deterioration of Austro–Russian relations. Throughout the Mediterranean basin, in fact, Italy's interests seemed to be drawing her closer to her allies. In the east Greece was already beginning to appear as a potential rival, and her aspirations in Crete and Asia Minor caused as much concern in Rome as in Constantinople. As early as 1910 Italy stood united with her allies in resisting efforts by the Triple *entente* powers to persuade the Turks to call off a boycott of Greek trade. In the western Mediterranean Italy's relations with France had certainly grown no closer since the agreements of 1902, from which few commercial or financial benefits had emerged; and it was France who, dominating the whole western Mediterranean coastline, was likely to be Italy's chief rival if she ever managed to realize her plans for a North African Empire. By 1911 these plans were finding increasingly vocal support from a growing and frustrated nationalist movement at home.

If France had been remarkably conciliatory during the Bosnian crisis, being anxious above all to prevent a war that could only spell disaster for her considerable financial interests in both the Ottoman Empire and the Balkan states, she had not ceased to pursue her own North African schemes. And changes were occurring at home that were to direct French policy into an altogether more nationalist and adventurous track. The anti-clerical crusade that had united the radical–socialist coalition since the Dreyfus affair had ended with the separation of church and state in 1905, and the two wings of the *Bloc des Gauches* were by 1909 engaged in a quarrel over priorities, fiscal or social reform. The financial and commercial *Intérêts* wanted neither, and finding their erstwhile allies now not only useless but dangerous, began to search for another issue to unite the nation and stave off reform. This they were eventually to discover in nationalism. The second Moroccan crisis was to lead to a transformation of French political life and to a nationalist wave that was to sweep France into far-reaching commitments, not only to Britain, but, more dangerously, to Russia in the Near East.

The British, after their exertions in 1908–89, had lapsed into passivity, almost rigidity: the Triple *Entente* contained Germany, and that was enough. As Grey insisted,

an attempt to isolate Germany by setting Austria against her might precipitate a conflict. On the other hand, . . . if Germany dominated Europe, the result would also be war. We have to steer between these two dangers. At present, there is a fair equilibrium.

Hence his stubborn rejection of all suggestions for winning over Italy or Austria-Hungary from the opposing camp. At the same time he was desperately anxious to hold on to France and Russia at all costs: the Triple *Entente* and what Grey saw as the balance of power were Britain's guarantees against a continental league or a *Dreikaiserbund* that might deflect Russia into reactivating her Asian ambitions – hence his indifference to British radical protests about Russia's brutal interference in the affairs of Persia; hence his determination to back France to the hilt in North Africa. Indeed, to the foreign office the chief danger in Anglo-German naval rivalry lay not so much in the continuing deadlock (Britain could always outbuild Germany in the last resort) but in German efforts to seduce the cabinet into accepting an agreement on the basis of an unconditional pledge of British neutrality in the event of a continental war. Such a withdrawal would obviously leave the way open for a *Dreikaiserbund*; or it would be fatal, as Grey preferred to put it, for the balance of power and for peace. But his very insistence on seeing the European states system in terms of a balance between two armed camps was not without dangers of its own.

Moreover, Grey's assumptions about Germany's overweening power bore little relation to reality. By 1909 the whole grand concept of rallying the nation behind the ruling élite through *Weltpolitik* lay in ruins. Its exponents had started with certain financial and diplomatic assumptions: that the costs of their programme would be kept within strict limits – the emancipation of the government from dependence on the Reichstag was, after all, central to the whole scheme; and Britain must continue on bad terms with France and Russia, leaving Germany to hold the balance and extract concessions in return for her goodwill. By 1906 these fundamental assumptions had proved erroneous. Just as the first Moroccan crisis had given the lie to German diplomatic assumptions, so the adoption by Britain of the Dreadnought programme raised the cost of naval competition to heights undreamed of by Tirpitz. The government was forced to approach the *Reichstag* with proposals for new taxes, including a controversial inheritance tax: the result by 1909 was the breakdown of the liberal–conservative coalition. The programme devised to unite the nation had plunged it into political deadlock. After this the government could only limp along with *ad hoc* majorities in the *Reichstag,* while the tensions between the establishment and the new forces in German society continued unresolved. Nor could the government retreat: confronted with the product of its own propaganda, a Navy League of over one million, it could never admit that its whole policy had been a mistake. It was condemned to go on, pouring out money for a fleet that was not only useless, but which deprived the army of much-needed funds. *Weltpolitik* had in fact only made Germany's difficulties worse; and although in 1911 a last attempt was made to snatch some prestige in North Africa, when this too failed, Germany turned to a narrower, and infinitely more dangerous, concentration on south-east Europe and Asia Minor.

This was only one aspect of the startling deterioration of the international situation that occurred about 1911. For fifteen years or so after the middle 1890s the powers had had to divide their attention between their relations with each other in Europe and the problems that had arisen to confront them in the decaying empires of the world, from China and Persia to North Africa. The international system had proved flexible enough to cope with all these extra-European problems, allowing of bilateral agreements which left less interested powers unaffected, and which on no occasion produced a serious confrontation involving the whole of Europe. This is not to say that even crises originating outside Europe could not assume a dangerous aspect when they appeared to present a threat to the existence and independence of a great power within the European states system – witness the British support for France in 1906. The year 1911, however, saw the start of a chain of such crises, made increasingly dangerous by the reactions of the European powers themselves, both great and small – by their growing habit of resorting to sabre rattling, even to actual violence; and above all by the fatal tendency of the great powers to view even extra-European developments in terms of the balance within the European states system. The crises themselves were dangerous enough: starting on the Atlantic coast of Morocco, they swept through the Ottoman province of Tripoli to destroy the Ottoman Empire in Europe, and ended by posing a direct threat to the existence of Austria–Hungary, and hence to the established states system. The cataclysm of 1914 was the culmination of this sudden deterioration of the international situation.

This was perhaps hardly foreseeable when French troops occupied the Moroccan capital in April 1911, partly in order to tighten French control of Morocco, but also to assist the sultan against disorderly elements who were also a constant nuisance to the French themselves in neighbouring Algeria. The initial German response too was reasonable enough: simply to point out that a prolonged occupation of Fez would violate the independence of Morocco as guaranteed by the powers in the Act of Algeciras. But, as in 1905, the Germans were not merely – if at all – interested in upholding the legal position. They were now rather less ambitious – there was this time no question of reordering the

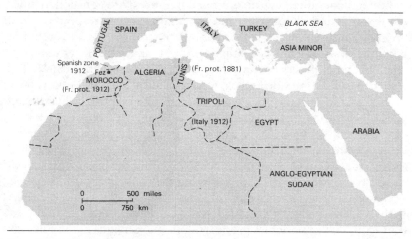

Map 6   North Africa in 1910

alignments of the powers under German direction – but they hoped to salvage something from the wreck of *Weltpolitik* and extract compensation for any French advance in Morocco. It was the size of the German claim – the whole of the French Congo – and Kiderlen's method of enforcing it by such crude devices as the *Panthersprung* that caused the international crisis. In London, German blustering was immediately interpreted as a calculated assault on the independence of France as a great power, and Lloyd George's Mansion House speech was designed both to stiffen France and to warn her against any separate deal with Germany. In fact the danger was less than the British imagined: neither Austria–Hungary nor Russia felt moved to give their ally the slightest encouragement; and as the Kaiser was from the start determined that Germany should in no circumstances go to war, the upshot was one of those compromise arrangements typical of the imperialist era: the Germans accepted French plans for a protectorate in Morocco in return for some modest slices of French territory in Central Africa. As a genuine compromise the settlement was greeted with howls of indignation in both France and Germany.

It was, moreover, to be the last of the old-style compromises; and if the immediate threat had been less serious than the British imagined, the long-term consequences of the second Moroccan crisis were extremely grave. The degeneration of the complex and flexible states system of the later 1890s into a crude confrontation between two blocs had proceeded a stage further. The British became more accustomed to the idea of fighting alongside France in a continental war: the autumn of 1911 saw a further round of Anglo-French military conversations; and if the decisions taken by Britain and France in 1912 to concentrate their naval forces in the North Sea and the Mediterranean respectively did not amount to a formal obligation, they came close to a moral commitment to defend each other's interests against Germany and her allies. In France the crisis fanned the flames of nationalism and helped to alter the whole tone of French foreign policy. When the Lorrainer Poincaré was swept into the premiership in January 1912 the *Intérêts* had at last secured their nationalist alliance against social reform. '*Ce n'est pas un homme qui triomphe, ce n'est pas un parti, c'est une idée nationale*', the moderate *Le Journal* declared. Caillaux was more prophetic: '*C'est la guerre*'. Finally, in Germany, the crisis, or rather the public reaction to the outcome, was seen as demonstrating the bankruptcy of *Weltpolitik* as the solution to Germany's problems. True, desultory negotiations with Britain about the Baghdad Railway, Persia, and the future of Portugal's African colonies produced some agreements in the summer of 1914. But the Germans had really lost interest in *Weltpolitik* in 1911;

or, at least, they decided to give priority to the more relevant, and infinitely more explosive, issue of Germany's position in Central Europe and the Near and Middle East.

More immediately, the French move in Morocco determined the Italians to lose no time in seizing Tripoli in September 1911. Admittedly, the ensuing Italo-Ottoman War was acutely embarrassing for all the other powers, especially as the belligerents were the two most delicately poised components of the European balance. But the endless stream of mediation proposals, all made with an eye to avoiding offending either of the belligerents rather than to forcing them to come to terms, and all consequently abortive, was a devastating comment on the paralysing division of Europe into two camps. The Concert had ceased to exist. In the end the Germans decided that the Triple Alliance was worth more than a Turkish *entente*; and even forced the Austrians to swallow their objections to anything that might bring the war to the Balkans, and to countenance an Italian occupation of the Dodecanese Islands. All this contrasted sharply with the behaviour of the Triple *Entente* Powers: Britain, increasingly sensitive to Moslem feeling in India, and dismayed by the establishment of a great power in the eastern Mediterranean within striking distance of Egypt; France, on the verge of war with Italy over the arrest of two French steamers in January 1912; and Russia, in October 1911 actually offering Turkey an alliance if she would join a Balkan league. Not surprisingly the Tripoli War saw the return of Italy into the bosom of the Triple Alliance.

In the long run the Central Powers lost more than they gained from the Tripoli War. In so far as it precipitated the collapse of the Ottoman Empire in Europe, it was the precursor of the collapse of their own position in the Near East. The Ottoman Empire's embarrassments encouraged the Balkan states to unite, by a network of agreements, some of which had Russia's approval, in a Balkan League – a League which the Russians hoped would serve as a defensive barrier against the Habsburg Empire, but which the Balkan states intended to use to seize the European provinces of the Ottoman Empire. By July 1912 defeats in North Africa had helped to bring down the Young Turk régime at Constantinople. Its successors carried out a purge of Young Turkish officers that left the army thoroughly disorganized; and their attempts to conciliate their Christian subjects, together with well-meaning but misguided efforts by some of the powers to encourage them in this path, only determined the Balkan states to strike down the empire lest it be reformed. Fully aware of the divisions paralysing the Concert, the Balkan states ignored all restraining advice, even a joint admonition from Russia and Austria-Hungary acting as spokesmen of the two camps (itself an admission of the bankruptcy of the Concert) and went to war in October. By December they had overrun virtually all of the Ottoman Empire in Europe except for three fortresses. The inert power-structure that had served for so long as the great shock-absorber of the European states system had ceased to exist.

The immediate consequence of the Balkan War was a sharp increase in international tension. Vital interests of great powers were in jeopardy: the Austrians were determined to prevent Serbian expansion to the Adriatic, where a Serbian port might some day become a Russian port; and in this they had Italian and German support. A large increase in the Austro-Hungarian army – the first since 1888 – gave the Russians food for thought, as did the premature and demonstrative renewal of the Triple Alliance in December 1912. The Russians, for their part, had retained with the colours the levy of troops due to return home in October; and they continued to support Serbian claims until well into December. Britain and France had no sympathy for the Serbs, but the solidarity of the Triple *entente* was another matter. These months saw Britain and France draw still closer as their new naval arrangements went into force; and, most significant of all, the Franco-Russian alliance was extended to cover the case of a general war resulting from a Russian attack on Austria-Hungary. It is true that these alarming portents were apparently counterbalanced by an even more dramatic revival of the Concert of Europe, when all six powers agreed to take in hand the broad lines of a peace settlement through informal conferences of ambassadors at London. But the very manner and timing of this revival were themselves symptomatic of the rift that now existed within the European states system. It was Britain and Germany who arranged the conferences, acting, significantly, as spokesmen of the two blocs; and German co-operativeness must be seen in the light of the conference of 8 December between the Kaiser and his military and naval advisers. There it was agreed that a war at that moment would be untimely; but that Germany's chances would improve if the government could not only educate public opinion to a sense of the importance of Balkan issues, but also improve Anglo-German relations to the extent that Britain might stay neutral in a continental war. To this extent Germany's willingness to co-operate with Britain in reviving the Concert of Europe was intended to facilitate, not prevent, a war with France and Russia.

Equally deceptive was the apparent revival of the Concert of Europe in the London negotiations. Peace was preserved; but at the cost of a very heavy mortgage on the future. Although at their very first meeting the ambassadors decided on an independent Albania stretching from

Montenegro to Greece and denying Serbia access to the Adriatic, this only solved half the problem. After this, the British blindly followed Russia in assigning to Serbia large tracts of undoubtedly Albanian territory inland, regardless of the merits of the issue; the Germans, anxious to humour the British, pressed Austria-Hungary to give way; and the Italians were more concerned about Greek expansion in the south than Serbian in the north. The Austrians were thus isolated, and had to settle for a puny Albania that fell far short of their intended solid barrier against Slav expansion. Worse, even when the Concert did take a decision in favour of Albania, it was unable to enforce it. It was not the comic opera international naval demonstration that forced the Montenegrins to hand over Scutari to Albania, but the threat of single-handed action by Austria-Hungary. In sum, the Concert's record in the Balkan Wars led Vienna to the dangerous conclusion that vital interests could not be entrusted to the Concert, whereas single-handed action brought results. For the present, there was not much the Austrians could do. Indeed, the waywardness of their allies only prolonged their isolation and helplessness when war broke out between the Balkan states over the spoils, and when the Kaiser supported the cause of his Greek and Romanian relatives, allies of Serbia, against Austria-Hungary's would-be protégé Bulgaria. The Treaty of Bucharest, coming in the midst of reports that Serbian nationalists were now avowedly preparing for a 'second round' against Austria-Hungary, was greeted in Vienna with impotent, but undoubtedly genuine, rage. Whether the Austrians would remain impotent would depend on their allies.

In fact, the dangers of confrontation increased in the autumn, as the Germans took alarm at the appalling state of Austro-German relations, and as Italy and Austria-Hungary both fell into the habit of resorting to single-handed action. Thus in October 1913 it was an Austro-Hungarian ultimatum that cleared Serbian forces out of territory assigned by the London conference to Albania; and, ominously enough, this ultimatum had German and Italian support. In the same month, and in March 1914, separate Austro-Italian *démarches* ordering Greece to evacuate territory that had not even been definitively assigned to Albania convinced the British that the Adriatic powers evidently did not consider 'that the Concert of Europe is any longer intact'. True, Germany, who was again developing a Near Eastern strategy of her own, based on Greece, Romania, and even Serbia, did not support her allies; and in Albania she even supported the Triple *entente* against them. But she was given no credit for this in London. There, the worst possible interpretation was put on her desperate efforts to avoid offending either Greece or Turkey in the endless negotiations over the fate of the Greek and Italian-occupied Aegean Islands. This marked the end of the policy of co-operation between England and Germany and the relapse on Germany's part into the cynical policy of promoting discord among other powers for the purpose of acquiring a position of advantage for herself.

The Anglo-German agreement to differ on the naval question, and their agreements over the Baghdad Railway and Portuguese colonies in the summer of 1914 were, after all, peripheral to the main issue. If extra-European questions had never been a serious threat to the peace of the European states system, they could provide no effective remedy when the system itself was threatened from within. It was perhaps no coincidence that the Anglo-German *detente*, like the halting Concert of the Balkan Wars, ceased to function when the crisis reached the very borders of the Habsburg Empire.

A particularly dangerous feature of the situation was Germany's increasing and direct involvement in the Near East. By the middle of 1914 the deterioration of Russo-German relations more than made up for any slight improvement in Anglo-German relations. Viewed from London, the crisis of July 1914 might well have blown up in a clear sky; but not when viewed from St Petersburg. The fall of the Ottoman Empire in Europe had made the Germans anxious for their investments in Asia; and the return to power of the Young Turks and the army in January 1913 had offered them a chance – eventually taken in the autumn, with the Liman von Sanders mission to reform the Ottoman army – to secure their position: after all, according to the German ambassador at Constantinople, whichever power controlled the Ottoman army, controlled the empire. Although the British were relatively unaffected (and, holding a similar position with regard to the Ottoman navy, were hardly in a position to object) the Russian reaction was violent and insistent enough to force Berlin to confine the mission to a very limited supervisory role. But the peaceful outcome of the affair could not conceal the fact that for the first time Germany and Russia had clashed over the Near East directly, and not merely in relation to Austria-Hungary. The prospect of German control of the Straits had given the Russians a tremendous fright; and crown councils in St Petersburg at the beginning of 1914 resolved to develop the Black Sea fleet in preparation for fighting for control of the Straits. By the spring Russia's armaments were causing something of a scare in the German press; and the insistence of German agrarians on prolonging the extremely favourable commercial treaties extracted from Russia during the Russo-Japanese war reopened other old wounds. At any rate, the Kaiser became convinced that Russia and France were preparing to attack Germany as soon as their armaments programmes were complete, possibly in 1917; and he concluded that 'Russo–German relations are dead for ever'.

Moreover, if Russia and her French backers were now declared opponents of Germany in the Near East, Germany was not having much success in confronting them by conventional diplomatic means. The reasons were fundamental. That very rate of industrialization that had made Germany the strongest power in Europe had resulted by 1914 in an acute shortage of capital for investment abroad. France, by contrast, while industrially backward partly because her investors had always preferred to concentrate on lucrative foreign loans, enjoyed enormous financial power and influence in the Near East. Consequently German diplomacy, lacking adequate financial resources, suffered one defeat after another. A French loan to Greece at the end of 1913 was regarded in Berlin as more than cancelling out any residual German dynastic influence at Athens. At Sofia, France and Russia even had British diplomatic support in pressing King Ferdinand to accept a French loan and instal a Russophile government; and it was only at the last minute, in July 1914, that the Germans, after enormous difficulty, managed to find the money to forestall them. As for the Turks, they were in fact genuinely neutral: the British even reckoned that they had gone over to the Triple Alliance. But the Germans drew the gloomiest conclusions from the unpopularity of the tactless Liman at Constantinople, and from the visit paid by a few Turkish dignitaries to the tsar at Livadia in May. Indeed, Bethmann decided that it was not only difficult, but positively undesirable, to lend money to Turkey: 'Why should we sharpen the sword of the Triple *Entente*?'. Finally, in Romania, although Grey, out of respect for the balance of power, would do nothing to weaken Romania's links with her allies; and although British and German oil companies were in fact co-operating against American competition, France and Russia scored a resounding success with the tsar's state visit to Constantsa in June. Already for some months the Austrian press had been sounding the alarm about the dangers of a new Balkan league under Franco–Russian auspices: this would be 'a dagger pointed at the heart of Austria–Hungary'.

Even so, it must be said that the startling diplomatic successes of France and Russia in 1914 were due in no small measure to the confusion of their opponents. The Triple Alliance powers perceived the threat, but they could devise no effective counter-strategy. Indeed, they were often more at odds with each other than with their opponents. If the Austro-Hungarian government's unimaginitive handling of South Slav and Romanian questions had poisoned its relations with its Balkan neighbours, the Hohenlohe decrees of August 1913 (removing Italian nationals from local government office in Trieste) brought to a sudden end the recent improvement in Austro-Italian relations. And if the Adriatic powers were united in resisting *entente*, and even German, influence in Albania, their own rivalry there was so intense that by June the Germans were beginning to fear for the future of the Triple Alliance. Not that the Germans were doing much to strengthen the Alliance themselves. They combined with Italy to frustrate Austrian attempts to secure – exclusively for prestige reasons – a sphere of influence in Asia Minor; they were exasperatingly slow to recognize any South Slav threat to Austria-Hungary – as late as March the Kaiser declared that Vienna would be 'completely crazy' to consider using force to prevent Serbia's gaining access to the Adriatic by means of a union with Montenegro; and their stubborn encouragement of an alignment of Serbia, Romania and Greece played directly into the hands of France and Russia. It was, therefore, no wonder that by June the Austrians had decided that a final effort must be made, even if Italy was for the present unapproachable, at least to win German support for a coherent diplomatic offensive to halt the decline by getting Romania to show her colours and by working for an alliance with Bulgaria and Turkey. This was the argument of the Matscheko memorandum, drawn up for dispatch to Berlin on 24 June. Even at this stage the Austrians, far from scanning the horizon for a pretext to attack Serbia, were still thinking in terms of security through a diplomatic counter-offensive within the framework of the European states system.

This was not to be. The Sarajevo murders of 28 June, presenting an open challenge to the dynastic-territorial Habsburg state, and demonstrating that the half-measures of 1909 had failed to contain South Slav nationalism in Serbia, made the Austrians revise their policy. It now seemed clear that patient secret diplomacy as recommended by the Matscheko memorandum would be interpreted abroad as yet another demonstration of Habsburg helplessness and would be bound to fail: Serbia must be reduced, once and for all, to that satellite status she had held in the 1880s, either by intimidation (through the note of 23 July) or by a punitive expedition. In a sense, this was a defensive move to restore Austria-Hungary's position within the European states system. But, at the same time, if Russia were compelled to remain a helpless spectator of such a sudden reversal of recent trends, the blow to Russian prestige would be irreparable. Indeed, Berchtold admitted that the consequence would be the elimination of Russian influence from the Balkans 'for a long time'. And as the Austrians were now demanding far more than in 1909, and as Russia was incomparably stronger, militarily and diplomatically, than in that year, she was unlikely to remain a passive spectator. As the deadlock at the end of July showed, when the Austrians refused to halt their invasion of Serbia even under pressure of a Russian mobilization, no compromise diplomatic solution was possible. The assassins of Sarajevo had contrived a situation in which either Russia or Austria–Hungary faced total diplomatic defeat.

Russia, like Austria–Hungary, was pursuing a defensive aim, not in itself incompatible with the European states system – indeed, designed to preserve her position within it; but the means she was compelled to adopt raised the dispute to a level where it was no longer manageable in terms of that states system. The Russian mobilization, albeit intended as a means of bringing Austria–Hungary to reason, precipitated the German declaration of war on Russia and France. Historians have argued that Germany was intent on war in 1914, pointing to German pressure on Vienna to attack Serbia with all possible speed. But this pressure was exerted in the calculation that the sooner any attack came after the assassinations, the greater the chance would be that shocked monarchical feeling might restrain Russia from intervention. The German ideal was, in fact, a diplomatic victory, a decisive shift of the balance of influence in the Near East in favour of the Central Powers, and possibly even Russia's abandonment of *ententes* which had demonstrated their uselessness for a second time in favour of a restoration of a *Dreikaiserbund*. As in 1905, the Germans were seeking the diplomatic supremacy in Europe; and they were understandably encouraged by the circumstance that, on a Balkan issue at least, Austria–Hungary would be reliable; and by the belief that Germany's chances could only deteriorate in the future. France and Russia were arming remorselessly – the French army, destined for elimination in weeks according to the Schlieffen plan, was already as big as the German; and rumours of impending Anglo-Russian naval talks convinced Berlin that Anglo-German relations were about as close as they were ever likely to be. Even if the German bid failed, compromise was not ruled out – witness the Kaiser's reaction to the Serbian reply to Austria–Hungary. But one thing the Germans would not tolerate was a further diplomatic defeat, leading to the possible collapse or desertion of their strongest ally. Here, the Russian mobilization was crucial. It is true that Russia had no intention of attacking Germany; but the tsar's promise that no Russian soldier would cross the German frontier was immaterial. The simple fact was that, as Germany's defence rested entirely on the Schlieffen plan, if the Russian army once stood fully mobilized on the German frontier, Germany would simply be unable to fight, and would have to accept any diplomatic solution France and Russia might care to dictate. The Russian mobilization confronted the Germans with the prospect of a colossal diplomatic defeat. Germany opted for war.

The entry of Britain transformed the continental war into a world conflict. It is true that Grey's failure over the years to keep the public informed as to the drift of his policy at first made it uncertain whether he and his supporters in the cabinet and foreign office would be able to carry the country with them. But waverers in the cabinet were finally persuaded by the argument that a split over the issue would mean an interventionist-Unionist coalition and the end of the Liberal Party; and talk of the German threat, not only to the balance of power but to gallant little Belgium, had the desired effect in parliament. Even so, given that the Royal Navy was more than adequate to cope with the German fleet, and that no one in the *entente* capitals in 1914 was prophesying the collapse of Russia and the near German victory that followed by 1917, one may question, if not the sincerity, at least the simplicity of Grey's belief in a German threat. It seems that British policy-makers were less afraid of a German military victory than of a German diplomatic victory leading to German control of the European states system, the formation of a continental league, or at least a *Dreikaiserbund,* and the reactivation of Russian policy in Asia. If Russia, betrayed by Britain, were forced to turn away from the Balkans, what price the British Empire? The British ambassador in St Petersburg warned Grey explicitly on 25 July that 'if we fail [Russia] . . . now, we cannot hope to maintain that friendly co-operation with her in Asia that is of such vital importance to us'. Grey may have had something similar in mind when he told the Commons on 3 August that 'if we are engaged in war, we shall suffer but little more than . . . if we stand aside'. His emphasis on the German threat only makes sense in the context of an ever greater Russian threat. Where interests 'of vital importance' were at stake, Britain was no more, but also no less, egoistic and amoral than the other members of the European states system; her participation in the system, like theirs, was in the last resort a matter of self-preservation; and if in 1914 as in the 1740s or the 1930s the security of the British Empire demanded the sacrifice of third parties in Central Europe, there could be no hesitation in London.

The war that broke out in 1914 marked the end of the European states system that had prevailed for the preceding two hundred years. The wartime diplomacy of all the belligerents was characterized by a search for total security through total victory, as opposed to the adjustment of differences within an agreed system of independent units.

With the establishment of totalitarian régimes in east and central Europe in the decades after 1917 the continent was riven with fundamental ideological divisions, and diplomacy became once more, as in the age of the wars of religion, not a method of adjusting differences according to generally accepted rules, but simply an additional means in pursuit of an end – total domination – that was the negation of any states system. As for a 'European' system, this was a thing of the past. The peace of 1871 had been a European peace and reflected European realities. It was the entry of the United States that determined the outcome of the First World War, just as their withdrawal, leaving France and possibly Britain to sustain unaided what only a great coalition had been able to construct, doomed the peace. Not surprisingly, France and Britain, confronted with the triumph of hegemonial forces in the Soviet Union and Germany, their energies sapped by the rise of anti-European nationalism in Africa, Asia and the Far East, proved unequal to the task. Their failure demonstrated that the days were gone when Europe could claim to be the world.

Bibliography

This bibliography is intended to be a guide to further reading. It is necessarily selective and it concentrates on books in English. Articles in scholarly journals have in general been excluded on the grounds that their inclusion would swell the list beyond reasonable limits. Exceptions have been made for those articles which contain information and points of view not otherwise available. Most of the books listed below contain bibliographies of a more specialist nature which should be consulted for further reading on particular topics. The bibliography is arranged chapter by chapter for ease of reference. Many of the books are of value for chapters other than those under which they are listed.

CHAPTER ONE

The problems and themes outlined in this chapter can be studied in some of the general surveys of European history in the fifty years after the Congress of Vienna. Excellent introductions to the problems of the period can be found in the following books: E. J. Hobsbawm, *The Age of Revolution* (London 1962); M. S. Anderson, *The Ascendancy of Europe* (London 1972); and W. E. Mosse, *Liberal Europe 1848–1875* (London 1974). An older account which still contains useful information and ideas, particularly on the problems of international relations, is E. L. Woodward, *War and Peace in Europe 1815–1870* (London 1931). The fundamental issues in great-power politics and contemporary attitudes towards international relations are discussed in a stimulating way in F. H. Hinsley, *Power and the Pursuit of Peace* (Cambridge 1963); Carsten

Holbraad, *The Concert of Europe* (London 1970); and C. H. D. Howard, *Great Britain and the casus belli from Canning to Salisbury* (London 1961). The volume edited by Alan Sked, *Europe's Balance of Power 1815–1848* (London 1979), contains short essays on the foreign policies of each of the great powers and on major diplomatic problems. The period after 1848 is dealt with in considerable detail and with great skill in A. J. P. Taylor, *The Struggle for Mastery in Europe 1848–1919* (Oxford 1954). The best general survey of great-power politics from a French point of view is P. Renouvin, *Histoire des relations internationales,* vols V, 1815–71, and VI, 1871–1914 (Paris 1954). J. Joll, *Europe Since 1870* (London 1973), treating international relations in the context of the development of European society as a whole, is an invaluable introductory survey. As far as individual powers are concerned there is a disappointing lack of general surveys of their foreign policies in the first half of the nineteenth century. The one exception is Great Britain. Kenneth Bourne, *The Foreign Policy of Victorian England 1830–1902* (Oxford 1970), is an indispensable study which also contains valuable documentary material, as does H. W. V. Temperley and Lillian M. Penson, *Foundations of British Foreign Policy 1792–1902* (Cambridge 1938). The second half of the century is better provided for in this respect. A. F. Pribram, *England and the International Policy of the European Powers 1871–1914* (Oxford 1931), is still worth reading as a general survey of trends in the policies of all the powers. L. Albertini, *The Origins of the War,* vol. I, 1878–1914 (London 1965), provides a very detailed, but still readable, account, from an Italian point of view; P. Milza, *Les relations internationales de 1871 à 1914* (Paris 1966), a concise survey from a French point of view. The foreign policies of several powers over fairly long periods are treated in some detail in the volumes so far published by Routledge & Kegan Paul, London, in the series *Foreign Policies of the Great Powers,* all of which volumes contain supplements of documents from the relevant archives: C. J. Lowe, *The Reluctant Imperialists, British Foreign Policy 1878–1902,* 2 vols (1967); C. J. Lowe and M. L. Dockrill, *The Mirage of Power, British Foreign Policy 1902–1922* (1972); C. J. Lowe and F. Marzari, *Italian Foreign Policy 1870–1940* (1975); F. R. Bridge, *From Sadowa to Sarajevo, The Foreign Policy of Austria-Hungary 1866–1914* (1972); I. Geiss, *German Foreign Policy 1871–1914* (1976); and I. H. Nish, *Japanese Foreign Policy 1869–1942* (1977). The diplomatic problems which arose in the Near East in the nineteenth century are lucidly explained in M. S. Anderson, *The Eastern Question 1774–1923* (London, 1966), and those which arose East of Suez in D. Gillard, *The Struggle in Asia 1828–1914* (London 1977). Numerous aspects of the diplomacy of imperialism in Africa are illuminated in two volumes of essays edited by P. Gifford and W. R. Louis, *Britain and Germany in Africa* (New Haven, Conn,. 1967), and *France and Britain in Africa* (New Haven, Conn., 1972). The military and naval policies of the powers can be studied in the following books: Gordon Craig, *The Politics of the Prussian Army* (Princeton 1955); J. S. Curtiss, *The Russian Army under Nicholas I 1825–1855* (Durham, New Hampshire, 1965); Douglas Porch, *Army and Revolution: France 1815–1848* (London 1974); and C. J. Bartlett, *Great Britain and Sea Power 1815–1853* (Oxford 1963). The financial and commercial relations between the powers are dealt with in D. C. M. Platt, *Finance, Trade and Politics in British Foreign Policy 1815–1914* (Oxford 1968); in W. O. Henderson, *The Zollverein* (London 1959); and in R. E. Cameron, *France and the Economic Development of Europe* (Princeton, New Jersey, 1961). All the major treaties of the period are usefully gathered together in Michael Hurst (ed.), *Key Treaties for the Great Powers* (2 vols) (Newton Abbot 1972).

CHAPTER TWO

Very full accounts of the Fourth Coalition and of the abortive peace negotiations with Napoleon can be found in C. K. Webster, *British Diplomacy 1813–1815* (London 1921); and in the same author's *The Foreign Policy of Castlereagh 1812–1815* (London 1931). H. V. Gulick's *Europe's Classical Balance of Power* (New York 1955) examines the relationship between eighteenth-century theories of the balance of power and the practice of diplomacy in the years from 1812–15. The same author's chapter 'The Congress of Vienna' in *The New Cambridge Modern History,* vol. X, ed. C. W. Crawley (Cambridge 1965) is a particularly useful short account of congress diplomacy. The classic survey of peacemaking is C. K. Webster, *The Congress of Vienna* (London 1920). The two outstanding recent monographs which substantially alter accepted views on the period of reconstruction, particularly as far as Russian diplomacy is concerned, are P. K. Grimsted, *The Foreign Ministers of Alexander I* (Berkeley, California, 1969) and C. M. Woodhouse, *Capodistria* (Oxford 1973). A somewhat controversial analysis of peacemaking and of the eight years of postwar diplomacy can be found in H. A. Kissinger, *A World Restored* (New York 1964). Two accounts in French of congress diplomacy and postwar rivalry between the powers deserve close scrutiny; J. H. Pirenne, *La Sainte Alliance,* vol. i, 1814–1815, vol. ii, 1815–1818

(Neuchâtel 1946); and Maurice Bourquin, *Histoire de la Sainte Alliance* (Geneva 1954). C. K. Webster, *The Foreign Policy of Castlereagh 1815–1822* (London 1925) is a very comprehensive record of British diplomacy in the postwar period. A. W. Palmer, *Metternich* (London 1972), contains a general account of the character and policies of the Austrian chancellor. G. Bertier de Sauvigny, *Metternich and his Times* (London 1962), is a valuable thematic study of Metternich and contains many interesting extracts from documents. The same author's *Metternich et la France après le congrès de Vienne*, vol. i, 1815–1820, vol. ii, 1820–1824, vol. iii, 1824–1830 (Paris 1968, 1970, 1974) contains indispensable documentary material and a useful commentary. Paul Schroeder, *Metternich's Diplomacy at its Zenith 1820–1823* (Austin, Texas, 1962) gives an admirably clear and concise account of a crucial period of Austrian diplomacy. Anglo-French rivalry in the Iberian peninsula and Anglo-Russian rivalry in the Near East in the 1820s is fully covered in H. W. V. Temperley, *The Foreign Policy of Canning* (London 1926). A shorter account of Canning's foreign policy can be found in *George Canning* (London 1973) by Wendy Hinde. The South American repercussions of the French intervention in Spain can be followed in H. C. Allen, *Great Britain and the United States* (London 1954); D. Perkins, *A History of the Monroe Doctrine* (London 1960); and C. K. Webster, *Britain and the Independence of Latin America*, 2 vols (Oxford 1938). The biography by W. Bruce Lincoln, *Nicholas I Emperor and Autocrat of All the Russias* (London 1978), contains an authoritative account of thirty years of Russian foreign policy. Two books by Douglas Dakin, *The Unification of Greece 1770–1923* (London 1972), and *The Greek Struggle for Independence 1821–1823* (London 1973), provide excellent accounts of great-power rivalries in the eastern Mediterranean in the 1820s. Derek Beales, *The Risorgimento and the Unification of Italy* (London 1971), contains short but useful surveys of Italian problems in the restoration period, and V. J. Puryear, *France and the Levant* (California 1968), contains an account of French Mediterranean policy during the Bourbon Restoration.

CHAPTER THREE

British policy towards Europe in the 1830s is covered in great detail in C. K. Webster, *The Foreign Policy of Palmerston 1830–1841*, 2 vols (new impression London 1969). Donald Southgate, *'The Most English Minister'* . . . *The Policies and Politics of Palmerston* (London 1966), contains a shorter survey of Palmerston's early diplomacy. J. R. Hall, *England and the Orleans Monarchy* (London 1912) is still a useful book. No modern survey has yet been published in English of the foreign policy of the July Monarchy. For the 1830s J. M. S. Allison, *Thiers and the French Monarchy* (London 1926), contains information not easily available elsewhere. Roger Bullen, 'France and the problem of intervention in Spain 1834–1836', *Historical Journal* 20, 2 (1977), examines Thiers' attempted change of direction in the mid 1830s. The chapter on foreign policy in A. J. Tudesq, *Les grands notables en France*, 2 vols (Paris 1964) is illuminating and important. The international repercussions of Italian problems in the 1830s can be followed in C. Vidal, *Louis Phillippe, Metternich et la crise italienne* (Paris 1938). E. Kossman, *A History of the Low Countries 1789–1945* (Oxford 1978), contains an authoritative account of the Belgian revolution and of the great-power negotiations which followed it. A good survey of Austro-Prussian relations in the 1830s and 1840s can be found in Agatha Ramm, *Germany 1789–1919* (London 1967). The two Near Eastern crises of the 1830s have both been subjected to close scholarly scrutiny: G. H. Bolsover, 'Nicholas I and the partition of Turkey', *Slavonic and East European Review* XXVII (1948–49) is an important article; as is also F. S. Rodkey, 'Lord Palmerston and the rejuvenation of Turkey' *Journal of Modern History* I (1929). P. E. Moseley, *Russian Diplomacy and the Opening of the Eastern Question in 1838 and 1839* (Cambridge, Mass. 1934), is an excellent account. The best survey of French policy in 1840 is the article by C. H. Pouthas, 'La Politique de Thiers pendant le crise orientale de 1840', *Revue Historique* CLXXXII (1938). Douglas Johnson, *Guizot: Aspects of French History 1787–1874* (London 1963), examines the French retreat from the brink of war in 1840 and also provides a valuable account of the principles and methods of Guizot's foreign policy. Two books by E. Jones Parry, *The Spanish Marriages 1841–1846* (London 1936), and Roger Bullen, *Palmerston, Guizot and the Collapse of the Entente Cordiale* (London 1974), provide full accounts of Anglo-French co-operation and conflict from 1841 to the revolution of February 1848. Mediterranean rivalry in the 1840s is discussed at length in F. R. Flournoy, *British policy towards Morocco in the Age of Palmerston 1830–1865* (London 1935). The diplomatic complications raised by Swiss and Italian problems in 1847 can be studied in Roger Bullen, 'Guizot and the Sonderbund Crisis', *English Historical Review* LXXXVI (1971); and in A. J. P. Taylor, *The Italian Problem in European Diplomacy 1846–49* (Manchester 1934), which takes the story down to the collapse of the Italian war effort in 1849. The chapter on international relations by J. P. T. Bury in F. Fejtö (ed.), *1848: The*

Opening of an Era (New York 1948), is an excellent short summary of the main diplomatic problems raised by the revolutions. L. Jennings, *France and Europe in 1848* (Oxford 1973), is an authoritative account. E. Eyck, *The Frankfurt Parliament* (London 1968), contains useful comments on Austro-Prussian relations, and C. A. Macartney, *The Hapsburg Empire 1790–1918* (London 1969), is an invaluable account of the political and diplomatic problems faced by the Austrian government in the period 1848–51. W. E. Mosse, *The European Powers and the German Question 1848–1871* (Cambridge 1958), contains useful chapters on German problems in the revolutionary period and is an indispensable book for the diplomacy of the 1850s and 1860s. The best short account of French foreign policy under Napoleon III is that in J. P. T. Bury, *Napoleon III and the Second Empire* (London 1964). There are many studies of the origins of the Crimean War. H. W. V. Temperley, *England and the Near East: The Crimea* (London 1936), is a wide-ranging survey. Gavin Henderson, *Crimean War Diplomacy* (Glasgow 1947), contains a number of important essays. Paul Schroeder, *Austria, Great Britain and the Crimean War* (London 1972), is a stimulating discussion of prewar diplomacy. Kingsley Martin, *The Triumph of Lord Palmerston* (revised edn London 1963), examines the impact of the press and public opinion on British foreign policy; and L. M. Case, *French Opinion on War and Diplomacy during the Second Empire* (Philadelphia 1954), deals with the same subject from the French point of view. It also provides very useful background to French diplomacy in the late 1850s and in the 1860s.

CHAPTER FOUR

The diplomatic history of the Crimean War and of the peace settlement of 1856 is thematically treated in W. E. Mosse, *The Rise and Fall of the Crimean System* (London 1963). H. Seton-Watson, *The Russian Empire 1801–1917* (Oxford 1967), has useful contributions on Russian diplomacy and on military policy during the war. T. W. Riker, *The Making of Roumania* (Oxford 1931), remains the best account of Romanian independence. F. Charles-Roux, *Alexander II, Gortchakoff and Napoleon III* (Paris 1913), is still the standard account of Franco-Russian relations in the late 1850s and early 1860s. The best short introduction to the complex political and diplomatic issues raised by the Italian question can be found in D. Mack Smith, *Italy – A Modern History* (Ann Arbor 1959). The same author's *Cavour and Garibaldi in*

1860 (Cambridge 1954) is very important, and a more recent collection of essays, *Victor Emmanuel, Cavour and the Risorgimento* (Oxford 1971), contains a number of useful essays on the diplomacy of the late 1850s and 1860s E. E. Y. Hales, *Pio Nono* (London 1954), has a good account of papal policy. D. E. D. Beales, *England and Italy* 1859–1860 (London 1961), succinctly analyses British policy. The diplomatic complications raised by the Venetian and Roman questions in the 1860s are dealt with in R. Blaas (ed.), *Il Problemo Veneto e l'Europa 1859–1866* (Venice 1966), and in Noel Blakiston, *The Roman Question* (London 1962). O. Pflanze, *Bismarck and the Development of Germany 1815–1871* (Princeton 1963), is a very thorough and judicious account of Bismarck's policy in the 1860s. Two shorter studies, A. J. P. Taylor, *Bismarck* (London 1955), and W. N. Medlicott, *Bismarck and Modern Germany* (London 1965), are also very useful. H. Boehme, *The Foundations of the German Empire* (Oxford 1973), is extremely important for the relations of the members of the *Bund* in the 1860s. H. Friedjung, *The Struggle for Supremacy in Germany* (London 1935), is also valuable. The diplomatic problems raised by the Danish attempts to alter the *status quo* in the duchies are admirably dealt with in L. D. Steefel, *The Schleswig Holstein Question* (Cambridge, Mass., 1932). An excellent study of the background to the conflict can be found in W. Carr, *Schlewsig-Holstein 1815–1864* (London 1963). The best analysis of Austrian policy in 1866 is F. R. Bridge, *From Sadowa to Sarajevo* (London 1972). E. Ann Pottinger, *Napoleon III and the German Crisis 1865–66* (Oxford 1968), fully examines French policy. H. Oncken, *Napoleon III and the Rhine* (New York 1928), covers the same ground but takes the story down to 1870. The origins of the war of 1870 were a matter of fierce historical and national controversy in both France and Germany before the outbreak of the First World War. Beginning in 1910 the French government published twenty-nine volumes of documents, *Les Origines diplomatiques de la guerre de 1870–71*. In 1932 the Germans began to give their own 'official' version of the same events in ten volumes of documents, *Die auswärtige Politik Preussens 1858–1871*. R. H. Lord, *The Origins of the War of 1870* (Cambridge, Mass., 1924), was the first attempt at a calm and scholarly appraisal. G. Bonnim (ed.), *Bismarck and the Hohenzollern Candidature for the Spanish Throne* (London 1957), contains important new documents. R. Millman, *British Policy and the Coming of the Franco-Prussian War* (Oxford 1965), is useful. Michael Howard, *The Franco-Prussian War* (London 1961), is an invaluable study of the military conflict.

CHAPTERS FIVE AND SIX

International relations in the Bismarckian era are very fully treated in W. L. Langer, *European Alliances and Alignments 1871–90* (2nd edn, New York 1950), which contains very full bibliographies. There are numerous shorter studies illuminating the foreign policy of Bismarckian Germany. The most manageable and most readable is still W. N. Medlicott, *Bismarck and Modern Germany* (London 1965); A. J. P. Taylor, *Bismarck* (London 1955), is provocative; E. Eyck, *Bismarck and the German Empire* (London 1950), is clear and straightforward; while W. Richter, *Bismarck* (London 1964), presents a German view and places more emphasis on Bismarck's relations with Russia than most English works. Bismarck's Russian policy in the later 1880s is among several important aspects of imperial Germany covered in a series of essays edited by M. Stürmer, *Das Kaiserliche Deutschland, Politik und Gesellschaft 1870–1918* (Düsseldorf 1970). On Austro-Hungarian policy, in addition to the works mentioned in the bibliography to Chapter One, the sections concerned with foreign policy in A. J. P. Taylor, *The Habsburg Monarchy* (London 1941), still make lively reading, although those in C. A. Macartney, *The Habsburg Empire* (London 1968), are fuller. S. Verosta, *Theorie und Realität von Bündnissen* (Vienna 1971), provides a modern, detailed and thought-provoking analysis of Austro-German relations between 1879 and 1914. The sections concerned with foreign policy in C. Seton-Watson, *Italy from Liberalism to Fascism* (London 1967), contain illuminating insights into the motivations of Italy's actions on the European and colonial stage; and H. Seton-Watson, *The Russian Empire 1801–1917* (Oxford 1967), renders an equally valuable service to the student of Russian foreign policy. B. Jelavich, *A Century of Russian Foreign Policy* (Bloomington, Indiana, 1964), is a most useful and illuminating survey. Particular aspects of the Eastern question in the 1870s and 1880s are treated in authoritative detail in E. Kofos, *Greece and the Eastern question 1875–8* (Salonica 1975); W. N. Medlicott, *The Congress of Berlin and after* (London 1938); C. and B. Jelavich, *Tsarist Russia and Balkan Nationalism* (Berkeley, California, 1958), and B. Jelavich, *The Great Powers, the Ottoman Empire and the Straits question 1870–1887* (Bloomington, Indiana, 1973). W. N. Medlicott, *Bismarck, Gladstone, and the Concert of Europe* (London 1956), and B. Waller, *Bismarck at the Crossroads, 1878–80* (London 1974), are likely to remain the definitive accounts of the tortuous diplomacy of the three eastern powers between the Congress of Berlin and the conclusion of the Three Emperors' Alliance.

CHAPTERS SEVEN AND EIGHT

The most detailed general account of the relations of all the European powers with each other after the fall of Bismarck is still W. L. Langer, *The Diplomacy of Imperialism 1891–1902* (2nd edn, New York 1950), which includes full bibliographies. On German policy J. Röhl, *Germany without Bismarck* (London 1967), is a seminal work which treats foreign policy in the context of domestic developments; V. R. Berghahn, *Germany and the Approach of War in 1914* (London 1973), develops the theme in the light of the latest research and ranges far more widely than the title suggests. M. Balfour's lively *The Kaiser and his Times* (London 1964) is a mine of information and essential reading. On British policy, the best recent survey is Zara Steiner, *Britain and the Origins of the First World War* (London 1977), while the same author's *The Foreign Office and Foreign Policy* (Cambridge 1969) looks more deeply into the mechanics of foreign policy-making in the early twentieth century. There are detailed studies of the development of British policy in the diplomatic revolution of 1895 to 1905 in J. A. S. Grenville, *Lord Salisbury and Foreign Policy* (London 1964); C. H. D. Howard, *Splendid Isolation* (London 1967); and G. W. Monger, *The End of Isolation* (London 1964). C. M. Andrew, *Théophile Delcassé and the Making of the Entente Cordiale* (London 1968), is lucid and authoritative, and one of the very few recent works to treat French foreign policy in the late nineteenth and early twentieth centuries in any detail. The Eastern question in the early twentieth century is the subject of F. R. Bridge, 'Izvolsky, Aehrenthal and the end of the Austro-Russian entente', in *Mitteilungen des österreichischen Staatsarchivs, 1976*. Extra-European developments are fully treated in G. N. Sanderson, *England, Europe and the Upper Nile* (Edinburgh 1965); L. K. Young, *British Policy in China 1895–1902* (Oxford 1970); and I. H. Nish's monumental studies, *The Anglo-Japanese Alliance 1902–07* (London 1966), and *Alliance in Decline, 1907–22* (London 1972).

On the European states system in the last years of peace L. C. F. Turner, *The Origins of the First World War* (London 1970), provides a good introduction and emphasizes Russia's share of responsibility. The essays edited by H. W. Koch, *The Origins of the First World War* (London 1972), tend to reflect the ideas of the modern German school and emphasize Germany's responsibility – a theme which is fully developed in the light of events after 1911 in F. Fischer, *War of Illusions* (London 1973). British policy in these years is illuminated in detail by K. G. Robbins, *Sir Edward Grey* (London 1971); and in the latest volume of the New Cambridge History of British Foreign Policy edited by F. H.

Hinsley, *British Foreign Policy under Sir Edward Grey* (Cambridge 1977). P. G. Halpern, *The Mediterranean Naval Situation 1908–14* (Cambridge, Mass., 1971); B. E. Schmitt, *The Bosnian Crisis* (New York 1937); and E. C. Helmreich, *The Diplomacy of the Balkan Wars* (Cambridge, Mass., 1938), are long likely to remain the standard works in their respective fields.

Chronology

1813

28 Feb.	Treaty of Kalisch
24 June	Treaty of Reichenbach
12 Aug.	Austria enters the war
18 Oct.	French defeat at Leipzig

1814

Feb.	Four allies offer peace terms to Napoleon
9 March	Treaty of Chaumont
31 March	Allied armies enter Paris
30 May	First Peace of Paris
Oct.	Congress of Vienna opens

1815

3 Jan.	Secret treaty between Austria, Great Britain and France
1 March	Napoleon lands at Cannes
8 June	General Act of the Congress of Vienna
18 June	Battle of Waterloo
26 Sept.	Holy Alliance
20 Nov.	Quadruple Alliance
20 Nov.	Second Peace of Paris

1818

Sept.–Nov.	Congress of Aix-la-Chapelle

1819

Aug.	Carlsbad meetings of German rulers
20 Sept.	Carlsbad decrees sanctioned by the Diet at Frankfurt

1820

Oct.   Congress of Troppau starts

19 Nov.   Protocol of Troppau

1821

Jan.–April   Congress of Laibach

Feb.–March   Risings against Turks in Wallachia, Moldavia and the Morea

Oct.   Metternich and Castlereagh meet at Hanover

1822

Oct.–Dec.   Congress of Verona

1823

April   French intervention in Spain

3–9 Oct.   Polignac memorandum

1826

4 April   St Petersburg Protocol (on Greek affairs)

1827

6 July   Three-Power Treaty of London (on Greek affairs)

20 Oct.   Battle of Navarino

1828

26 April   Russia declares war on Turkey

1829

Sept.   Polignac plan

14 Sept.   Treaty of Adrianople

1830

March–June   French expedition to Algiers

July   Revolution in France

Aug.   Chiffon of Carlsbad

Aug.–Oct.   Belgian revolt

Nov.   Polish revolt

Nov.   London Conference on Belgium begins

1831

March	Austrian intervention in Papal States
15 Nov.	Treaty of London confirms Belgian independence
	Mehemet Ali invades Syria

1832

Feb.	French occupation of Ancona
April	Ottoman Empire goes to war with Mehemet Ali
21 Dec.	Turkish defeat at Koniah

1833

8 July	Treaty of Unkiar Skelessi
18 Sept.	Münchengrätz agreement
15 Oct.	Convention of Berlin

1834

22 April	Quadruple Alliance
May	Convention of Evora Monte (exiles Dom Miguel from Portugal)
18 Aug.	Additional articles to the Quadruple Alliance

1839

19 April	Treaty of London (Belgian neutrality)
21 April	Sultan atttacks Mehemet Ali
24 June	Turkish army defeated at Nizib
Sept.–Dec.	Brunnow Missions to London

1840

15 July	Four-Power Treaty of London (closure of Straits and settlement of Mehemet Ali crisis)
27 Nov.	Mehemet Ali submits to the Four Powers

1841

13 July	Straits Convention

1844

June	Moroccan crisis
	Visit of Nicholas I to England

1847

Sept.–Dec.   Great-power negotiations on Switzerland

1848

Feb.   Revolution in France
4 March   Lamartine's circular on Treaties of 1815
13 March   Metternich resigns
17 March   King of Prussia appoints liberal ministry
22 March   Outbreak of war in Northern Italy
April   Prussian troops enter Schleswig and Holstein
May   Palmerston offers British mediation between Austria and Piedmont
24 July   Radetzky defeats Piedmontese at Custozza
2 Dec.   Louis Napoleon Bonaparte assumes presidency of Second French Republic

1849

12 March   War in Northern Italy renewed
23 March   Piedmontese defeated at Novara
28 March   Frankfurt parliament offers crown of a 'small Germany' to King of Prussia
25 April   French army enters Papal states
17 June   Russian army enters Hungary
June   Pope restored to his temporal power

1850

29 Nov.   Punctation of Olmütz

1852

May   French warship sent to Constantinople to force Turks to concede on Holy Places dispute
8 May   Treaty of London defines relationship of Schleswig and Holstein to Denmark

1853

Jan.–Feb.   Nicholas I discusses Near East with British ambassador (Seymour conversations)
Feb.–May   Menshikov mission to Constantinople
2 July   Russians occupy principalities of Moldavia and Wallachia

193

July–Aug.	Vienna Conference on Near East
7 Sept.	Russians repudiate Vienna Note
23 Sept.	British fleet ordered to Constantinople
4 Oct.	Ottoman Empire declares war on Russia
30 Nov.	Turkish fleet destroyed at Sinope

1854

3 Jan.	British and French fleets enter the Black Sea
28 March	Great Britian and France declare war on Russia
20 April	Austro-Prussian treaty
8 Aug.	Austria, Great Britian and France agree 'Four Points'; Russia evacuates principalities
2 Dec.	Triple Alliance of Austria, Great Britian and France

1855

26 Jan.	Piedmont enters Crimean War
2 March	Death of Nicholas I
March–June	Vienna Conference
June–Sept.	Siege of Sebastopol
28 Dec.	Austrian ultimatum to Russia

1856

Feb.	Russia agrees to preliminary peace conditions at Vienna
Feb.–March	Congress of Paris
30 March	Treaty of Paris

1858

14 Jan.	Orsini attempts to assassinate Napoleon III
20 July	Meeting of Napoleon and Cavour at Plombières

1859

March	Secret Franco-Russian Agreement
23 April	Austria sends ultimatum to Piedmont (outbreak of war in Northern Italy)
12 May	France enters the war
4 June	Battle of Magenta
14 June	Prussian mobilization begins

24 June	Battle of Solferino
11 July	Truce of Villafranca
10 Nov.	Treaty of Zürich

1860

23 Jan.	Cobden Free Trade Treaty between Great Britain and France
24 March	Piedmont annexes central duchies and cedes Nice and Savoy to France
11 May	Garibaldi lands in Sicily
22 Aug.	Garibaldi crosses the Straits of Messina
Sept.	Piedmontese troops occupy Papal States
Oct.	Warsaw meeting of Austrian, Prussian and Russian monarchs

1861

| 17 March | Victor Emmanuel II declared King of Italy |

1862

| 22 Sept. | Bismarck appointed minister-president of Prussia |

1863

Jan.	Warsaw uprising
8 Feb.	Alvensleben convention
7 June	French troops occupy Mexico City
18 Nov.	Christian IX signs new constitution affecting Schleswig and Holstein

1864

16 Jan.	Austro-Prussian alliance
Feb.	Austria and Prussia occupy Schleswig and Holstein
April–June	Conference of London
July	Austria and Prussia invade Denmark
Aug.	Schönbrunn meeting between Austria and Prussia
30 Oct.	Treaty of Vienna ends the war

1865

| 14 Aug. | Convention of Gastein |
| Oct. | Napoleon III and Bismarck meet at Biarritz |

1866

8 April	Italian-Prussian alliance
12 June	Austria agrees to cede Venetia to France
14 June	Outbreak of Austro-Prussian war
3 July	Austrian defeat at Sadowa
26 July	Preliminary Peace of Nikolsburg
23 Aug.	Peace of Prague

1867

April	Luxembourg crisis
May	London Conference on Luxembourg (Treaty of London, 9 Sept.)
19 June	Execution of the Emperor Maximilian in Mexico

1870

June–July	Hohenzollern candidature crisis
19 July	Outbreak of Franco-Prussian war
1 Sept.	Italians occupy Rome
31 Oct.	Russians denounce Black Sea clauses of Treaty of Paris 1856

1871

18 Jan.	German Empire proclaimed at Versailles
Feb.	Preliminary peace terms negotiated between France and Germany
13 March	London Protocol
March–May	Paris Commune
10 May	Treaty of Frankfurt

1872

Sept.	Meeting of the three emperors in Berlin

1873

6 May	Russo-German military convention
6 June	Austro-Russian Schönbrunn Convention
Oct.	Germany accedes to Schönbrunn Convention: Three Emperors' League formed

1875

April–May	'War in Sight' crisis

July Outbreak of insurrection against Ottoman
rule in Herzegovina, then Bosnia
25 Nov. Disraeli buys Suez Canal shares
30 Dec. Andrássy Note

1876
13 May Berlin Memorandum
May–Sept. Insurrection in Bulgaria
30 June Serbia declares war on Turkey
8 July Reichstadt Agreement
Dec.–March 1877 Constantinople Conference

1877
15 Jan.–18 March Budapest Convention
24 April Russia declares war on Turkey
10 Dec. Fall of Plevna

1878
15 Feb. British fleet arrives at Constantinople
3 March Treaty of San Stefano
13 June–13 July Congress of Berlin

1879
4 Sept. Dual control (Britain and France)
established in Egypt
7 Oct. Austro-German alliance (Dual Alliance)

1880
3 July Madrid Convention on Morocco

1881
12 May Treaty of Bardo establishes French
protectorate over Tunis
18 June Three Emperors' Alliance signed
28 June Austro-Serbian alliance
Winter Rising in Bosnia: Skobelev tours Europe
(1881–82)

1882
20 May Triple Alliance
11 July British bombard Alexandria

13 Sept.   Battle of Tel-el-Kebir, leading to British occupation of Egypt

1883
Feb.–April   Germans established at Angra Pequeña (South West Africa)
30 Oct.   Austro-Romanian alliance (Germany acceding 30 Oct., Italy 13 May 1888)

1884
15–17 Sept.   Skiernewice meeting of three emperors
15 Nov.–26 Feb.1885   Berlin West Africa conference

1885
26 Jan.   Mahdi takes Khartoum
April–Sept.   Penjdeh crisis
28 June–Aug. 2   London conference on Egyptian finances
18 Sept.   Revolution in Eastern Roumelia
13 Nov.   Serbia declares war on Bulgaria

1886
3 March   Treaty of Bucharest between Serbia and Bulgaria
14 July   General Boulanger appointed minister of war in France
7 Sept.   Russians force abdication of Alexander of Battenberg in Bulgaria

1887
12 Feb.   First Mediterranean Agreement between Great Britain and Italy (Austria-Hungary accedes 24 March; Spain 4 May)
20 Feb.   Triple Alliance renewed
20 April   Schnaebelé incident
22 May   Drummond-Wolff Convention
18 June   Reinsurance Treaty signed
7 July   Ferdinand of Saxe-Coburg-Koháry elected Prince of Bulgaria
Nov.   *Lombardverbot*
12 Dec.   Second Mediterranean Agreement

1888
29 Oct.   Suez Canal Convention

1890
18 March Bismarck dismissed
1 July Anglo-German Heligoland-Zanzibar treaty

1891
6 May Premature renewal of Triple Alliance
4 July William II's state visit to London
21,27 Aug. Franco-Russian diplomatic agreement

1892
1 Aug. Mission of General Boisdeffre to
St Petersburg

1893
July Anglo-French crisis over Siam
15 July German military bill passed by *Reichstag*
13 Oct. Russian squadron visits Toulon
27 Dec.–4 Jan. 1894 Franco-Russian exchange of notes

1894
12 May Congo Treaty between British and
Leopold II
1 Aug. Outbreak of war between China and Japan
Aug.–Sept. Armenian massacres

1895
17 April Treaty of Shimonoseki
Oct. Armenian massacres and
Anglo-Franco-Russian scheme of
reforms

1896
3 Jan. Kruger telegram
1 March Italians defeated at Adua by Ethiopians
March British begin advance in Sudan

1897
17 April–18 Sept. War between Greece and Turkey
May Franz Joseph's visit to St Petersburg,
Austro-Russian *status quo* agreement
14 Nov. German forces land at Kiao-Chow

1898

27 March	Russians secure lease of Port Arthur
28 March	First Naval Law passed by *Reichstag*
24 April–10 Dec.	Spanish-American War
30 Aug.	Anglo–German agreement on Portuguese colonies
Sept.–March, 1899	Fashoda crisis
21 Nov.	Franco–Italian commercial agreement

1899

18 May–29 July	First Hague Peace Conference
9 Oct.	Outbreak of Boer War
1 Nov.	Anglo–German Samoa agreement
25 Nov.	German syndicate secures Baghdad Railway concession

1900

13 June–14 Aug.	Boxer Rising and siege of legations in Peking
16 Oct.	Anglo–German Yangtse Agreement
9 Nov.	Alexeieff-Tseng agreement on Manchuria
14 Dec.	Franco–Italian agreement (Visconti Venosta-Barrère)

1901

March–April	Crisis over Russian activities in Manchuria
May	End of Anglo–German alliance negotiations
Nov.-Dec.	Ito's visit to St Petersburg

1902

30 Jan.	Anglo–Japanese Alliance
31 May	Boer War ends: Treaty of Vereeniging
1 Nov.	Franco–Italian agreement (Prinetti-Barrère)

1903

Feb.	Austro–Russian scheme of reforms for Macedonia
1–4 May	Edward VII's visit to Paris
2 Oct.	Mürzsteg Punctation

1904

4 Feb.	Outbreak of Russo-Japanese War
8 April	Anglo–French agreements

Oct.	Austro-Russian neutrality agreement
Oct.–Nov.	Russo-German alliance negotiations
Dec.	St René Taillandier mission to Fez

1905

31 March	William II's visit to Tangier
6 June	Fall of Delcassé
24 July	Treaty of Björkö
5 Sept.	Treaty of Portsmouth ends Russo-Japanese War

1906

10 Jan.	Start of Anglo-French military and naval conversations
16 Jan.–7 April	Algeçiras Conference
10 Feb.	First Dreadnought launched

1907

16 May	Anglo-Franco-Spanish agreement on Mediterranean *status quo*
15 June–18 Oct.	Second Hague Peace Conference
31 Aug.	Anglo-Russian Convention

1908

27 Jan.	Sanjak Railway project announced
9 June	Edward VII and Nicholas II meet at Reval
24 July	Constitution of 1876 restored in Turkey
16 Sept.	Buchlau Conference
5 Oct.	Proclamation of Bulgarian independence
6 Oct.	Proclamation of annexation of Bosnia and Herzegovina

1909

12 Jan.	Austro-Turkish agreement about Bosnia
8 Feb.	Franco-German agreement about Morocco
21 March	German 'ultimatum' to Russia leads to end of Bosnian crisis
24 Oct.	Russo-Italian Racconigi agreement

1910

4–5 Nov.	Nicholas II and William II meet at Potsdam

1911

April–May	French advance in Morocco
June–Nov.	Second Moroccan crisis
1 July	*Panther* arrives at Agadir
28 Sept.–18 Oct. 1912	Italo-Ottoman War
4 Nov.	Franco-German agreement on Morocco
11 Nov.	Russian ultimatum to Persia

1912

13 March	Serbo-Bulgarian treaty
29 May	Bulgarian-Greek treaty
July	French naval agreements with Russia and Britain
21 July	Fall of Young Turkish government at Constantinople
8 Oct.	Outbreak of first Balkan War
17 Dec.	First meeting of ambassadors at London

1913

April	Scutari crisis
30 May	Treaty of London
29 June	Outbreak of war between Balkan states
10 Aug.	Treaty of Bucharest
18 Oct.	Austro-Hungarian ultimatum to Serbia
30 Oct.	Austro-Hungarian-Italian *démarche* at Athens
Nov.–Jan. 1914	Liman von Sanders crisis

1914

14 June	Tsar's visit to Romania
28 June	Sarajevo assassinations
23 July	Austro-Hungarian note to Belgrade
28 July	Austria-Hungary declares war on Serbia
1 Aug.	Germany declares war on Russia (on France 3 August)
4 Aug.	Great Britain declares war on Germany
6 Aug.	Austria-Hungary declares war on Russia
12 Aug.	Great Britain and France declare war on Austria-Hungary

Indexes

Index of persons

General index

Index of topics

Indexes